After Mahler

The music of Gustav Mahler repeatedly engages with romantic notions of redemption. This is expressed in a range of gestures and procedures, shifting between affirmative fulfilment and pessimistic negation. In this ground-breaking study, Stephen Downes explores the relationship of this aspect of Mahler's music to the output of Benjamin Britten, Kurt Weill and Hans Werner Henze. Their initial admiration was notably dissonant with the prevailing zeitgeist – Britten in 1930s England, Weill in 1920s Germany and Henze in 1950s Germany and Italy. Downes argues that Mahler's music struck a profound chord with them because of the powerful manner in which it raises and intensifies dystopian and utopian complexes and probes the question of fulfilment or redemption, an ambition manifest in ambiguous tonal, temporal and formal processes. Comparisons of the ways in which this topic is evoked facilitate new interpretative insights into the music of these four major composers.

STEPHEN DOWNES is Professor of Music at Royal Holloway, University of London. He is the author of two books on the music of Karol Szymanowski and won the Wilk Prize for Research in Polish Music (University of Southern California) and the Karol Szymanowski memorial medal. He is also the author of *The Muse as Eros* (2006), *Music and Decadence in European Modernism* (2010) and *Hans Werner Henze: Tristan* (2011).

After Mahler

Britten, Weill, Henze and Romantic Redemption

STEPHEN DOWNES

CAMBRIDGE
UNIVERSITY PRESS

CAMBRIDGE
UNIVERSITY PRESS

University Printing House, Cambridge CB2 8RU, United Kingdom

Published in the United States of America by Cambridge University Press, New York

Cambridge University Press is part of the University of Cambridge.

It furthers the University's mission by disseminating knowledge in the pursuit of
education, learning, and research at the highest international levels of excellence.

www.cambridge.org
Information on this title: www.cambridge.org/9781107008717

First published 2013

Printed in the United Kingdom by CPI Group Ltd. Croydon CR0 4YY

A catalogue record for this publication is available from the British Library

Library of Congress Cataloguing in Publication data
Downes, Stephen C., 1962–
After Mahler : Britten, Weill, Henze, and romantic redemption / Stephen Downes.
  pages   cm
Includes bibliographical references and index.
ISBN 978-1-107-00871-7 (alk. paper)
1. Britten, Benjamin, 1913–1976 – Criticism and interpretation.   2. Weill, Kurt,
1900–1950 – Criticism and interpretation.   3. Henze, Hans Werner,
1926–2012 – Criticism and interpretation.   4. Mahler, Gustav, 1860–1911 – Criticism
and interpretation.   5. Mahler, Gustav, 1860–1911 – Influence.   6. Music–20th
century – History and criticism.   I. Title.
ML197.D68   2013
780.9′04–dc23

2013026054

ISBN 978-1-107-00871-7 Hardback

Ich komm' zu dir, traute Ruhestätte!
Ja, gib mir Ruh, ich hab' Erquickung not!
(I come to you, beloved resting place!
Yes, give me rest, I have need of reviving.)

'Der Einsame im Herbst' (Hans Bethge/Tchang-Tsi, alt. Mahler)

For Alice Marianne

Contents

Music examples

Acknowledgements

I was very fortunate to have world leaders in Mahler and Britten studies as colleagues in the School of Arts at the University of Surrey. Jeremy Barham was a constant source of information and advice as I repeatedly pestered him on all things Mahlerian; the Britten scholar, Chris Mark, read a draft of Chapter 2 with characteristically meticulous thoroughness and made many valuable comments and corrections.

Parts of the final section of Chapter 1 were given as a paper at the conference 'Gustav Mahler: Contemporary of the Past?', University of Surrey, July 2011 and at the International Nineteenth-Century Music Conference, University of Edinburgh, June 2012.

I am grateful to Lucy Walker and Nicholas Clark for their help during my visit to the Britten-Pears Library in October 2011 and for subsequent email correspondence. They answered all my queries and requests with speed, efficiency and warmth. Thanks again to Victoria Cooper and to her assistant Fleur Jones at Cambridge University Press for all their expert guidance in the final stages of preparing the manuscript.

The musical examples were prepared with consummate skill by Jake Willson. The cost of licensing and preparing musical examples was supported by the School of Arts, University of Surrey. The extracts from the following works are reproduced by permission.

Benjamin Britten:

Serenade for Tenor, Horn and Strings © Copyright 1944 by Hawkes & Son (London) Ltd. Reproduced by permission of Boosey & Hawkes Music Publishers Ltd.

Winter Words © Copyright 1954 by Boosey & Co Ltd. Reproduced by permission of Boosey & Hawkes Music Publishers Ltd.

On this Island © Copyright 1938 by Boosey & Co Ltd. Reproduced by permission of Boosey & Hawkes Music Publishers Ltd.

Peter Grimes © Copyright 1945 by Boosey & Hawkes Music Publishers Ltd. Reproduced by permission of Boosey & Hawkes Music Publishers Ltd.

Sinfonia da Requiem © Copyright 1942 by Hawkes & Son (London) Ltd. Reproduced by permission of Boosey & Hawkes Music Publishers Ltd.

During the period of work on this project I have, as always, been sustained by the love, patience and support of my wife Rachel. Our daughter Alice Marianne was born as I started to write my first drafts, and it is to her that I dedicate this book.

1 | Mahler's moment

I: After Mahler: influence or intertext?

if you weren't you, who would you like to be?
Paul McCartney Gustav Mahler
Alfred Jarry John Coltrane
Charlie Mingus Claude Debussy
Wordsworth Monet Bach and Blake   Adrian Henri, 'Me'[1]

Henri's poem, first published in 1967, can be read as a litany or genealogy.[2] It confers iconic status on a conglomeration of artists. The opening of this list of a few of the Liverpudlian poet's favourite things grants especially high status to Mahler by provocatively pairing him with McCartney, the hometown popular hero and by the poem's year of publication one of the world's most famous musicians. It is a poem which, as Bernice Martin has noted, mixes categories and tastes with no care for chronology, but most crucially carries the 'weight of implicit knowledge; all those names have to trigger a shared memory and understanding of multiple traditions'. It is also in several ways a 'parasitic' poem: its apparent 'anti-structure' depends upon poetic traditions of metre and rhythm; its wilfully scatty inventory recalls biblical verses of begetting.[3] Up front, the poem projects McCartney and Mahler as on-trend *alter egos* for the modern, artistically aspirant subject.

Many would warm to Henri's homage. It is widely appreciated that Mahler's music raises aesthetic, expressive, technical and political issues that are subsequently extended, interrogated, transformed and challenged in fascinating and diverse ways in the work of a broad range of composers.[4]

---

[1] Adrian Henri, Roger McGough and Brian Patten, *The Mersey Sound*, Penguin Modern Poets 10 (Harmondsworth: Penguin, 1967), 27.

[2] See Bernice Martin, *A Sociology of Contemporary Cultural Change* (Oxford: Blackwell, 1981), 95. Henri's complete poem is a list (totalling over eighty names) dominated by white males.

[3] *Ibid.*, 96.

[4] For an overview, see 'Mahler and Posterity' in Jens Malte Fischer, *Gustav Mahler*, trans. Stewart Spencer (New Haven: Yale University Press, 2011), 691–706, and my essay 'Musical Languages of Love and Death: Mahler's Compositional Legacy', in Jeremy Barham (ed.), *The Cambridge Companion to Mahler* (Cambridge University Press, 2007), 226–42.

1

Our understanding of these issues and their significance for music of the past one hundred years remains, however, partial.[5] An important critical task remains to be done. This book seeks to do some of this critical work through examining three composer case studies: Benjamin Britten, Kurt Weill and Hans Werner Henze. In particular, it interprets their work in the light of Mahler's complex engagement with romantic notions of redemption or fulfilment.

The proposition that the music of Mahler was greatly admired by Britten, Weill and Henze is neither provocative nor revelatory. They each frequently expressed their appreciation of Mahler's achievement and described its personal significance for their artistic outlook. This has predictably led to ascriptions of direct or indirect influence. The critical literature on these three composers is littered with descriptions of their music as more or less explicitly 'Mahlerian', or 'post-Mahlerian'.[6] And yet the interpretative potential of exploring their music in the

---

[5] In Lisa Brooks Robinson's thesis *Mahler and Postmodern Intertextuality*, unpublished PhD, Yale University (1994) works by Lukas Foss, George Rochberg, Luciano Berio and Alfred Schnittke are discussed as case studies demonstrating how aspects of Mahler's music – stylistic pluralism, including juxtaposition of high and low materials, irony, allusion – were attractive to composers working within the 'postmodern aesthetic'. Robinson emphasizes that this is just one aspect of Mahler's impact on twentieth-century music. Hermann Danuser's study of the post-1960 reception of Mahler is couched in oppositional notions – regression/progression; late romanticism/new music; nostalgia/advanced art – which he argues are present in Mahler's music: *Gustav Mahler und seine Zeit* (Laaber-Verlag, 1991). Hans Keller concluded that 'the diagnosis, however tentative, cannot be avoided that it was in fact Mahler, rather than the more revolutionary Schoenberg, who was the widest influence on twentieth-century music – just because he was less of a revolutionary'; 'The Unpopularity of Mahler's Popularity', in Christopher Wintle (ed.), *Essays on Music* (Cambridge University Press, 1994), 69–70. See also Leon Botstein, 'Whose Mahler? Reception, Interpretation and History', in Karen Painter (ed.), *Mahler and His World* (Princeton University Press, 2002), 1–53.

[6] To exemplify the proliferation of such comments, and to take just Britten, the 'Messalina' section of *Our Hunting Fathers* (1936) is described as Mahlerian by both Philip Rupprecht, *Britten's Musical Language* (Cambridge University Press, 2001), and Donald Mitchell, 'What do we Know about Britten Now?', in Christopher Palmer (ed.), *The Britten Companion* (London: Faber, 1984), 31. Arved Ashby's 'Britten as Symphonist', in Mervyn Cooke (ed.), *The Cambridge Companion to Britten* (Cambridge University Press, 1999), 217–32, offers many subtle but passing comments on both 'Mahlerian' and 'non-Mahlerian' aspects. For Eric Roseberry, the *War Requiem* (1961) suggests a Mahlerian 'embracing of the world', and the treatment of climax in the 'Libera me' is comparable with Mahler's apocalyptic visions in the Sixth and Ninth Symphonies; 'A debt repaid? Some Observations on Shostakovich and his Late Period Reception of Britten', in David Fanning (ed.), *Shostakovich Studies* (Cambridge University Press, 1995), 229–53. The promisingly titled Philip Reed (ed.), *On Mahler and Britten* (Woodbridge: Boydell Press, 1995) is divided between essays on these two composers with no sustained attempt to bring the two together beyond passing comparative comment. Many essays both here and elsewhere point to thematic or expressive similarities between the composers' works without getting beyond surface allusions or parallelisms.

context of Mahler's work remains underdeveloped. To address this through positioning these composers with regard to Mahler's negotiation with versions of redemption and transcendence from the romantic tradition may seem to be an unexpected strategy. But the music of Britten, Weill and Henze is part of a narrative thread in the story of twentieth-century music which tells of repertory which is non-conformist and anti-dogmatic and yet also firmly entwined with traditions elsewhere considered outworn, irrelevant or ideologically suspect. Their music overtly raises the issue of tradition – sometimes to celebrate it, sometimes to recalibrate it. It has become a commonplace of criticism (rightly) to align aspects of their work with notions of anti-romanticism, neoclassicism, new objectivity or realism, but they repeatedly displayed profound concern for how music might evoke – through both affirmation and negation – a redemptive or transcendent mode that so preoccupied the Romantics but which seemed, to many of their contemporaries, to be indisputably redundant, dismissible or disreputable. This aspect of their work remains under-explored. It is especially interesting that their initial admiration for Mahler's music was in each case notably dissonant with the prevailing zeitgeist: Britten in 1930s England, Weill in Germany of the 1920s and Henze in Germany and Italy in the 1950s. Each occupied an acutely felt position as cultural and social outsider and explored the resistance of the individual to subjugating social forces through expressions of alienation, assimilation and reconciliation. In a century of cataclysm and horror, in which the utopian–dystopian polarity became extreme, the music of Britten, Weill and Henze frequently seems to inhabit a precarious position between cultural entrenchments. Mahler's music struck such a profound chord with these composers because of the powerful way in which it raised and intensified dystopian and utopian complexes and probed the possibility of fulfilment or redemption, an ambition manifest in ambiguous tonal, temporal and formal processes. In all these ways, it is valid and valuable to explore their music as being 'after Mahler'.

'After Mahler': this unavoidably raises the spectres of epigonism and mannerism (the perpetuation of a once vigorous artistic style beyond its 'normal' lifespan). Whether such relationships are signified by the suffix 'esque' or by the prefix 'post' the implications are, as I have stated elsewhere, 'ambiguous, suggesting either stylish evocation of a prestigious predecessor or the perilous dangers of pale imitation'. The implied 'borrowing' or 'emulation' may at best suggest 'homage or compliment, but at worst might be viewed as parasitical, a weak imitation which actually drains the artistic life out of the revered source of inspiration'.[7] The impression can all too readily evoke latecomers furtively sweeping up discarded materials after the glory and brilliance of the Lord Mayor's show has long passed by. The idea of influence, once a respected topic of study (with perhaps the classic twentieth-century text being T.S. Eliot's famous essay on 'Tradition and the Individual Talent'[8]), is now highly problematic. Studies which focus on the relationship of an artist, or group of artists, to a single, immediate predecessor of high cultural status have perhaps been recently avoided because this critical strategy is felt to be suspiciously reductive or in danger of lapsing into discredited ideology. Such pitfalls can be avoided by challenging conventional notions of artistic influence. With musicology's rather belated and uncertain flirtation with Harold Bloom's once influential idea of the anxiety of influence now some time past and theories of intertextuality well established in the discipline, the time seems ripe for studies which identify and interrogate points of comparison between the work of an artist or artists and that of a venerated antecedent and develop these to inform critical interpretation and analysis.[9]

For Michael Baxandall the traditional notion of influence is 'a curse of art criticism'. He argues that we need to turn the conventional critical direction on its head: 'If one says that X influenced Y it does seem that one is saying that X did something to Y rather than that Y did something to X. But in the consideration of good pictures and paintings the second is always the more lively reality.' Baxandall continues:

If we think of Y rather than X as the agent the vocabulary is much richer and more attractively diversified: draw on, resort to, avail oneself of, appropriate from, engage

---

[7] Stephen Downes, *Music and Decadence in European Modernism: The Case of Central and Eastern Europe* (Cambridge University Press, 2010), 227.

[8] T.S. Eliot, 'Tradition and the Individual Talent' [1920] in *The Sacred Wood: Essays on Poetry and Criticism* (London: Methuen, 1950), 47–59.

[9] Two key texts of 'Bloomian' musicology from the early 1990s were Joseph N. Straus, *Remaking the Past: Musical Modernism and the Influence of the Tonal Tradition* (Cambridge, Mass.: Harvard University Press, 1990) and Kevin Korsyn, 'Towards a New Poetics of Musical Influence', *Music Analysis* 10 (1991), 3–72. For a devastating critique see Richard Taruskin, 'Revising Revision' [1993], in *The Danger of Music and Other Anti-Utopian Essays* (Berkeley: University of California Press, 2009), 354–81. Mark Evan Bonds, *After Beethoven: Imperatives of Originality in the Symphony* (Cambridge, Mass.: Harvard University Press, 1996), which includes an extended discussion of Mahler's Fourth Symphony, sets out its territory in Bloomian terms. Bloom also informs the final chapter of Michael Klein's *Intertextuality in Western Art Music* (Bloomington: Indiana University Press, 2005). Jonathan Cross's *The Stravinsky Legacy* (Cambridge University Press, 1998), which is closely comparable in aim to the current book (it seeks to analyse the legacy of Stravinsky's modernism, though the discussion is broadly organized by topic rather than composer case study) uses the word 'influence' rather casually, although it contains three passing references to Bloom.

with, react to, quote, differentiate oneself from, assimilate oneself to, align oneself with, copy, address, paraphrase, absorb, make a variation on, revive, continue, remodel, ape, emulate, travesty, parody, extract from, distort, attend to, master, subvert, perpetuate, reduce, promote, respond to, transform, tackle . . . – everyone will be able to think of others. Most of these relations just cannot be stated the other way round – in terms of X acting on Y rather than Y acting on X. To think in terms of influence blunts thought by impoverishing the means of differentiation.[10]

Baxandall's example is Picasso's *Les Demoiselles d'Avignon* (1906–7) and its relationship to the work of Cézanne (who died in the autumn of 1906), in particular to the series of *Baigneuses* canvasses (*c.* 1900). Picasso's creative engagement with Cézanne's works explored their contribution within a particular notion of, or story within, the history and techniques of modern painting. In Cézanne's *Baigneuses*, Picasso identified both an artistic problem which he decided to address or tackle and a 'resource', a place to find and adapt techniques or 'tools for solving problems'. Baxandall exhorts that 'to sum all this up as Cézanne influencing Picasso would be false: it would blur the differences in type of reference, and it would take the actively purposeful element out of Picasso's behaviour to Cézanne'. Picasso was highly selective, approaching Cézanne's work from a markedly particular, 'tendentious' angle, and through this 'rewrote' Cézanne's place in art history. The consequence is that 'we will never see Cézanne undistorted by what, in Cézanne, painting after Cézanne has made productive in our tradition'.[11]

Even where the rhetoric of traditional criticism remains more intact, there has been a concern to avoid creating a passive portrait of the younger artist. The keynote essay in the catalogue of an exhibition exploring the relationship of Picasso to the work of a range of modern British artists (Duncan Grant, Wyndham Lewis, Ben Nicholson, Henry Moore, Francis Bacon, Graham Sutherland and David Hockney) posed it not as a 'question of influence as a passive acceptance but of study and appropriation as a conscious strategy in each artist's practice'.[12] And yet, as the art critic of *The Observer* noted, such a 'comparison is frequently cruel', and too often is one which 'ends up shrinking the art'.[13] Comparative studies of this kind can all too often be doubly reductive. They reduce the complexity of the possible

---

[10] Michael Baxandall, *Patterns of Intention: On the Historical Explanation of Pictures* (New Haven: Yale University Press, 1985), 58–9.

[11] *Ibid.*, 61–62.

[12] James Beechey, 'Picasso and Britain', in James Beechey and Chris Stephens (eds.), *Picasso and Modern British Art* (London: Tate, 2012), 16.

[13] Laura Cumming, 'Picasso and the Borrowers', *The Observer*, 19 February 2012.

meaning and intertextual character of the work and reduce the place of the artist to a singular, dominant and unequal relationship. They also remain too often informed by lingering anxieties over supposed originality. In his widely read essay 'On Originality', the late Edward Said, that famous scholar of lateness, wrote that 'the writer thinks less of writing originally, and more of rewriting'.[14] All art is to some degree a form of palimpsest or type of afterthought. As the author and critic Jonathan Lethem has more recently commented, 'it has become apparent that appropriation, mimicry, quotation, allusion, and sublimated collaboration consist of a *sine qua non* of the creative act'. Lethem urges us to get over modernism's 'contamination anxiety' and celebrate the 'ecstasy of influence' and the 'strange beauty of second use'.[15]

The influence of the traditional notion of influence on critical work has recently come under the most scathing scrutiny from Lawrence Kramer. For Kramer, influence is ineluctably tied up with romantic hang-ups over notions of the 'great work', genius, maturation, originality and progress. It places a 'dreadful constraint on intertextual potential' because 'the richness of cultural production' is 'condensed into a single controlling and limiting antecedent'. Kramer argues, furthermore, that any hope of developing a new, improved theory of influence is doomed for, unlike the 'plural, heterogeneous relations' which inform theories of intertextuality, it would necessarily be restricted to the study of a younger artist 'seeking to transcend the tutelage of the older'.[16] The notion of influence which Kramer rejects is not one to which this study adheres. But there is deliberate intertextual 'constraint'. Its aim is to generate interpretations of Britten, Weill and Henze through focusing discussion of their musical materials and procedures around certain structural, aesthetic and expressive characteristics of Mahler's output. These characteristics, which are identified in the final part of this introductory chapter, relate to the music of Britten, Weill and Henze as prominent parts of its 'cultural memory'. They do so sometimes overtly, sometimes latently, and often in ambiguous, ambivalent ways. As Kramer has put it, the 'presence of the past in the presentness of the musical work can be heard in the form of oddly familiar, uncanny figures, as ghosts in the material'. Kramer reads the '*Freund Hein spielt auf*' violin solo of the second movement of Mahler's Fourth Symphony as a 'trope for the curiously memorial function of all composed, all written music, the mere

---

[14] Edward Said, *The World, The Text, and the Critic* (Cambridge, Mass.: Harvard University Press, 1983), 135.
[15] Jonathan Lethem, *The Ecstasy of Influence* (New York: Doubleday, 2011), 93–120.
[16] Lawrence Kramer, *Interpreting Music* (Berkeley: University of California Press, 2011), 118–19.

performance of which according to the score constitutes an attempt to reanimate something always already fleeting, disappearing, lost, dead. All such music is memorial; all such music is necromantic. Even where it mourns, it forms an attempt to transcend or undo mourning.' Kramer focuses on the 'revenant', that is, a 'specter, a ghost, a phantom, one who haunts, who returns, who walks again'. Such figures may be 'genial' or 'ghastly':

> The spectre of death – realized by Schubert, whose revenants, snatches of song transplanted to instrumental works, are all imbued with the melancholy of absent voice and nearly all topically laden with themes of loss: a beautiful world now vanished; the solitude of the wanderer for whom the world has no beauty left; the meeting of Death and the Maiden. These revenants seem to summon up a melancholy latent in all forms of citation, even self-citation.[17]

It would be equally insightful to substitute Mahler for Schubert in Kramer's paragraph.

Mahler's music has long been heard to raise questions concerning the value, relationship and meaning of reminiscences, quotations, musical reuse, recycling and allusion.[18] It technically develops and expressively intensifies the allusive qualities that are a characteristic aspect of romantic musical compositional practice and reception. In a study of this practice, Christopher Alan Reynolds notes how compositional allusions may be assimilative or contrastive. They are materials invoked in forms of artistic play which may involve transformation, elevation, concealment, contradiction or irony. The significance and effect, Reynolds rightly asserts, is profoundly conditioned by the manner in which an allusion is 'framed' or 'presented'. Merely spotting allusions to past or borrowed material in a game of musical 'snap' is a pastime of little import. Allusions need to be recognized as significantly relating to artistic and critical engagements with notions including creativity, meaning, subjective identity, politics and tradition.[19] Allusions alert listeners to the possibility of more embedded or subtle intertextual associations; they might tell of the relation of a work to a version or rendering of history. Identifying and exploring these cultural or

---

[17] Lawrence Kramer, *Musical Meaning: Towards a Critical History* (Berkeley: University of California Press, 2002), 261; from whom the term 'cultural memory' is also borrowed (see p. 265.)

[18] See Henry-Louis de La Grange, 'Music about Music in Mahler: Reminiscences, Allusions, or Quotations?' in Stephen Hefling (ed.), *Mahler Studies* (Cambridge University Press, 1997), 122–68.

[19] Christopher Reynolds, *Motives for Allusion: Context and Content in Nineteenth-Century Music* (Cambridge, Mass.: Harvard University Press, 2003), xi, 15, 21.

historical themes can provide context for a central topical focus and ensure a move beyond myopic allusion spotting, which, as John Daverio warns in the final pages of his study of intertextual relationships between the music of Schubert, Schumann and Brahms, can lead to restrictive emphasis on striking moments at the expense of the larger interpretative and historical picture.[20]

At the broadest level, allusion to things past can raise intertwined notions of historicism and modernism. The work of Walter Frisch has been especially important in unpacking this ambiguity in late nineteenth- and early twentieth-century German repertory. In an essay on Brahms, he argues that 'historicism really becomes indistinguishable from [Brahms's] ... own style'.[21] In a study of Reger, Frisch includes 'late Mahler' as part of a privileged repertory that characteristically led to a focus on 'chromaticism and atonality as the barometers of emergent modernism' in Austro-German music between the death of Wagner and the start of the First World War. By contrast, Frisch raises the importance of 'historicist modernism' in music from around 1900, which had a 'deep and sophisticated engagement with music of the past', in a manner which must be differentiated from later neoclassicism, and in which the music of Brahms played a crucial role.[22] The differentiation Frisch demands between the attitude towards the past exhibited by pre-war historicist-modernists and the neoclassicists who flourished from the 1920s points up the requirement for critical subtlety. But his characterization of Mahler, even if limited to 'late' Mahler, is too one-dimensional. In a widely read essay, Carl Dahlhaus distinguished various forms of historicism through evoking notions of inclusion and exclusion, nature and history, and the naïve and sentimental, all of which are particularly apposite to Mahler, Britten, Weill and Henze. Tradition can be sustained yet critiqued artistically through controlled estrangement. Such critical work reveals what was 'natural' to be historical, and raises the problem of assimilation. An artistic project of restoration seeks to renew contact with a tradition after an interruption; such restorations are by their very nature reflective (unlike traditions which can be unreflective, naïve), as they are based on

---

[20] John Daverio, *Crossing Paths: Schubert, Schumann and Brahms* (Oxford University Press, 2002), 7–8, 245.

[21] Walter Frisch, 'Bach, Brahms, and the Emergence of Musical Modernism', in Michael Marissen (ed.), *Bach Perspectives III: Creative Responses to Bach from Mozart to Hindemith* (Lincoln: University of Nebraska Press, 1998), 119.

[22] 'Reger's Bach and Historicist Modernism', *19th-Century Music* 25 (2002), 296–312. Frisch's 'historicist modernism' may relate as a subset to J. Peter Burkholder's broader notion of 'The Historicist Mainstream in Music of the Last Hundred Years', *The Journal of Musicology* 2 (1983), 115–34.

the recovery of the lost in the manner of the Schillerian sentimental. Conservatism, unlike restoration, seeks to preserve traditions that are considered to be current but 'endangered'. It is nonetheless reflective, latently polemical. Conservatism turns into overt historicism when the presentness of the past and that material's very 'pastness' is subjected to scrutiny. This position contrasts with the naïve traditionalist who, Dahlhaus explains, clings to the 'metaphysics' of a timeless, unchanging and abstract notion of beauty. The Schillerian sentimental leanings of historicism facilitate the appreciation of 'past things for being past, in a form of recollection that figures as an essential feature of the present moment. The remote is perceived as such but experienced as near; the foreign is recognized as alien yet also felt to be familiar.'[23] The complex, shifting tone of Mahler's music, across and within works, at various times evokes all these variant forms of historicism, in part depending on what tradition is evoked. Mahler's historicism embraced the tensions between assimilation and alienation, obligation and freedom, conservation and restoration, naïvety and sentimentality.[24]

As Arnold Whittall has pointed out, an important aspect of the mid twentieth-century 'rediscovery' of Mahler was that his music sounded new yet 'familiar' because of its 'evident relationship with traditional genres and aesthetic codes'. Composers such as Britten 'who were most highly regarded for their ability to combine individualism and accessibility ... were often perceived as having Mahlerian traits'. Furthermore, in a century of '*angst*', scepticism and even anarchy, Mahler's music was often heard to evoke 'the vulnerability of faith and hope in a time of continuing political uncertainty, complemented by the possibility of a triumphant reassertion of control'. It did this as a form of 'Art' music (with all the romantic, transcendent baggage attached to that capitalized term still in tow, if on an extendable leash) which engaged with tradition 'as sacred, or as corrupt, or as something to be acknowledged with scepticism, even irony: and if, in the interests of accessibility, it welcomes a close relation to tradition, because it believes tradition remains open to individual reinterpretation, then these elemental states of joy and sorrow so palpably present in Mahler are likely to remain the principal sites of creative

[23] Carl Dahlhaus, *Foundations of Music History*, trans. J.B. Robinson (Cambridge University Press, 1983), 64–70.
[24] On the historicism at work in Mahler's performance practice, see Reinhold Kubik, 'Mahler's Revisions and Performance Practice' in Jeremy Barham (ed.), *Perspectives on Gustav Mahler* (Aldershot: Ashgate, 2005), 402–5.

activity'. Whittall calls this 'moderate music' (as a contrast to radical avant-gardism), repertory which is pervaded by generic and topical evocations 'in which pessimism and Utopianism might intersect'.[25]

II: Mahler, romanticism and redemption in an age of scepticism

In an essay written for the BBC celebrations of the centenary of Mahler's birth, Deryck Cooke declared that Mahler 'was a romantic, and therefore suspect; but he was a romantic with a difference, which complicates matters considerably'. This romantic difference or complication Cooke identifies with Mahler's lateness: 'first of all he was a late romantic', the 'late romantic who speaks most clearly to our age'. For Cooke, Mahler spoke to the twentieth century because he combined the idealist, revolutionary freedom of the early Romantics with the resignation, laments and temptations of the retreat into an imaginary idyll of the late Romantics: 'he was intensely preoccupied with this discrepancy between aspiration and weakness'.[26] More recently, Morten Solvik argued that Mahler harboured a 'tortured soul that maintained a tenuous balance between idealism and nihilism', manifest in the contrast between redemptive symphonic conclusions such as the Second, Third and Eighth Symphonies and the 'anti-heroic' endings of the Sixth and Ninth. Mahler's music repeatedly suggests an ideal world and a unity of inner and outer realms, 'but the transcendental vision' was 'highly problematic': it is 'rife with conflict and unsettling questions'. In an age of scepticism, Mahler's agnostic idealism is 'hard won' and not as anachronistic as it may seem, for many of Mahler's generation 'maintained a transcendental streak in their thinking'.[27] Ultimately, Mahler was no nihilist. He retained a visionary aspect in a time of widespread unbelief. Mahler was also, in the religious sense, no fundamentalist. For Cooke, 'Mahler's inner conflict was the eternal one between innocence and experience, idealism and realism, affirmation and denial . . . But there was more to it than romanticism. What affronts the idealist – the cruelty, vulgarity,

[25] Arnold Whittall, 'Individualism and Accessibility: The Moderate Mainstream', in Nicholas Cook and Anthony Pople (eds.), *The Cambridge History of Twentieth-Century Music* (Cambridge University Press, 2004), 364–94.

[26] Deryck Cooke, 'Mahler as Man and Artist' (1960), reprinted in *Gustav Mahler: An Introduction to his Music* (London: Faber, 1980), 3–18.

[27] Morten Solvik, 'Mahler's Untimely Modernism', in Barham (ed.), *Perspectives on Gustav Mahler*, 153–71.

triviality and apparent meaninglessness of life – he stared boldly in the face.' This is the 'difference'. 'If half of him was a romantic the other half was that characteristic twentieth-century figure: the restless seeker for the naked truth (whether "beautiful" or "ugly"), ridden with doubt and perplexity, ill-at-ease in an unfriendly cosmos.'[28]

Cooke's 1960 essay has long been overshadowed in Mahler criticism by Adorno's more extensive (and certainly more intellectually demanding – he was writing for a different readership of course) 'musical physiognomy' of the same centennial year.[29] After Adorno, recent Mahler scholarship has been particularly engaged with scrutinizing and affirming Mahler's modernist credentials. Modernist ambiguity is identified in what Julian Johnson calls its 'broken' tone: after Adorno's emphasis on fractured material and Mahler as a 'poor yea-sayer', the cracked voice speaks denial of closure and wholeness, which are nonetheless often strongly implied in music which appears to 'expose its own artificiality and conventionality while, at the same time, apparently affirming its expressive gestures as authentic and non-ironic'. In short, Mahler's music engages with an 'aspiration' to a 'grand unity' which persists 'alongside an increasing sense of its own impossibility'.[30] The formal and expressive materials of romanticism which exist in Mahler's music are likely to be heard as remnants or residues, as memories or echoes on the edge of extinction, or as specimens preserved in a jar of musical formaldehyde for sceptical or ironic scrutiny. In John Williamson's view, Mahler's music in *Das Lied von der Erde*, for example, includes 'expressive gestures that remember the style of musical romanticism without reproducing it'. And again turning to the metaphor of a complex voice, Williamson hears the music displaying 'numerous links' with 'the Romantic and Post-Romantic past, even if the links are themselves rendered subtly problematic by a critical internal voice'.[31] In this kind of hearing, one commonly described in response to Mahler, the romantic material is held at a distance, or placed in the quarantine of 'scare' quotation marks. Perhaps most 'hazardously', for those who might prefer a more decidedly modernist Mahler, his music frequently raises the issue of romantic redemption. Robert Samuels has suggested that the Fifth, Sixth and Seventh

[28] Cooke, 'Mahler as Man and Artist', 18.
[29] Theodor W. Adorno, *Mahler: A Musical Physiognomy*, trans. Edmund Jephcott (Chicago University Press, 1991).
[30] Julian Johnson, 'The Breaking of the Voice', *Nineteenth-Century Music Review* 8 (2011), 179–95. See also Johnson's *Mahler's Voices: Expression and Irony in the Songs and Symphonies* (Oxford University Press, 2009).
[31] John Williamson, 'Fragments of Old and New in "Der Abschied"', *Nineteenth-Century Music Review* 8 (2011), 197–217.

Symphonies 'pose the Dostoevskian question of whether some sort of redemption of their material is possible'. The possibility of redemption may or may not be fulfilled but certainly exists as a 'genuine possibility'. On the 'semiotic content' of redemption, Samuels continues:

> The idea seems to involve several characteristics simultaneously: a sense of history, or extension through time; an originating, negative state; a final, positive state; connectedness between these states, so that the last is a transformation of the first, but one which affirms the fact that its potential always existed; and lastly, this transformation is often (though not always) attributable to an outside agency.

In the Fifth Symphony, for example, the negative state of Part 1 is transformed in the finale, with the Adagietto, in Samuels's reading, 'acting as, or at least symbolizing, the "external" agency effecting this change'.[32]

This notion of external agency suggests that the manner through which Mahler's music explores redemptive aspirations and expirations can be related to key aspects of Adorno's 1960 Mahler monograph. As is well known, Adorno identified three formal types in Mahler's music: breakthrough (*Durchbruch*), suspension (*Suspension*) and fulfilment (*Erfüllung*).[33] Mahler scholarship after Adorno has rather neglected the last of these types and particularly emphasized the notion of breakthrough.[34] Adorno related fulfilment closely to the *Abgesang* of bar form, where fulfilment is achieved through the introduction of intensifying and closing material. As examples he cites the close of the exposition of the first movement of the Third Symphony, the end of the recapitulation in the finale of the Sixth (before the final reappearance of the introduction), and the third stanza of the first movement of *Das Lied*. He identifies fulfilment with the 'unleashing of accumulated power, an unfettering, a freedom', for example, as in the beginning of the recapitulation in the first movement of the Eighth, the *fortissimo* repeat of the main theme in the first movement of the Ninth, or the end of the second subject in the exposition of the finale of the Sixth. These are the formal functions and sections where fulfilment is explicitly evoked, but Adorno emphasizes that 'the idea of fulfilment is at work throughout the whole symphonic structure.

---

[32] Robert Samuels, 'Narrative Form and Mahler's Musical Thinking', *Nineteenth-Century Music Review* 8 (2011), 237–54.

[33] Adorno, *Mahler*, 41.

[34] See James Buhler, '"Breakthrough" as a Critique of Form: The Finale of Mahler's First Symphony', *19th-Century Music* 20 (1996), 125–43, which is subjected to critique in Warren Darcy, 'Rotational Form, Teleological Genesis, and Fantasy Projection in the Slow Movement of Mahler's Sixth Symphony', *19th-Century Music* 25 (2001), 49–74.

Everywhere the obligation of expectation is honoured.' In romantic music the increased chromatic tensions weakened the potential function of tonal return as the 'conventional means for simulating fulfilment'. It is for this reason, Adorno argues, that Mahler invested in diatonicism, because it might 'resolve the tensions more energetically than the means of *Tristan* permitted'. But as he could no longer rely simply on tonality, fulfilments therefore became a task of purely musical form: 'fulfilment fields achieve by form, by their relation to what preceded them, what the breakthrough promised itself from outside'. In this way Mahler's music 'keeps its promise', is 'consummated'. In this way 'yearning is fulfilled'.[35]

The negation which sounds in direct conflict with this promise of fulfil-ment was a key marker of Mahler's modern musical authenticity for Adorno. This is how Mahler's work ultimately avoids falling into kitsch even while it clearly makes selected use of kitsch materials. In the dystopian nightmares of modern times, anachronistic Utopian dreams are, according to Adorno, the characteristic aspect of 'every great, authentic piece of kitsch' which is 'capable of acting as the accompaniment to imaginary catastro-phes'. But kitsch 'is the depraved reflection of an epiphany vouchsafed only to the greatest works of art'.[36] Adorno identified the 'authenticity' of the fulfilment expressed by the main theme of the slow movement of Mahler's Fourth as guaranteed by the fact that it is 'counterpointed' and negated by the movement's 'lamenting' second theme. Tones of grief coexist with those of restful peace. A more extreme type of negation lies in the 'negative fulfilment' in passages of collapse and disintegration (for example, at the end of the development of the first movement of the Ninth), which, crucially for Adorno, function not as transitions but as goals. 'If at first glance' Mahler's images seem 'Romantic' through their pastoral nostalgia, this 'extending' of the 'idyll' is only possible, Adorno argues, because of the 'brokenness' of the images. Mahler's 'Romanticism negates itself through disenchantment, mourning, long remembrance.' Ultimately, in the ending of the 'seraphic' Fourth Symphony, for example, Adorno believes that 'the phantasmagoria of the transcendent landscape is at once posited by it and negated. Joy remains unattainable, and no transcendence is left but that of yearning.'[37] As Richard Leppert explains, in Adorno's view 'great' art 'stares history directly in the face and speaks the unspeakable – and sometimes the unbearable'. But, furthermore, 'great art knows how to evoke kitsch for the

---

[35] Adorno, *Mahler*, 43–4.

[36] Theodor W. Adorno, 'Motifs' [1929], in *Quasi una fantasia: Essays on Modern Music*, trans. Rodney Livingstone (London: Verso, 1992), 16, 43.

[37] Adorno, *Mahler*, 45–7, 57.

utopia that inhabits its shadows – Mahler generally; Berg occasionally'. Kitsch and *Kunst* thus exist in 'impure mixtures'.[38] Such an 'impure' aesthetic leads to idiomatic complexity which can evoke the suspect utopias and beauties of kitsch in an age of horror.

The role of utopianism in the thinking of the famously pessimistic Adorno has recently been thoroughly scrutinized. Richard Wolin identifies the 'utopian motif', after Leo Lowenthal, as that which inspired the messianic thoughts of a generation of Central European Jewish thinkers in the early twentieth century. Utopian longing was a fundamental impulse in the work of, for example, Ernst Bloch and Walter Benjamin as well as Adorno. Adorno raised aesthetic modernism as a type of 'this-worldly salvation' from the disenchanted, alienated, rationalized life described by Max Weber. In this view art 'takes on a compelling utopian function as a prefiguration of reconciled life': artistic works are 'ciphers of reconciled life'. This 'aestheticist solution' sustains aspects of the romantic tradition through forms of remembrance and utopian projection in which the absolute appears partially, enigmatically, indirectly. As Adorno wrote in his incomplete *Aesthetic Theory*: 'Art works talk like fairies in tales: if you want the absolute, you shall have it, but only in disguise.'[39] Adorno would need no reminding of the dangers of Utopian projects.[40] For John Sheinbaum, the profoundly qualified utopianism of Adorno's criticism mirrors the profound quality of Mahler's music. Specifically, in the context of his post-holocaust writings, Adorno's 1960 Mahler monograph can be read as offering a musical critique of the totalitarian impulse. The subjection of the individual and the abjection of the outsider is critically examined and paralleled with the artistic use of exoteric voices which break into the 'autonomous' structure of the artwork and thus imperil its organic, unifying impulse, or (better) the illusion of unity. In Adorno's thinking and Mahler's music 'disintegration' and 'unity' are poles in a dialectic in which the dangers of totalization are

---

[38] Richard Leppert, 'Music "Pushed to the Edge of Existence" (Adorno, Listening, and the Question of Hope)', *Cultural Critique* 60 (2005), 125–6.

[39] Richard Wolin, 'Utopia, Mimesis, and Reconciliation: A Redemptive Critique of Adorno's *Aesthetic Theory*', *Representations* 32 (1990), 33–49. Theodor W. Adorno, *Aesthetic Theory*, trans. Robert Hullot-Kentor (Minneapolis: University of Minnesota Press, 1997), 183.

[40] As Klára Móricz notes, 'the more perfect the utopia is – and perfection is one of the main characteristics of utopian sites – the more inhuman it becomes'. 'The goal of utopia is total unity, accomplished through total order' – so it turns into a nightmare. 'Utopias and dystopias have always existed side by side as complementary genres. In the twentieth century, however, dystopias became more prevalent . . . [artists] preferred the satirical and disillusioned mood of dystopia to the naïve idealism of utopia', for 'utopia's perfection restrains rather than liberates'. *Jewish Identities: Nationalism, Racism, and Utopianism in Twentieth-Century Music* (Berkeley: University of California Press, 2008), 202–4.

avoided.[41] Polarity strongly informs Adorno's categories of Mahlerian form. As Sheinbaum points out, breakthrough, suspension and fulfilment operate to various extents and to different effect through the invoking of an external agency or exoteric material. Nonetheless they each work in a dialectical relationship with traditional, closed formal procedures. Fulfilment, by contrast with breakthrough and suspension, invokes coherent conclusion in a manner closely comparable with traditional formal process. But its closure is not simply the end-game of an immanent and developmental process; it possesses a sense of newness or quality of outsideness. Fulfilment is often combined with the effect of culmination, most powerfully in the moment of recapitulation in the first movement of the Eighth Symphony, which Adorno included in his list of examples. But though this culmination is combined with a traditional formal event to suggest positive fulfilment, both Sheinbaum and Adorno nonetheless remain sceptical of its affirmative, resolving quality – Sheinbaum pointing to its 'overwhelming forcefulness' as a mask for a resolution which remains problematic'.

The arts of suspicion, to use Gabriel Josipovici's term, were extensively developed by the romantic pessimists to whom Adorno's work is so frequently – and correctly – compared. But, as Josipovici states, the 'genuine negative thinker' of the nineteenth century (Nietzsche or Kierkegaard, for example) 'always recognizes how easy it is for suspicion itself to harden into a new conviction'. Early twentieth-century modernists who sustain this romantic melancholy, such as Franz Kafka or Thomas Mann, might seem from the vantage point of the 'postmodernist' to be engaged in a pointless lamenting for 'fraudulent absolutes' and a 'false transcendent'. But their work reveals that 'suspicion' both has a history and is tied to a sustained dialectic. It achieves this through evocation of pairs of terms which stand as alternatives for 'trust' and 'suspicion' –for example, through pursuing contrasts between 'lightness and earnestness' or scrutinizing the implications of Schiller's naïve and sentimental.[42] In a sceptical modern age, the utopian aspects of the redemptive myths of romanticism and the Enlightenment notion of rational progress both seem 'unbearable' but remain enormously potent, acting in frequent conflict with

[41] John J. Sheinbaum, 'Adorno's Mahler and the Timbral Outsider', *Journal of the Royal Musical Association* 131 (2006), 38–82 (at 40). Sheinbaum highlights the 'Jewish impulse' in Adorno's thought, its anti-totalizing heterogeneity, exposing the falseness and dangers of total identity. He quotes Peter Franklin: Adorno's 'ambivalence and worry about the experience of affirmative music derives from a cultural position and intellectual personality arguably so close to Mahler's own as to render his interpretations an almost documentary historical significance'. Peter Franklin, '"... His fractures are the script of truth"', in Hefling (ed.), *Mahler Studies*, 286.

[42] Gabriel Josipovici, *On Trust: Art and the Temptations of Suspicion* (New Haven: Yale University Press, 1999), 22–4.

the darker arts of modernity and modernism.[43] The pragmatic, parodistic, pluralist or nihilist aspects of modernism, created through a loss of confidence in the 'totalizing religious and political frameworks of the nineteenth century', coexist with modernism's search for new forms of a redemptive or transcendent mode (manifest, for example, in aspects of symbolism, expressionism and Kandinsky's abstraction).[44] Mahler's music reflects this wide artistic, cultural and philosophical concern in the early twentieth century to find new modes of the redemptive amongst the fractured perspectives of modernist art.

In his *Geist der Utopie* (1918), Ernst Bloch writes of Mahler entering an 'empty, insipid, sceptical age'. He describes Mahler in redemptive metaphors: 'nobody has previously been borne closer to Heaven with the force of a most soulful, effervescent and visionary music than has this yearning, holy, hymnic man'.[45] Bloch urged for a new kind of listening, one which could open up the promise of a redemptive utopia which he deemed to be beyond philosophical enquiry but not beyond musical expression. There is a clear debt to Schopenhauer, but though Bloch did not share Schopenhauer's pessimism, he did share much with Adorno in asserting that the redemptive can only emerge out of a 'labour of the negative'. Through this he sought to avoid the illusions and comforts of a facile optimism, the lapse into kitsch. Bloch also insisted, by contrast with much romantic thinking, that music is allegorical through and through. This was an important part of his concern to demystify and rigorously test all notions of hope, in order to evade the trappings of naïve utopianism.[46] Benjamin shared with Bloch the notion that a work of art can offer moments of breakthrough, of 'now-time' (*Jetztzeiten*) which, for Bloch, were anticipatory utopian images. In Benjamin's 1925 study, *The Origin of German Tragic Drama*, the *Trauerspiel* is raised as timely and true for the way images of death, decay and decline pointed 'all the more vehemently', if negatively, to salvation.[47] The *Trauerspiel* exemplified the potentially redemptive function of the allegorical amongst an art riddled with ruins and corpses. Wolin has noted the parallels between Benjamin's 'conception

---

[43] See David Roberts and Peter Murphy, *Dialectic of Romanticism: A Critique of Modernism* (New York: Continuum, 2004).

[44] Christopher Butler, *Early Modernism: Literature, Music and Painting in Europe 1900–1916* (Oxford: Clarendon Press, 1994), 1–9.

[45] Ernst Bloch, 'Geist der Utopie', in *Essays on the Philosophy of Music*, trans. Peter Palmer, with an introduction by David Drew (Cambridge University Press, 1985), 37.

[46] Christopher Norris, 'Utopian Deconstruction: Ernst Bloch, Paul de Man and the Politics of Music', in Norris (ed.), *Music and the Politics of Culture* (Lawrence & Wishart, 1989), 309, 335, 341–3.

[47] Walter Benjamin, *The Origin of German Tragic Drama*, trans. John Osborne (London: Verso, 1998).

of literary works of art as hieroglyphs of the redeemed life and the Kabbalistic idea of a state of redemption which can be intuited through a linguistic analysis of sacred texts'. Benjamin argued that although since the expulsion from paradise 'pure' language has been corrupted and eroded into a condition of fragmentation and plurality, the lost unity of paradise can still be dimly, darkly perceived. The critical task lay in rescuing or remembering the transcendent image in the unredeemed historical age, in which, according to Benjamin, man's relation to the absolute is precarious, anxious and ambivalent. In such times an authentic artwork is one constructed of fragments or ruins rather than one exhibiting perfect wholeness or total unity. However, 'the more manifestly historical life appears destitute of salvation, the more inexorably it presents itself as a ruin, the more it refers to that sphere *beyond* historical life where redemption lies in store'.[48] Benjamin's critical thinking not only suggests formal aspects of the modern artwork (wholeness and unity versus fragment and ruin) but also suggests two contrasting temporalities – historical, progressive time, and a 'messianic' breakthrough which is sudden and revelatory – which coexist in tensed or dissonant relationship. In both these ways Benjamin's thinking relates strongly to the work of the early Romantics, and as we shall see, bears close parallels with central aspects of Mahler's music.[49]

Martin Geck points out how the legacy of romantic pessimism chimes with Adorno's view that in Mahler's music 'entire complexes' (*ganze Komplexe*) were meant to be 'taken negatively' (*negativ genommen*) and that they must be heard 'as it were, against themselves' (*gleichsam gegen sie*). Fragment, disintegration, brokenness, irony and decay are the characteristics of Mahler's music often raised as manifestations of this negation. But Geck also perceptively writes that

this is not all that can be perceived in Mahler's music: an *order* is also perceptible, one that does not only pretend to be an order; a sense that it is not solely the negation of itself, a consolation that does not wish only to be heard as false. As brilliant and unsurpassed as Adorno's Mahler interpretation is, it is just as obviously the product of a (burnt) child of the Enlightenment who, whilst identifying a significant aspect of Mahler, does not truly accept it; the dream as the paradigm of artistic experience.[50]

---

[48] Richard Wolin, *Walter Benjamin: An Aesthetic of Redemption* (New York: Columbia University Press, 1982), 25–62.

[49] One need only recall the frequently cited letter to Joseph Steiner of June 1879; Knud Martner (ed.), *Selected Letters of Gustav Mahler* (London: Faber, 1979), 54–7.

[50] 'Doch nicht nur dies ist in Mahlers Musik wahrzunehmen: Zugleich ist eine Ordnung spürbar, die nicht nur Ordnung zu sein vorgibt; ein Sinn, der nicht lediglich die Negation seiner selbst ist, ein Trost, der nicht allein als ein falscher gehört warden will. So glänzend und

Geck cites the letter to Max Marschalk of 26 March 1896, where Mahler famously wrote: 'The need to express myself musically – in symphonic terms – begins only on the plane of obscure feelings, at that gate that opens into the "other world", the world in which things no longer fall apart in time and place.'[51] The key phrase here is 'at that gate': Mahler pictures his symphonic position as one on the threshold; the transcendent realm is tantalizingly in view yet remains a step beyond. This liminality is reflected in the sustained conflicts between early romanticism and idealism that Geck argues inform Mahler's 'symphonic dreamtime' (*Sinfonische Traumzeit*). Romanticism in its radical early form considered it impossible to depict ideal or absolute unity, and 'strove for the infinite in forms that bore the visible marks of finiteness' ('die sichtbar das Zeichen der Endlichkeit trugen, nach Unendlichkeit strebten'). Mahler's music strains to similar ends. In this way Mahler, for Geck, is *the* German romantic composer. After the example of the early Romantics, Mahler's irony destroys the illusion of beautiful unity. But Geck points out that there are also passages of 'blissful music-making, and their attraction lies in the uncertainty as to which parts of them can be "believed" and which cannot'.[52]

Geck's subtle insights into Mahler's ambiguous 'symphonic dreamtime' relate to aspects of Mahler's extensions of the romantic *lied*. Marjorie W. Hirsch has discussed the nineteenth-century *lied*'s characteristic longing for paradise lost as stemming principally from Schiller and Goethe. Schiller's 'On Naïve and Sentimental Poetry' (1795), although, as Hirsch points out, an often inconsistent and unclear text, proposed an immensely significant dualism. Schiller's essay provided a key source on the search for a

---

unübertroffen Adornos Mahler-Deutung ist, so ersichtlich stammt sie doch von einem – gebrannten – Kind der Aufklärung, das ein wesentliches Moment bei Mahler zwar benennt, nicht aber wahrhaft gelten lässt: den Traum als Paradigma für künstlerisches Erleben.' Martin Geck, *Von Beethoven bis Mahler* (Reinbek: Rohwolt, 2000), 423.

[51] Martner, *Selected Letters*, 179.

[52] 'Mahler kennt lange Passagen, ja ganze Sätze seligen Musizierens, deren Reiz in dem Zweifel besteht, was man ihm davon "glauben" kann und was nicht.' Geck, *Von Beethoven bis Mahler*, 411, 419. Elsewhere I have shown how the Sixth is a work whose complex tone moves between opposing worldviews. Its first movement presents a conflict between redemptive and pessimistic narratives, manifest in polarized affects and contradiction between two possible endings, until the final section of the finale crushes any lingering hope that the vigorous, apparently redemptive close of the first movement might return to save the day. *Music and Decadence in European Modernism*, 194–202; see also my essay 'Mahler's Fifth and Sixth Symphonies: Idyllic Fantasies, the Sublime, Formal Mastery, and Processes of Mourning and Reparation' in *The Muse as Eros: Music, Erotic Fantasy and Male Creativity in the Romantic and Modern Imagination* (Aldershot: Ashgate, 2006), 112–46. Seth Monahan describes the end of the first movement of the Sixth as one in which 'the sonata has been redeemed' by material which has a false ring, a feverish, strained character, positing an uneasy victory which is doomed: 'Success and Failure in Mahler's Sonata Recapitulations', *Music Theory Spectrum* 33 (2011), 52.

transcendent or second naïvety, for a new and beautiful synthesis. It was recognized that an ideal reconciliation might only be approached through the imaginative and aesthetic impulses of artistic creativity. Thus redemptive hopes are placed in romantic Art. But optimism coexists with pessimism; affirmation with resignation; images of the idyllic with elegiac tones of melancholy and despair.[53] Hirsch's final example is Mahler's 'Ging heut' Morgen übers Feld', the second of the *Lieder eines fahrenden Gesellen* (1883–4), which she poses as a pessimistic 'deflation of Romantic ideals'.[54] But a more complex reading is possible in the manner of Hirsch's introductory discussion. The opening paragraph of the song is exclusively set in diatonic D major, in music expressive of naïvety and shaped by graceful melodic simplicity of scales, undisguised sequences and 'folk' drone fifths. The structural dominant (b. 15) marks the first use of chromaticism on the repeated question of the finch to the wandering protagonist, 'schöne Welt? Schöne Welt?' (repeatedly asking: is the natural world not beautiful?); the rising, scalic melodic figure is here enriched by D♯–E and E♯–F♯ inflections (Example 1.1, bb. 15–18). These chromatic elements are then more playfully exploited in the tweeting finch's answer to its own question. The second stanza proceeds in similar fashion until its closing bars where the playful chromaticisms are extended to allow the only modulation in the song, from D to B major (b. 56ff.; the E♯–F♯ semitone drives the move to the dominant of B). The final stanza is set in this new key, the major submediant of D. It is a significant recomposition of the music of the first two stanzas, particularly in that the repeated chromatic enunciation of the 'Schöne Welt' is replaced by diatonic material in the vocal line, combining with pentatonic accompaniment to suggest a more carefree, naïve quality and the return to a pastoral idyll (Example 1.2, bb. 96–9).

In its presentation of a new tonality and intensifying processes moving towards anticipated closure, the final stanza seems at first to be a promising example of Adorno's fulfilment category of form. But the punctuation at the end of the final couplet's first line, 'Nun fängt auch mein Glück wohl an?!' (Will my happiness now begin?!), encapsulates a curious coexistence of exclamation and inquisition. It thereby alludes to the two contrasting modes of expressing 'schöne Welt' in Examples 1.1 and 1.2: it is a double punctuation mark which summarizes, in a wordless binary sign of contradiction, the coexistence of hope and doubt that is a defining double character

[53] Marjorie W. Hirsch, *Romantic Lieder and the Search for Lost Paradise* (Cambridge University Press, 2007), 16–17.
[54] *Ibid*, 242–3.

Example 1.1 Gustav Mahler, 'Ging heut' Morgen übers Feld', *Lieder eines fahrenden Gesellen*, bb. 15–18.

Example 1.2 Mahler, 'Ging heut' Morgen übers Feld', bb. 96–9.

of Mahler's music. Significantly, the whole couplet is set over an unresolved dominant in a retarded tempo (Example 1.3). The melodic line of the opening is recalled but with one simple yet telling change: the falling B–A♯ replaces the expected rising B–C♯ to create a neighbour-note A♯–B–A♯ figure (b. 105). This phrase is then repeated a fourth higher to form, at its tail, the neighbour-note D♯–E–D♯ motion (bb. 110–11). Before the final vocal line, the lower chromatic part in the instrumental repetitions of semitonal neighbour-notes in parallel sixths recalls the chromatic motive of the 'schöne welt?' from Example 1.1. Chromatic neighbour-note oscillations continue as the final line begins: 'Nein! Nein! Das ich mein, mir nimmer blühen kann!' (No! No! The happiness I mean will never bloom!'). The gesture of bars 119–21 has an especially poignant effect. It combines the chromatic rising motive from 'schöne welt' with an aspiring pentatonic upper line (G♯–A♯–C♯–G♯–F♯, shared between instrument and voice) which is a permutation of the naïve expression of 'schöne welt' in Example 1.2. This leads to the song's most excruciating dissonance over the unfulfilled new tonic of B, created as the

Example 1.3 Mahler, 'Ging heut' Morgen übers Feld', close.

upper E♯ is harmonized by the leading-note triad on A♯. This is a richer version of the chromaticism engendered in bars 15–16 but the top note, instead of rising (as E♯ did on the statement of 'schöne welt' in b. 16), falls to generate the falling two-note motive which dominates the song's closing bars.

Example 1.4 Mahler, 'Ich hab' ein glühend Messer', *Lieder eines fahrenden Gesellen*, bb. 68–71.

The technical skill with which relatively simple diatonic and chromatic elements are deployed in these final lines creates semantic ambiguity between the overt, and perhaps overdeterminedly repeated, nay-saying and a persistent, remnant hope suggested by the aspiring, pentatonic rise to G♯ (b. 120). This latter quality, a yes to the question of the beauty of the natural world and also to the lingering prospect of happiness, is also suggested by the song's tonal move from D to a B major of brighter resonance. This occurs within a cycle in which the keys of G minor (song 1), E♭ minor (song 3), and E minor and F minor (song 4) are arrayed around the central key of D and create possible expressive meanings. Berthold Hoeckner considers the second song to express an idyllic episode which is negated by the protagonist and fails to reach closure. The following song, 'Ich hab' ein glühend Messer', sounds what Hoeckner has called a 'negative moment' in the cycle.[55] The recollection of the opening bars of 'Ging heut' Morgen übers Feld' at the poetic evocation of the protagonist's broken dreams (b. 45) is fleeting and quickly dispersed by intense chromaticism. Adorno traced the category of collapse (*Einsturzes*) back to this third song's closing passage. The collapse, the negative fulfilment, itself (Example 1.4, bb. 68ff.) recalls the more ambivalent moment in bars 119–21 of the second song through its rising opening and gradual descent within the context of an elaboration of the unresolved dominant of the final key of the song. The affirmative aspects of Example 1.3 are darkly recalled and catastrophically negated as the music collapses abysmally into apparent disorder.

[55] Berthold Hoeckner, '*Music as a Metaphor of Metaphysics: Tropes of Transcendence in 19th-century Music from Schumann to Mahler*', unpublished PhD, Cornell University (1994), 384–417.

Zygmunt Bauman has described how, after the collapse of the 'divinely ordained world', when order is 'reflected upon' in a self-conscious practice, an intolerance and fear of ambivalence raises its head. An urge to eliminate ambivalence sustains a quest for utopian order but one which merely generates yet more ambivalence and intensifies the horror and abjection felt in the presence of the other, figured as the abnormal, exiled, banished, unassimilated, the stranger or the wanderer.[56] The final song of the *Lieder eines fahrenden Gesellen* opens with a suggestion of the coexistence of expulsion from, and nostalgia for, home: 'Die zwei blauen Augen von meinem Schatz / Die haben mich in die weite Welt geschickt. / Da mußt ich Abschied nehmen vom allerliebsten Platz!' ('The two blue eyes of my beloved / Have sent me into the wide world. / I had to bid farewell to the dearest place of all!') The wandering protagonist is a dejected and rejected homesick nomad. But, as Lydia Goehr has written, on the 'double life' in exile, the ambivalence between adaptation and resistance, inclusion and exclusion, might be experienced as a state of mind which creates critical and potentially artistically productive detachment. Furthermore, home and estrangement need not always be presented as mutually exclusive opposites. The Weill of the Weimar years can be considered an outsider on the inside (he composed 'American' music before he was exiled there).[57] Britten's ambiguous position with regard to English societal 'norms' was hardly resolved on his return from exile in the United States. Henze used the term *'innere Emigration'*.[58] If, on his move to Italy in 1953, Henze was geographically able to distance himself from the dogmatic hegemony he perceived in German post-Second World War musical culture, it also allowed him artistically to reassess and creatively revisit the traditions of his *Heimat*. Mahler's music, with its ambivalent position with regard to that tradition, proved an enormously stimulating example.[59] Henze then felt able to pursue what he called a 'personal path outside the "acceptable"

[56] Zygmunt Bauman, *Modernity and Ambivalence* (Cambridge: Polity Press, 1991), 4, 195. Bauman exemplifies this with the assimilatory pressures on Central European Jews, citing Mahler as one of the 'most perceptive' of those working during the 'intense assimilatory obsessions in central Europe at the beginning of the twentieth century'.

[57] Lydia Goehr, *The Quest for Voice: Music, Politics, and the Limits of Philosophy* (Oxford University Press, 1998), 179–80, 186. On outsiders in Weimar culture, Goehr cites Peter Gay, 'The Outsider as Insider', in D. Fleming and B. Bailyn (eds.), *The Intellectual Migration: Europe and America 1930–1960* (Cambridge, Mass.: MIT Press, 1969), 11–93.

[58] Hans Werner Henze, 'German Music in the 1940s and 1950s', in *Music and Politics: Collected Writings 1953–81*, trans. Peter Labanyi (London: Faber, 1982), 35.

[59] On Mahler as outsider, see, for example, Henry A. Lea, *Gustav Mahler: Man on the Margin* (Bonn: Bouvier, 1985) and K.M. Knittel, *Seeing Mahler: Music and the Language of Anti-Semitism in Fin-de-Siècle Vienna* (Aldershot: Ashgate, 2010).

aesthetic course of the mainstream of self-styled modern music'.[60] The stylistic contradictions, garish colours, allusions to tonal formulae, the old and the banal are all employed to express obsessions with love, death, renewal and redemption at the individual and social level. In the 1960s, Henze cut an ambiguous figure. At times greatly feted by prestigious and venerable musical institutions, at other times allied with radical left-wing politics, Henze's position as an insider (as member of the establishment or counter-establishment) always seemed questionable. In this way there is much that parallels Britten's predicament as pacifist and homosexual outsider who nonetheless sought and gained wide public acceptance. That there was, as Philip Brett puts it, always a 'dark side of [Britten's] feelings as a potential victim of persecution and as an outsider in an established society',[61] could equally be said of Henze.

As is well known, the paradoxical coexistence of inwardness and distance pervades romantic aesthetics.[62] The distant realm might be the remembered past, the glimpsed horizon, the longed-for future, the lost home, the heavenly or promised land. In a 1926 review of Mahler's Ninth Symphony for *Der deutsche Rundfunk*, Weill described the musical evocation of an array of such 'distant lands'. In this symphony, he argued, Mahler

reaches far into our era, anticipating most of what musical development has achieved in recent years. The wondrous interweaving of deeply expressive melodic lines; the unfettering of harmonies, occasionally taken right to the limit; the soloistic, almost chamber music-like treatment of the orchestra that conjures forth heavenly sounds of unimagined beauty; and the completely new form that grows out of the clear shaping of the most profound content – these have all become the principles of contemporary music. The work of great artists reaches a point where they grow beyond themselves, where the premonition of death guides their hand, where the prophetic view of the dying mind encompasses distant lands. The florid beauty of reminiscence, the total calm that goes far beyond even resignation, fills us with an agitation that keeps us in its thrall for days. The slow first and last movements of this symphony breathe the calm of a man who is no longer aware of earthly time, who has already been assimilated by the eternities.[63]

[60] Hans Werner Henze, *Language, Music and Artistic Invention*, trans. Mary Whittall (Aldeburgh: Britten-Pears Library, 1996), 7.

[61] Philip Brett, 'Britten and Grimes', in *Music and Sexuality in Britten: Selected Essays*, ed. George E. Haggerty (Berkeley: University of California Press, 2006), 23.

[62] For a full exploration of the hermeneutic potential, see Berthold Hoeckner, 'Schumann and Romantic Distance', *Journal of the American Musicological Society* 50 (1997), 55–132.

[63] 'Die Neunte dagegen ragt weit hinein in unser Zeitalter, sie nimmt bereits das meiste von dem voraus, was die musikalische Entwicklung in den letzten Jahren erreicht hat. Die wundersame

Weill describes the prophetic character of Mahler's symphony in terms of new technical freedoms – the emancipation of harmony, the move away from the obligations of traditional forms towards formal nominalism driven by the character of specific content. But this aspect coexists with a more metaphysical dimension. There is a twofold focus on beauty: the celestial beauty generated by Mahler's orchestration, and the beauty of remembrance; the sensing, under the sign of death, of remote regions and especially prominently the notion of a restfulness which is not bound by the experience of 'earthly time'. In a perhaps unexpectedly romantic interpretation of Mahler's symphony from Weill, the music's beauty evokes a transcendent realm, one pervaded by reminiscences of things past, but also which possesses a rest beyond quotidian time and space, a state which, as we will see, was a defining characteristic of the romantic symbol. Weill's reading of Mahler's symphony highlights many of the themes explored in some of his own compositions from the mid 1920s and early 1930s. These will form the focus of Chapter 3.

Britten's music sustains a complex, often ambivalent relationship to romanticism and particularly to notions of redemption which relate to the romantic tradition. In *The Rape of Lucretia* and other works, there is an explicit suggestion of Christian salvation, but Britten's relationship with Christianity is far more complex than that of a confirmed believer,[64] and the question of redemption is not one simply to be explored within churchly precincts. It is a question ineluctably tied up with music's metaphysical ambitions and art's wider claims to transcendence. Philip Brett has explored Britten's position within the post-romantic cultural context in which the dualism of the transcendent and worldly is discussed in terms of issues of

Durchflechtung ausdrucksvollster melodischer Linien, die bisweilen bis zur letzten Konsequenz durchgeführte Entfesselung der Harmonien, die solistische, fast kammermusikalische Behandlung des Orchesters, die jenseitige Klänge von nie geahnter Schönheit hervorzaubert, dazu die vollkommen neue, aus eindeutiger Gestaltung tiefster Inhalte erwachsende Formgebung – das alles sind die Grundlagen für die heutige Musik geworden. Das Schaffen grosser Künstler gelangt bis zu einem Punkte, wo sie über sich selbst hinauswachsen, wo Todesahnung ihnen die Hand führt, wo der prophetische Blick des sterbenden Geistes ferne Länder umfasst. Die blühende Schönheit des Rückschauens, die völlige Stille, die selbst die Resignation weit hinter sich lässt, löst in uns eine Erschütterung aus, die uns tagelang in ihrem Banne hält. Die beiden langsamen Ecksätze dieser Sinfonie atmen die Ruhe eines Menschen, der die irdische Zeit nicht mehr kennt, den die Ewigkeiten bereits aufgenommen haben.' Kurt Weill, *Musik und musikalisches Theater: Gesammelte Schriften*, ed. Stephen Hinton and Jürgen Schebera (Mainz: Schott, 2000), 314–15.

[64] See Stephen Arthur Allen, '*Benjamin Britten and Christianity*', unpublished PhD, University of Oxford, 2002; Graham Elliott, *Benjamin Britten: The Spiritual Dimension* (Oxford University Press, 2005).

autonomy and engagement. His thoughts are worth quoting in some length because they are so apposite:

Coded as feminine, art and musical works were placed on a pedestal, giving them almost religious significance to counterpoise the age's increasing industrialization and materialism. Although a modernist reaction occurred against many aspects of Romanticism at the opening of the twentieth century, artists and composers were not willing to forfeit the attention that the autonomous state of art thrust upon them. Style had to change, of course. In place of the mercurial genius, coattails and hair a-flying, like Liszt, or clothed in enigmatic and androgynous satin brocade, like Wagner, appeared the magisterial bank teller as embodied in T.S. Eliot or the wizard-like craftsman image promulgated by Stravinsky. But except in a few exceptional areas, such as theatre, the artistic content of art continued to predominate in the minds of both artists and critics. Interpretation, shying away from disclosing any real or practical meaning in an art-for-art's sake climate, continued to focus on aesthetic effect in spite of, or perhaps in answer to, the evils of the twentieth century ... In this climate, how was the artist, schooled in the autonomy of art, to experience and show the effects of any of the twentieth-century's cataclysmic events without being dismissed as a charlatan or traitor to art?[65]

The response could be to pursue the path to lofty abstraction, the retreat to ivory towers or dreaming spires, or the open engagement of the 'committed' political artist. Brett suggests a third, mediating response, a 'negotiation' that defines Britten's 'canny ability to have the traditional cake of autonomy and at the same time to eat it away'. Britten's comparably ambiguous relation to redemption is reflected in the fact, as Whittall explains, that Britten never escaped the sense of 'profound sadness that any celebration of peace, or love, which he might undertake, had to be tinged with regret, with the acknowledgement that such blissful states were unstable, if not utterly unreal'.[66] In Britten's work, alongside passages of redemptive promise, there are powerful examples of a dark negation or collapse – for example, the scherzo from the *Sinfonia da Requiem* (1939–40), often called a 'dance of death'. As Brett describes in an interpretation of the movement's climax:

[r]ather than being sustained and progressing to a further heroic apotheosis, as it would likely have done in a symphony of the nineteenth century, the music self-destructs through overassertive gestures of a hysterical kind which, becoming self-conscious of their very extremity, seem limply to collapse on to each other, like so

---

[65] Brett, 'Pacifism, Political Action, and Artistic Endeavor', in *Music and Sexuality in Britten*, 173.

[66] Arnold Whittall, 'Britten's Lament: The World of *Owen Wingrave*', *Music Analysis* 19 (2000), 148–66 (at 165).

many hollow men, and to die off in impotence. The gesture, as so much else in this work, owes a good deal to the musical irony of one of Britten's heroes, Gustav Mahler, a composer then hated and reviled in Britain. The young composer fortunately worked his way through this influence towards a unique and unmistakable idiom.[67]

In those last sentences, Brett evokes a concept of influence (it was Britten's 'good fortune' to come out from the 'debt' to Mahler with something unique) which many would now wish to abandon. There are, however, many passages in Britten where complex, ambiguous negotiations within the utopian–dystopian duality and gestures of collapse and their counterpoles, fulfilment or redemption, lend themselves to rich interpretation through deploying Mahler's music as point of comparison (the very end of the *Sinfonia da Requiem* being one such example). Before embarking on this task in Chapter 2, in the final section of this chapter typical, shifting features of the redemptive or transcendent mode in Mahler will be considered. This topical examination is pursued through exploring the dualism between allegory and the romantic symbol, in particular to analyse significant and characteristic cadential gestures.

III: Mahler, allegory and symbol

The distinction between symbol and allegory is a key issue in romantic art. The romantic symbol was proposed as a replete, self-sufficient, sensuous revelation of the super-sensuous and universal. Allegory, by contrast, was considered an artificial, constructed particular. In the late twentieth century, 'new allegorists', inspired principally by Paul de Man, debunked the organic and transcendental romantic symbol as illusory and explored the potential of allegory as a subversive, deconstructive mode. More recent literary theory has developed the potential of modal interplay between symbol and allegory. This notion is far from new. It rekindles aspects of early romantic thought and practice which were very important for Mahler. In Mahler's music the symbol–allegory dualism can be seen as a crucial aspect of his sustained engagement with the question of art and the transcendent. This final part of the chapter will consider examples in which cadences evoke what Robert Hatten has called 'arrival' or 'salvation' dominant six-four harmonies.[68] In their characteristic coincidence of harmonic harbinger of

---

[67] Brett, 'Pacifism, Political Action, and Artistic Endeavor', in *Music and Sexuality in Britten*, 176.

[68] See Robert S. Hatten, *Musical Meaning in Beethoven* (Bloomington: Indiana University Press, 1994) 15, 97; *Interpreting Musical Gestures, Topics and Tropes: Mozart, Beethoven, Schubert*

formal closure with thematic recapitulation and rhetoric of apotheosis, these events are, in romantic terms, redolent of the absolute self-sufficiency and apparently transcendent, most beautiful artistic content which was so often ascribed to music itself. They can be heard as musical particulars which aspire to the condition of a romantic symbol.

For Goethe, the symbol 'represented the Universal, not as a dream or shade, but as a vivid and instantaneous revelation of the inscrutable'.[69] The symbol was the point of contact between a finite particular and the infinitely meaningful whole. Goethe relegated allegory as transitive, functional, utilitarian, conventional and arbitrary. The symbol, by contrast, was promoted as intransitive, intuitive, laconic and condensed. In allegory, the poet is seeking access to the general *through* the particular. In symbol, it is *in* the particular.[70] Symbol and allegory are distinguished by both their mode of evocation and their content. Allegory merely points to something other than itself; symbols really *are* what they represent. Nicholas Halmi has revealed how the romantic symbol was generated through critical attitudes of historical specificity. He begins by asking whether the idea of the symbol was constructed to 'compensate' for allegory's apparent loss of 'numinosity' and founded upon the desire to overcome fragmentations, disenchantments and dualisms. Halmi writes:

The theorization of the symbol in the Romantic period may be understood as an attempt ... to foster a sense of harmony of the human mind with nature, of the unity of seemingly disparate intellectual disciplines, and of the compatibility of individual freedom with a cohesive social structure – all for the sake of reducing anxiety about the place of the individual in bourgeois society ... and about the increasing dominance of mechanistic science.

In short, the romantic symbol was a momentary 're-enchantment of the world'.[71] The ideal status of the romantic symbol reflects the desire for deep spiritual content in art, one to rival and exceed the content of both redemptive religion and totalizing philosophical systems. In such thinking lies the essence of the notion of 'Great' art, produced by the spirit of genius and raised as a symbolic expression of a higher, absolute, transcendent ideal.

(Bloomington: Indiana University Press, 2004), 24–9. Klein has explored later nineteenth-century transformations of Hatten's notions – for example, a 'tragic' six-four in the pastoral topic which he interprets as a critique of the hopes for a return to the pastoral idyll in Chopin's Fourth Ballade (b. 195); Klein hears the climactic C major six-four in Liszt's Piano Sonata (bb. 205ff.) as an anticipation of the breakthrough event as postulated in Adorno's famous reading of Mahler's First Symphony: *Intertextuality*, 66, 68.

[69] Goethe, *Maxims and Reflections* [1827], trans. Bailey Saunders (New York: Macmillan 1906), no. 202, p. 102.

[70] *Ibid.*, no. 435, p. 159.

[71] Nicholas Halmi, *The Genealogy of the Romantic Symbol* (Oxford University Press, 2007), 7, 25.

Thus, the 'idealist aesthetic contemplation of the artwork demanded that the imagination mediated between the senses and the spirit', in a 'reverent contemplation', to enter a redemptive or transcendent sphere in which the phenomenal and noumenal are unified in a realization of the beautiful and Absolute.[72]

A complication soon emerges in romantic aesthetics, however, for previous conceptions of wholeness are no longer considered available or 'true'. Schlegel highlighted the contrast between Classical 'natural' harmony and the modern consciousness of internal discord in which the Classical ideal is impossible, and posed the importance of the struggle to unite two worlds. Consequently, if the romantic artwork is to absorb the classic–modern opposition, 'a whole comes to figure as an element within itself'.[73] An image of perfect unity must be present, or perhaps alluded to or striven for, within an otherwise only partially complete work. In counterpoint, the allegorical impulse was ambivalently sustained even during the romantic espousal of the symbol. For Theresa M. Kelley, this dramatizes Romanticism's internal conflicts. The allegorical may mimic, ironize, dismantle or parody the romantic's voices of power, including the symbolic. In the romantic artwork, therefore, symbol and allegory can typically coexist in a subtle, dynamic relationship, in a kind of flux or floating between the two modes.[74]

Thomas Nelson's recent consideration of the 'fantasy of Absolute Music' aimed at revealing the allegorical nature of the romantic symbol. Nelson's thesis, which includes examples from Mahler, draws heavily on the *Frühromantik* metaphor of *Schweben*, a transcendent floating above a dialectical opposition, a provisional synthesis in an allegorical pastoral fantasy, a 'paradoxical simultaneity of *Sehnsucht* and *Ruhe*'. In this state

---

[72] Mark Evan Bonds, 'Idealism and the Aesthetics of Instrumental Music at the Turn of the Nineteenth Century', *Journal of the American Musicological Society* 50 (1997), 387–420.

[73] See Tzvetan Todorov, *Theories of the Symbol* [1977], trans. Catherine Porter (Oxford: Basil Blackwell, 1982), 189.

[74] Theresa M. Kelley, *Reinventing Allegory* (Cambridge University Press, 1997). Gunnar Berefelt suggested something similar in his essay 'On Symbol and Allegory', *The Journal of Aesthetics and Art Criticism* 28 (1969), 201–12. This pre-dates (just) the heyday of the neo-allegorists' dismantling of the romantic symbol, launched by Paul de Man's essay of the same year, 'The Rhetoric of Temporality'. Allegory became a hot critical topic in the 1970s and 1980s. In a powerful review of this scene from the early 1980s, Joel D. Black identifies the romantic's 'blindness to the historicity of symbolic forms'. But Black's review already notes the potential for rehabilitating the symbol after the highpoint of allegorical deconstruction, with the allegorical and the symbolic recognized as two potentially coexisting constructed realities that can interact in the text of the artwork: 'Allegory Unveiled', *Poetics Today* 4 (1983) 109–26; Review of Morton W. Bloomfield (ed.), *Allegory, Myth, and Symbol* (Cambridge, Mass.: Harvard University Press, 1981) and Stephen J. Greenblatt (ed.), *Allegory and Representation* (Baltimore: Johns Hopkins University Press, 1981).

of *Schweben*, Nelson argues, 'one always remains within the gravitational pull of the provisional and temporal, and this keeps one's transcendence grounded in the reality to which one must inevitably submit'. This evokes a 'fleeting pastoral moment', one which 'resonates with the elegiac idyll of a lost plenitude'. Nelson contrasts this ambiguity with how later 'sentimental' Romantics, 'infected by passive melancholy', were seduced by the 'opportunity to enter the timeless refuge of a structurally opposed alternative world of symbolic certainties', a religion of art of absolute value and 'ascetic purity'. Their art was in effect an 'escapism' that avoids acknowledging the structurality and fantasy of its symbolic representations. Wagner, characteristically of this species of later romanticism, embraced a transcendental organicism, in which 'contingent allegorical aspects' are 'to be crystallized into the Symbolic identity of universal and particular'. The Wagnerian *Gesamtkunstwerk* and the formalist purity of absolute music became two interlocking and self-generating fantasies of the symbolic status of music. Nietzsche's reaction to this late romanticism was crucial. He returned to rhetoric closer to that of the early Romantics, in imaginative fantasies whose allegorical character, interruptions, fragmentations and deconstructions revealed organic and symbolic unity as an illusion sterile by comparison with the ambiguous fluctuations of *Schweben*. In the 1886 preface to *The Birth of Tragedy*, written long after the earlier idolization of Wagner which informs the book itself had become more profoundly ambivalent, Nietzsche 'rejects the pessimistic structure of other-worldly metaphysics that exacerbate the hostility to real life by giving metaphysical comfort in the pastoral illusion of estrangement's reconciliation, be it in a Christian Heaven under the lawful hierarchy of God the Father, or romantically, within Apollo's "countless illusions of the beauty of mere appearance"'.[75]

As we have seen, in *The Origin of German Tragic Drama* (which includes a critique of Nietzsche's *Birth of Tragedy* somewhat after Nietzsche's own self-critique) Benjamin praised the *Trauerspiel* for the way in which its fractured character destroys or eschews the illusory pretensions of beautiful totality characteristic of works of art adhering to Classical aesthetics of unity. Benjamin identified two different temporalities. The symbol is found in the fulfilled mystical instant (*Nu*); allegory is presented in unfulfilled, potentially endless progression. For the symbolic artwork, the relation to redemption is immediate; for the allegorical work

---

[75] Thomas Nelson, '*The Fantasy of Absolute Music*', unpublished PhD, University of Minnesota (1998), 664, 690–1, 716.

of the post-paradisical age, it is 'infinitely removed'.[76] This accounts for the melancholic temperament that characterizes the allegorical world. Benjamin's *Trauerspiel* is a seductive model for interpreting Mahler, but would be a one-sided one, for in Mahler remnants of a symbolic art, the moments suggestive of repleteness and fulfilment, coexist with allegorical melancholy and fragmentation. In an apparently post-symbolic world, Mahler's music can be heard to propose glimpses of the redemptive and absolute, aspirations to the momentary recuperation of the romantic symbol coexisting with an allegorical sound world. Mahler's music may fracture the ideology of autonomy, the romantic idea of absolute music is often opposed by an 'empirical' rather than a 'spiritual' tone,[77] but it can also be heard to reveal that the redemptive pretensions of the symbolic are still of timely resonance, even after Nietzsche's condemnation of Wagner's decadent preoccupation with redemption in *The Case of Wagner* (1888). This redemptive aspiration embraced the sustained urge towards achieving, or imagining, some form of 'higher' unity. Indeed, as Karen Painter points out, though the '*fin-de-siècle* symphony was deeply resistant to forming an image of the whole' the 'tenet of unity was … too ingrained to be discarded outright'. Although stretched to breaking point, 'the principle of unity, if anything, bore more philosophical weight than before'. This might typically be manifest, for example, in the sustained if imperilled search for a unity of inner and outer, of sensuous materiality and the spiritual, of the perception of individual stimuli and some kind of metaphysical otherworld of stable symbolic relationships. It can be especially felt in the striving for fulfilment in an ultimate closure, in the investment in the mystique of the redemptive finale, and attempts at ever-greater processes of intensification (*Steigerung*), Goethe's term for striving towards the higher synthesis of polar opposites, in the aspiration to express the inexpressible, to point towards ultimate cohesion.[78]

The work of the strict allegorists amongst recent Mahler commentators, who include Nelson and Raymond Monelle (who wrote that music is not the 'prototypical Symbol but a particularly potent kind of allegory'[79])

---

[76] Benjamin, *The Origin of German Tragic Drama*, 165, 183; Wolin, *Walter Benjamin*, 68.

[77] See John Williamson's discussion of Geck, *Von Beethoven bis Mahler*, and Hans Heinrich Eggebrecht, *Die Musik Gustav Mahlers* (Munich: Piper, 1982) in 'New Research Paths in Criticism, Analysis and Interpretation', in Jeremy Barham (ed.) *The Cambridge Companion* to Mahler, 263–6.

[78] Karen Painter, *Symphonic Aspirations: German Music and Politics 1900–45* (Cambridge, Mass.: Harvard University Press, 2007), 65–71.

[79] Raymond Monelle, *The Sense of Music: Semiotic Essays* (Princeton University Press, 2000), 197. See the sections, 'Mahler and Gustav' and 'Allegory and Deconstruction', 170–226.

offers highly valuable insights, but the complexity of 'tone', the often conflicting array of 'voices' (a widely pursued metaphor in recent Mahler studies) includes the sound of the apparently unspeakable. Monelle finds Mahler's talk of romantic apocalypse and apotheosis unhelpful. But this musical voice should not be silenced. A symbolic mode is at play in Mahler's music as part of its sustained if often ambivalent engagement with romantic notions of transcendence, unity and redemption. The examples which follow demonstrate this quality through discussion of a special symbolic variant of the 'salvation' six-four with pentatonic added sixth.[80]

The first part of Mahler's setting of the *Wunderhorn* text, 'Urlicht', the fourth movement of the Second Symphony, expresses longing for the as yet unattained higher realm: the second fulfilment, revelation, redemption.[81] A key expressive phrase in the first part is the C–B♭–A♭–F–E♭ melodic incipit to the poetic line 'Je lieber möcht' ich im Himmel sein' (Yes I'd rather be in Heaven) (bb. 22–4). It presents a falling pentatonic melodic cell over the dominant which is not immediately resolved (Example 1.5). This poetic line is then repeated as the rising cadential melody from the opening of the movement returns over a dominant six-four/five-three (bb. 27ff.). But resolution is again interrupted and is only achieved, by the orchestra alone, at the third attempt (bars 32–4). After the denunciation from the angel in the next section, this pentatonic cadential figure returns at the line 'wird mir ein lichtchen geben' (bb. 66–8; Example 1.6) – the light that will show this rejected subject the way to heaven. Again, the anticipated

[80] The symbol–allegory dualism informs essays on Weber, Schumann and Wagner (now there's an 'influential' triumvirate for Mahler) by John Daverio and Michael Spitzer. In Spitzer's reading of the Norns scene in the Prologue to *Götterdämmerung*, the symbolic is identified with closed and 'natural' form, allegory with openness and artifice; *Metaphor and Musical Thought* (Chicago University Press, 2004), 315–19. In the music of Schumann, to whom Daverio attributes 'a highly developed allegorical intuition', the 'false appearance of totality is extinguished'; in Daverio's readings the fragments and structural fissures in Schumann's cycles of miniatures and the larger-scale works reveal symbolic unity to be illusory or unachievable. In *Euryanthe*, Daverio writes that 'it is arguable that Weber, in addition to recognising music's symbolic potential, likewise imbued his work with a markedly allegorical dimension'. Allegory, the 'corrective to the utopian doctrine of the symbol' is raised by the 'tears and ruptures' in the operatic signification; *Nineteenth-Century Music and the German Romantic Ideology* (New York: Schirmer, 1993), 91–9. Berthold Hoeckner's reading of Mahler's setting of Rückert's 'Nun seh' ich wohl, warum so dunkle Flammen', the second of the *Kindertotenlieder*, offers the closest precursor to my own readings of Mahler which follow, in particular because of his recourse to Robert Hatten's notions of 'arrival' and 'salvation' six-four harmonies; *Programming the Absolute*; *Nineteenth-Century German Music and the Hermeneutics of the Moment* (Princeton University Press, 2002), 262–4.

[81] For a fascinating reading of the ideas of redemption/scepticism/rejection in this setting, see Martha C. Nussbaum, *Upheavals of Thought: The Intelligence of Emotions* (Cambridge University Press, 2001), 621–31.

Example 1.5 Mahler, 'Urlicht', Symphony no. 2, bb. 17–35.

resolution is interrupted, now chromatically to C♭ rather than C, in an
enharmonic echo of the B major/minor of the angel's preceding music. The
final dominant is reached (on 'ewig', b. 71) as the original cadential rising
figure returns, once more over a dominant six-four/five-three. The voice
now joins in the final resolution and its climactic F–E♭ ('Leben!') over
the closing tonic is continued in the upper part of the orchestra to form
F–E♭–B♭–A♭, under which an instrumental 'tenor' line rises from B♭ to C
to generate a passing statement of the pentatonic collection. The rising
tenor line then continues through the leading-note to tonic and the A♭

Example 1.6 Mahler, 'Urlicht', bb. 66–close.

resolves to G suggesting a 'hymnic' 4–3 suspension. The key elements here are the pentatonic association with closural dominant six-four/five-three gestures as signs of the redemptive which are questioned, denied but ultimately fulfilled in the final bars, affirming (at least in this moment) the legitimacy of the search for, and belief in, the transcendentally symbolic.

The romantic qualities of 'Urlicht' bear close comparison with Mahler's setting of Rückert's 'Liebst du um Schönheit' (Example 1.7, in the E♭ version for piano and voice).

Example 1.7 Mahler, 'Liebst du um Schönheit' (Rückert).

Liebst du um Schönheit,
O nicht mich liebe!
Liebe die Sonne,
Sie trägt ein gold'nes Haar!

Liebst du um Jugend,
O nicht mich liebe!
Liebe den Frühling,
Der jung ist jedes Jahr!

Example 1.7 (cont.)

Liebst du um Schätze,
O nicht mich liebe!
Liebe die Meerfrau,
Sie hat viel Perlen Klar!

Liebst du um Liebe,
O ja mich liebe!
Liebe mich immer,
Dich lieb' ich immerdar!

If you love for beauty,
Oh do not love me!
Love the sun,
For he has golden hair.

If you love for youth,
Oh do not love me!
Love the spring,
Which is young every year!

If you love for riches,
Oh do not love me!
Love a mermaid,
For she has many fine pearls!

If you love for love,
Oh yes love me!
Love me for ever,
I'll love you evermore!

The instrumental opening (bb. 1–3) moves through diatonic, pentatonic, chromatic and back to diatonic material. It establishes the importance of C–Bb at its midpoint, after which the chromatic counterpoint introduces Bb–A–Ab in the descant, Eb–Eb–F in the 'alto', and C–C#–D in the 'tenor' line. The second statement of this material (bb. 7ff.), contrapuntally and chromatically enriched, presages the first structural chromatic move, the shift to the tonic minor (eb) which introduces new chromatic elements, G–Gb and Cb–Bb, both of which are adumbrated, enharmonically, by the passing chromaticisms of bar 7. A third varied statement of the opening material leads towards the close of the first half of the song (bb. 13–14). The chromatics first heard in bar 2 are now reharmonized as decorations of the dominant of the dominant to facilitate the lead back to the tonic major. The two bars of piano material which link the two halves of the song (bb. 15–16) extend the chromatic material of the opening gesture (b. 2). (Note the motivating importance of C–C# in the tenor, B–A–Ab in the descant and Eb–Eb in the alto, all over a dominant pedal. The other chromatic pitches, Bb and F#, enharmonically recall the move to the tonic minor in bars 9–10.)

The music of the second half of the song is a reworking of the first. When the opening gesture first returns (bb. 22–3; equivalent to that in bars 7–8) it signals the lead into the final, closing, 'symbolic' paragraph.[82] The tenor D♭–C in bar 24 reverses and harmonically reinterprets the C–C♯ of bar 2 to suggest the traditional closing gesture of a harmonic move to the subdominant. This is deflected into a move towards V/V, driven in bars 25–7 by the tenor E♮–F, a reinterpretation of the chromatic content of the alto in bars 2–3. Over the final structural dominant (b. 28) the C–B♭ and harmony first heard on the key poetic word 'beauty' (b. 4) returns. In the climactic, clinching gesture, over a dominant six-four (bb. 29–31) the upper instrumental line picks up the C–B♭ and extends it into a falling pentatonic gesture C–B♭–G–E♭, generating the redemptive six-four with 'natural' added sixth. The voice ends tantalizingly on the added sixth. The short instrumental coda then offers the unity of diatonic, chromatic and pentatonic material for which the song has seemed to yearn since its opening gesture. As indicated by the analytical annotation (the beamed pitches in Example 1.7), the upper line is a chromatic embellishment of the C–B♭–G–E♭ falling pentatonic collection. This is superimposed over, or better, unified with, the chromatic inner motions that had been developing throughout the song from their initial 'genesis' in the song's opening gesture. The effect is one of a final synthesis of diatonic, pentatonic and chromatic over a clinching dominant pedal. The last bar echoes the parallel motion in thirds of C–B♭, A♭–G that was first heard on the word 'Schönheit', now as the resolution of a double suspension with quasi-religious resonance. These bars suggest the musical equivalent of the poetic suggestion of moving from the love of surface to ideal beauty, from sensuous particular to supersensuous, ideal wholeness, the primary characteristics assigned to the romantic symbol.

As Camilla Bork has noted, Rückert's 'Ich bin der Welt abhanden gekommen' is a text about artistic creation. The withdrawal from the world expressed in the last stanza is a move towards the state of inward rest in which love and art appear as one:

Ich bin gestorben dem Weltgetümmel
Und ruh' in einem stillen Gebiet.
Ich leb' allein in meinem Himmel,
In meinem Lieben, in meinem Lied.

---

[82] Stephen Hefling has described Mahler's setting of the final stanza as 'music of such simple transcendent beauty', a 'quiet apotheosis of the idealistic love he had always hoped for and wanted to believe in'. 'The Rückert Lieder', in Donald Mitchell and Andrew Nicholson (eds.), *The Mahler Companion* (Oxford University Press, 2002), 364.

I am dead to the world's bustle
And I rest in a tranquil realm.
I live alone in my heaven,
In my love, in my song.

The last three vocal statements are set over a pentatonically and chromatically inflected dominant six-four/five-three cadence so stretched as to almost approach stasis despite the harmony's progressive implications (Example 1.8). In the instrumental coda, Bork comments, the 'sonic character as well as the performance instruction "transfigured" suggests one of those post-Wagnerian transfiguration endings that possess an aesthetic, quasi-religious significance'. In this way Mahler's music offers 'the expression of a reflective shift toward the elevated sphere of art'.[83] The relationship of 'Ich bin der Welt abhanden gekommen' to the Adagietto of the Fifth Symphony is well-trodden ground, but considering them in the context of the romantic symbol allows a notable contrast to emerge. The final cadence of the Adagietto movement achieves an effect similarly suggestive of an idealized love of symbolic quality (both suggest a kind of state of ecstasy, if in the symphony it is certainly more passionately yearning than in the more restful ending of the Rückert setting[84]) which only the sensuous sounds of music can express (the Adagietto has the character of a song without words). The D–D♭ chromatic inflection in the details of the Adagietto's cadence is a microcosm of the tonal move of the whole symphony from C♯ minor to D major. The movement is positioned within the symphony as a symbolic riposte, perhaps, to the *Trauerspiel* of the preceding movements and as portal to the finale, in which the climactic, 'breakthrough' chorale of the second movement is often heard as somehow more successfully assimilated 'within' the process of the work. As we have noted, in Samuels's reading the negative state of Part 1 is transformed in the finale, with the Adagietto 'which constitutes its extended introduction acting as, or at least symbolizing, the "external" agency effecting this change'.[85] If this is so, then there is contrast with the inward move expressed in 'Ich bin der Welt abhanden gekommen'; the symbol promised by the Adagietto is proposed as something of a gift, not the product of a process of internalization.

More complex manifestation of the potentially external quality of the symbolic, redemptive gesture is found in the closing section of the slow

[83] Camilla Bork, 'Musical Lyricism as Self-Exploration: Reflections on Mahler's "Ich bin der Welt abhanden gekommen"', trans. Irene Zedlacher, in Painter (ed.), *Mahler and His World*, 159–72.
[84] Hefling, 'The Rückert Lieder', 358–9.
[85] Samuels, 'Narrative Form and Mahler's Musical Thinking', 237–54.

Example 1.8 Mahler, 'Ich bin der Welt abhanden gekommen' (Rückert), close.

movement of the Fourth Symphony. After the *Luftpause* and the breakthrough into E major there is melodic pentatonic descent G♯–F♯–E–C♯–B
in the upper register (bb. 320–5) comparable with the melodic descents in the
preceding examples. After this powerful, striking and arresting event in E, the
move back to the movement's tonic G is achieved via C, a harmony expanded
with pentatonic rising figures (bb. 332–7, Example 1.9). Over the tonic G
from bar 340 the descending pentatonic figure is presented in a
new, expanded form (F♯–E–D–B–A–G–E–D–B–A–G in the second
violins). The overall bass progression from bar 326 (fig. 13) to the end
expands the closing function of E–D (6–5) bass motives (established from

Example 1.9 Mahler, Symphony no. 4, third movement, bb. 326–close.

Example 1.9 (cont.)

the close of the opening section, bars 51–5) into an E–C–D–G motion. It is thus motivically 'explainable', and tonally too, with C functioning as an extension of the pre-dominant harmonic field. But the music over the bass C sounds like an expression of an alternative, ideal world, one whose musical materials are closely related to the opening of 'Ich bin der Welt abhanden gekommen', but here sounding as music from without, as a gift comparable with the Adagietto of the Fifth, rather than expressing an inward move of immanent provenance. The powers of 'organic' unity through bass motivic expansion and tonal progression for a moment seem close to breaking point. The music approaches the condition of a vivid if restful breaking through of the symbolic, in the Goethean sense of a momentary instance of revelation. The result is that the final section of the movement has two greatly contrasting, though related, breakthrough moments prior to the final cadence: the first (in E) is sublimely arresting; the second (in C) beautifully uplifting.

In the setting of Rückert's 'Um Mitternacht', the aspiration towards the redemptive state of the romantic symbol is glimpsed but then so deeply darkened by a negative, melancholic turn that the concluding resolution and affirmation is evoked in rhetoric that can suggest an overblown or bombastic tone. The redemptive symbol is evoked by the motive at the aspiration of the soul to heaven: 'Um Mitternacht hab' ich gedacht hinaus in dunkle Schranken' ('At midnight I sent my thoughts far to the bounds of dark space') (Example 1.10, bb. 24–5).[86] At the poetic confirmation of frustrated yearning ('no vision of light brought me hope'), the orchestra chromatically elaborates this motive (bb. 30–1) to create a melodic shape which, when picked up in a further version by the voice (end of bar 32 into bar 33, now with increasing whole-tone character) acts as a transition to the return of the falling scalic motive from the song's introduction. The pentatonic motive evocative of the yearned-for symbolic realm has been transformed, through chromatic then whole-tone versions, into the elegiac falling minor scale. The heavenly glimpse is also a transformation of the 'grell' motive which itself had plunged into the first chromatic element of the song (bb. 17–18 – the whole-tone fall articulated as dotted minim–crotchet is common, and the arpeggio of bar 25 effectively fills in the precipitous fall of the 'grell' motive). The pentatonic transformation alludes to the aspired peace or transfiguration, with the subsequent chromatic and whole-tone negation back to minor tonality at this point denying the

---

[86] Zoltan Roman's promisingly titled essay 'Allegory, Symbolism, and Personification in Selected "Night Songs" by Liszt, Mahler, and Strauss', which includes a discussion of Mahler's setting of 'Um Mitternacht', disappointingly offers no discussion of the allegorical or symbolic aspects of its examples. *Studia Musicologica Academiae Scientiarum Hungaricae* 41 (2000), 407–39.

Example 1.10 Mahler, 'Um Mitternacht' (Rückert), bb. 14–37.

'ascent' to symbolic redemption. The apparently redemptive ending in the song's final transformations in the diatonic major and the final vocal descent from G♯ is often heard as problematic in tone, whether ironic, hyperbolic or even bellicose.[87] The 'authenticity' of the redemptive ending

---

[87] For discussion of this ambiguous, to some ears troubling, ending, see Henri-Louis de La Grange, *Gustav Mahler Vol. 2 Vienna: The Years of Challenge (1897–1904)* (Oxford University Press, 1995), 794–5, who hears it as 'obviously a "Durchbruch"', and Hefling, 'The Rückert Lieder', 352–3.

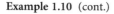

Example 1.10 (cont.)

seems to be in some doubt because of the complex, ambiguous shifts between aspiration towards affirmation and desperation generated by negation in the song's middle section.

The scream of painful awakening in 'Um Mitternacht' directly recalls a famous passage in Wagner's 1870 'Beethoven' essay, which was especially important for Mahler.[88] In this essay, Wagner writes of a symbolic inner dream world, 'through which we are directly allied with the whole of Nature, and thus brought into a relation with the Essence of things that eludes the forms of outer knowledge, Time and Space'. At the moment of waking we scream, the 'anguished will' first made manifest in the outer world as sound. Wagner argues that music arises from this scream and the various 'diminutions of its vehemence, down to the gentler cry of longing'. But though the profound dream contents of deep sleep 'can only be conveyed to the waking consciousness through translation into the language of a second, an allegorical dream which immediately precedes our wakening ... the *musician* is controlled, as it were, by an urgent impulse to impart the vision of his inmost dream'. This is possible because harmony, 'belonging to neither Space nor Time, remains the most inalienable element of Music'. Through

---

[88] See Stephen McClatchie, 'Mahler's Wagner', in Erich Wolfgang and Morten Solvik (eds.), *Mahler im Kontext/Contextualizing Mahler* (Vienna: Böhlau Verlag, 2011), 407–16.

Example 1.11 Mahler, Symphony no. 6, Andante, bb. 1–10.

the rhythmic organization of harmony through time, the 'musician reaches forth a plastic hand, so to speak, to strike a compact with the world of semblances' in a manner similar to the way that the allegorical dream establishes the link between symbolic and waking (temporal, spatial) worlds. The systematizing of rhythmic structure in periodicity moves music closer still to the characteristic of plastic forms, but it is possible, Wagner argues, to pierce these beautiful forms of periodic rhythmic structure and through these moments of rupture reveal music's true, sublime, symbolic essence.[89] All this may seem irredeemably flowery, metaphorical and speculative. But there are remarkable parallels with the opening theme of the Andante of Mahler's Sixth Symphony (Example 1.11). Its initial quasi-lullaby character and periodic symmetry is disturbed by what Warren Darcy calls the 'anguish' chord (b. 7)[90] which leads to motives suggestive of grief (b. 8). This dissonant chord can be heard as the screaming intrusion of the real into the dream-world of beautiful form. Grief motives and chromatic distortions follow instead of the perfectly possible 'salvation' dominant six-four (the anguish chord could potentially move to a second inversion E♭ triad through strong semitonal counterpoint). The codetta to the theme offers restful figures and the closing bars of the movement include pastoral-idyllic echoes of the pentatonic, but they are passing comforts. Despite its intimate, romantic and lyrical tone, the anguished,

---

[89] Richard Wagner, *Beethoven*, trans. William Ashton Ellis (London: Dodo Press, n.d.), 7, 11, 13.

[90] Darcy, 'Rotational Form, Teleological Genesis, and Fantasy-Projection', 49–74.

'symbolic' failure of the opening theme foreshadows the Sixth Symphony's dark, anti-redemptive finale.

Perhaps of all Mahler's symphonies it is the affirmatively redemptive Eighth which has generated the most questioning and negative critical reaction (famously, of course from Adorno). Henry-Louis de La Grange commented that 'there is indeed every reason to wonder how and why a composer born in an age of scepticism, whose work is filled with anxiety and ambiguity, should in the Eighth have needed so loudly to proclaim his faith'. But La Grange insists that the Eighth is far from untypical of Mahler, for 'there was always in Mahler an imperious sense of transcendence' and the symphony confirms the importance of 'Mahler's obstinate, categorical rejection of contemporary materialism and rationalism'.[91] That said, as John Williamson has noted, 'it is difficult not to be aware of the consummate but shameless materialism with which Mahler marshals his huge forces'.[92] The famous title 'Symphony of a Thousand', coined by the Munich agent Emil Gutmann, is no exaggeration: 858 singers and 171 instrumentalists took part in the premiere in Munich on 12 September 1910.[93] As La Grange summarizes, the second part of the symphony 'celebrates repose', yet the triumph of the work is also dependent upon 'effort'.[94] Goethe wrote in 1827: 'I should not know what to do with eternal beatitude unless it also presented me with tasks to carry out and difficulties to overcome ... Let us continue to work.' Mahler stated that 'for the right labourer it is always granted to collect an imposing little heap!'[95] In the Eighth Symphony (some little heap!), massive material forces and sheer performative effort can be closely related to Mahler's interpretation of Goethe's Eros as the generative force of both the creative spirit and the inexhaustible artistic labour. Gendered notions of work driven by longing (*Sehnsucht*) and the blessing found in rest (*Ruhe*) underpin a central collection of oppositions: physical material versus metaphysics, construction versus spontaneity, and the romantic symbol versus the work of allegory. These oppositions allow an interpretative reconsideration of the

[91] Henry-Louis de La Grange, 'The Eighth: Exception or Crowning Achievement?', in Jos van Leeuwen (ed.), *A 'Mass' for the Masses: Proceedings of the Mahler VIII Symposium, Amsterdam 1988* (Rijswisk: University of Rotterdam Press, 1992), 131.

[92] John Williamson, 'The Eighth Symphony', in Mitchell and Nicholson (eds.), *The Mahler Companion*, 418.

[93] Constantin Floros, *Gustav Mahler: The Symphonies*, trans. Vernon Wicker (Aldershot: Scolar Press, 1995), 213.

[94] La Grange, 'The Eighth: Exception or Crowning Achievement?' 131–44.

[95] *Erinnerungen von Natalie Bauer Lechner*, 33; this sentence is missing from the English translation. See McClatchie, 'Mahler's Wagner', 415.

relationship of the symphony's two parts. As Floros states, the 'spiritual unity of the two parts' includes in part the contrast between manly struggle and womanly rest, the contrast between appearance and the imperishable which can only inadequately be represented in appearance, and 'the idea of redemption "from the body of earthly inadequacy"'.[96]

Siegfried Lipiner's *On the Elements of a Renewal of Religious Ideas in the Present* (1878) was an important text for Mahler.[97] Lipiner rejected Nietzsche's anti-metaphysical turn. Through comparisons with and allusions to Goethe's *Faust*, he argued for the inadequacy of the material and that everything hints and strives towards the metaphysical. Symbol and strength both play important roles. Lipiner proclaimed 'Art' to be a '*symbolic* abbreviation of life', achieved in the most enlightened moments. But heroic strength is also required: 'Only a weakling endures in skepticism', he writes. He concludes with a call to action: 'reborn ourselves' we must 'vigorously engage our hands and help build the building of a new life'.[98] Wagner read Lipiner's essay and it surely informed and stimulated his own 'Religion and Art' (1880). Wagner argued that religion had become 'artificial' because of the continuous addition of 'allegorical accessories which hitherto have overlaid the noblest kernel of Religion'. These allegories are proclaimed as matter of fact; Art redeems religion by eschewing the 'alleged reality of the symbol', fulfilling 'her' role 'when, by an ideal presentment of the allegorical figure, she led to the apprehension of its inner kernel, the truth ineffably divine'. Wagner is advocating the move from phenomenal to noumenal, from the material, constructive effort of allegorical artifice to the revelatory, symbolic effect of Art. He makes the familiar Schopenhauerian claim of the supreme quality of music: 'of painting's most perfect forms we can say "That signifies"; But Music, completely removed from the world of appearances says "That is".' In short, if we recall Goethe's definitions, Wagner considered the plastic arts to be merely allegorical, music to be symbolic. Furthermore, the 'simplest and most touching' symbol reveals the

[96] Floros, *Gustav Mahler*, 216–18. Floros is quoting Mahler's letter to Alma of June 1909 (see note 98).

[97] See Stephen Hefling, 'Siegfried Lipiner's *On the Elements of a Renewal of Religious Ideas in the Present*', in Wolfgang and Solvik (eds.), *Mahler im Context*, 91–114. La Grange does not rate Lipiner highly: 'a strange, mystical and spiritualist, a "*raté*" genius, to whom Mahler remained attached all his life, and for whom he had a quite unjustified admiration'. *Mahler: Volume 1* (London: Gollancz, 1976), 68–9.

[98] Siegfried Lipiner, 'Über die Elemente einer Erneuerung religiöser Ideen in der Gegenwart / On the Elements of a Renewal of Religious Ideas in the Present', trans. Hefling, in Wolfgang and Solvik (eds.), *Mahler im Context*, 133, 147, 151.

knowledge of the 'Need of Redemption'.[99] This was explicitly stated in the 'Beethoven' essay when Wagner wrote, quoting lines from the final part of Goethe's *Faust*: 'Alles Vergängliche ist nur ein Gleichniss' (which can be translated as 'All that is transitory is but an allegory') 'we will interpret as the spirit of Plastic art', whilst 'Das ewig Weibliche zieht uns dahin' ('The Eternal Feminine beckons us there') 'we will read as the spirit of Music, which mounted from the poet's deepest consciousness, and, soaring over him, led his footsteps on the pathway to redemption'.[100]

Lipiner's 1894 dissertation on Goethe's *Faust*, now lost, was probably also important for Mahler, for it seems clear from existing secondary sources that it discussed a Schopenhauerian distinction between what is representable and the enigmatic workings of the will, and the conflict between materialism and idealism. Mahler's musical interpretation of Goethe's Eros as the driving force of artistic labour and the creative spirit reinforces overtly gendered imagery – masculine work, feminine intuition, manifest in yearning and peace (*Sehnsucht* and *Ruhe*) respectively. Goethe's lines 'He who always keeps on striving / Him we can redeem' are vitally important, but Goethe's text also highlights that this is not the only condition required for Faust's redemption, he also needs 'love' which is given 'from above'. The famous final stanza may state 'Alles Vergängliche ist nur ein Gleichnis' but Lipiner exhorts that 'we will joyfully sacrifice the transitory, for ours is the immortal'.[101] What remains is that which cannot be fully grasped, the symbolic, the *in*transitive, Goethe's figurative embodiment of which is 'Das Ewig-Weibliche', whom Mahler called that which is 'resting' (in that sense endless and motionless, lying outside time and space), the unattainable but always desired goal of man's striving.

An important letter to Alma of June 1909 reveals Mahler's understanding of Goethe's *Faust* as pertaining to the material and metaphysical, the artifice of hard work and spontaneous creation. He described Goethe's final stanza as 'the peak of that vast pyramid which constitutes the work as a whole and which expounds a world of characters, situations and developments'. The next part of Mahler's letter is worth quoting more fully:

---

[99] Richard Wagner, *Religion and Art*, trans. William Ashton Ellis (Lincoln: University of Nebraska Press, 1994), 213, 224, 249.

[100] Wagner, *Beethoven*, 56. On the importance of Wagner for Mahler, and for the Eighth in particular, see Stephen McClatchie, 'The Wagnerian Roots of Mahler's Eighth Symphony', in Elisabeth Kappel (ed.), *The Total Work of Art: Mahler's Eighth Symphony in Context* (Vienna: Universal Edition, 2011), 152–68, though McClatchie does not explore the symbol–allegory connections.

[101] Lipiner, 'Über die Elemente', 151.

Each scene ... points ever more clearly, if at first indistinctly, towards this one final, inexpressible, scarcely imaginable and most intimate of ideas. So here everything is an allegory, a means of expressing an idea, which is by definition inadequate to fulfil the requirements. While it may be possible to describe transitory things, we can feel or imagine but never approach what underlies them (i.e. all that which 'here is achieved'), for it is transcendental and unchanging, hence inexpressible. That which leads us forwards with mystical strength ... and which Goethe here calls Eternal Femininity – here too, an allegory – namely a fixed point, the goal, is the antithesis of eternal longing, striving, motion towards that goal – in a word, Eternal Masculinity.[102]

Mahler summarized Goethe's *Faust* as an endless hierarchy of allegories ('*eine unendliche Stufenleiter dieser Gleichnisse*') culminating with the Mater Gloriosa. Mahler's musical setting suggests a floating (*Schweben*) from the allegorical towards the symbolic. Its tonal relationships can be shown to underpin this exploration of the fluctuation between, on the one hand, the masculine/material/labours of allegory, and, on the other, the metaphysical/instantaneous/symbolic, figured in the highest of all allegories as the eternal feminine.

In Part One the text 'Infirma nostri corporis / Virtute firmans perpeti' ('Endow our weak flesh / with perpetual strength') is set in D minor with significant semitonal dissonance between D and E♭ (2 bars before fig. 20). This is an adumbration of later E/E♭ clashes and also a reminder that the passage's tonal centre is a semitone below the movement's tonic E♭. At fig. 21 the harmony settles back on the dominant of E♭, 'Sehr ruhig' ('Very still and restful'), preceding, at 'Firmans virtute' (the plea for perpetual strength; fig. 22), a long dominant pedal over which the climactic dissonance of E (enharmonic F♭) with added pentatonic sixth over E♭ (Example 1.12, 5 before fig. 23) leads to the cadential dominant six-four. There are at this moment fragmented anticipations of the Mater Gloriosa theme in both choir and orchestra. But there is no resolution on E♭; the cadence is interrupted. Overall, then, the section moves from 'infirmed' D minor to an unfulfilled or 'weakened' cadence in E♭. The available physical strength is proving to be insufficient. But the cadence also briefly includes suggestions of an alternative world of E and pentatonicism. The unstable, darkly negative orchestral passage which follows leads to the bass soloist's 'Infirma' in C♯ minor (fig. 30), continuing the broad semitonal sinking in the tonal structure (E♭ major–D minor–C♯ minor). At fig. 33 the music

---

[102] Henry-Louis de La Grange and Günther Weiss (eds.), *Gustav Mahler: Letters to his Wife*, trans. Antony Beaumont (London: Faber, 2004), 326–7.

Example 1.12 Mahler, Symphony no. 8, Part one, 5 before fig. 23.

which had previously introduced the dominant of E♭ (fig. 21) is now heard in D, 'Sehr zart und gehalten' ('very soft'), at the first enunciation of the words 'accende lumen sensibus' ('kindle our senses with light'). This leads, through G major, to C major (at fig. 36) in a series of sinking tonal moves towards the energetic low point, with melodic lines recalling the previously 'failed' peaceful cadence. The energetic and tonal levels have been gradually denuded. The famous 'sudden' (*Plötzlich*) E major at the next statement of 'Accende lumen sensibus' (fig. 37) then offers a bodily, sensuous revitalization, but also, as a call or demand, one indicative of doubt and desire after the apparent preceding failure of physical effort. It provides the drive, the re-energizing to build towards recapitulation. But the passage also has implications for Part two of the symphony. As Mahler revealed to Webern at the final rehearsal before the premiere in Munich, 'The passage *accende lumen sensibus* forms the bridge to the concluding section of *Faust*. This spot is the cardinal point of the entire work.'[103] Transformed returns of material from Part one of the symphony play a vital role in Part two.

In Part two the D minor 'infirmed' music returns (fig. 75) as the more perfect angels speak of the painful burdens of an earthly residue ('Uns bleibt ein Erdenrest, zu tragen peinlich'). The restful cadence on V/E♭ from Part one, fig. 21 returns at 3 before fig. 79 and an alto solo leads to the same climactic dissonance and dominant six-four as in Part one (recall Example 1.12), now (at fig. 80) on 'die ewige Liebe', textually a clearer hint of the Mater Gloriosa which the motive and E major musically more subtly foreshadow, as they did at the equivalent moment in Part one. But instead of the interrupted cadence heard at the parallel moment in Part one, the music this time cadences on E♭ minor ('Ich spur …'). The tenor, Dr Marianus, enters as the alternative voice to the bass solo at fig. 32 in Part one (fig. 84), first in G, then B, then E, in brightening, energetic contrast to the enfeebling harmonic movement heard in the parallel passage in Part one. There are passing returns of E♭, but the goal is the E major (fig. 106) statement of the Mater Gloriosa theme which figures the restful, redemptive goal ultimately beyond the labours of man. In the terms deployed by Wagner in *Religion of Art*, this is where 'her' (that is, Art's) role is fulfilled 'when, by an ideal presentment of the allegorical figure, she led to the apprehension of its inner kernel, the truth ineffably divine'. The passing E♭ phrases emphasize the sense of uplift to E, in opposition to the falling E♭ major to D minor in the parallel passages of Part one.

---

[103] Fischer, *Gustav Mahler*, 522.

The parallels and contrasts between the two parts of the symphony are therefore clear enough. They can be interpreted through invoking Adorno's notions of breakthrough and fulfilment. As we saw, according to Adorno, 'Mahler's fulfilment fields achieve by form, by their relation to what preceded them, what the breakthrough promised itself from outside.' In this way Mahler's music thereby 'keeps its promise', is 'consummated', its 'yearning is fulfilled'. And Adorno identified fulfilment with the 'unleashing of accumulated power, an unfettering, a freedom' at the beginning of the recapitulation in the first part of the Eighth.[104] The drive towards this 'fulfilment' was initiated, or rekindled, by a sudden, breakthrough moment at 'Accende'. Tentatively, one might suggest from these examples that an Adornian fulfilment, as partially achieved by working through internal relationships, tends to the allegorical mode while the Adornian breakthrough – instantaneous, given from without – tends to release the symbolic. The momentary intrusion of the symbolic at the breakthrough in a sense stimulates the progressive work of development towards a state of fulfilment. The Mater Gloriosa theme in Part two musically sounds as another fulfilment rather than a breakthrough (she gets a long introduction from Dr Marianus); Goethe's text, however, suggests Mater Gloriosa as pointing towards the symbol. Through the symphony, then, the two modes are in ambiguous interplay. The Mater Gloriosa theme's '*Schweben*' marking (Example 1.13) not only suggests a musical parallel to physical image of the floating body (she is weightless, timeless, a miraculous denial of the physical laws of nature) but also in Nelson's sense a floating between two modes. As the highest of all allegories her music brings us in touch with the symbolic. The setting of the opening words of the Chorus Mysticus (Example 1.14, 4 after fig. 202), confirms the work's floating position within the symbol/allegory dualism.

Alles Vergängliche
ist nur ein Gleichnis;
Das Unzulängliche,
Hier wird's Ereignis;
Das Unbeschreibliche,
Hier ist's getan;

A translation of these lines could read:

All that is transitory
Is but an allegory;

---

[104] Adorno, *Mahler*, 44.

Example 1.13 Mahler, Symphony no. 8, Part two, fig. 106.

The inadequate
Here is resolved;
The indescribable
Here is accomplished.

The text suggests ascending yet inadequate allegories function as preparation for 'Das Ewig-Weibliche', who figures the final move towards the
timeless symbolic. In the music overt surface echoes of the Mater Gloriosa

Example 1.13 (cont.)

theme coexist with a subtler subsurface, motivic expansion of the second phrase of her theme, over chromatic insinuations of E (her key) within E♭ (compare Examples 1.13 and 1.14). The text overtly alludes to the inadequacy of allegory; the music covertly to the music which previously evoked most closely the supremacy of the symbol. Yet Mahler, of course, 'constructs' this covert allusion to the unconstructable symbol through notably

Example 1.14 Mahler, Symphony no. 8, Part two, 4 after fig. 202.

high artifice (the rather clever motivic process and tonal ambiguity). Furthermore, tonalities appear also to slip across the allegory–symbol, work–rest dualisms. In particular, it is noteworthy that E major, the breakthrough key from without that inspires developmental, masculine 'work' in Part one ('Accende'), becomes the key of 'restful', feminine fulfilment in Part two (the Mater Gloriosa). This might suggest a glimpse of some kind of utopian androgyny, the highest fulfilment of the work of Eros. As Donald Mitchell noted:

E, after which the work (and mankind) aspires, represents the unattainable, and E♭ what realistically can be attained, i.e. the recognition of what leads us onward and upward, which is itself a triumph over doubt and scepticism, while necessarily falling a step (a semitone!) short of final enlightenment. If there is any merit in that idea, then the Eighth could never have ended in E, which can be glimpsed but never grasped.[105]

And in an essay on Mahler's 'gendered musical discourse', Franklin suggests that the Eighth can come 'to symbolize music itself engaged in a reflexively, perhaps posthumously, troubled celebration of all it had hoped itself to be (transcendent, unifying, supranational)'. Ultimately, the symphony is perhaps an acknowledgement that 'the *Unbeschreibliche* had still not really been *getan*; that the *Ewig-Weibliche* was a construction marked by the ideological residue of *Alles Vergängliche*; that the *Ereignis* remained *unzulänglich*'.[106]

Bruno Walter once described the first movement of the Ninth Symphony as a transcendent *Schweben*: 'an unparalleled hovering between the sadness of leave-taking and the vision of heavenly light (not floating fantasy, rather immediate emotion) lifts the movement into an atmosphere of utmost transfiguration'.[107] At the movement's closing cadential gesture, there is no dominant six-four, indeed the dominant is completely absent (reflecting the greatly reduced structural role of the dominant throughout the movement). Instead (see Example 1.15) E♭ and B harmonies echo their important preceding structural functions as precursors of return to the tonic D; one shadowy, *Schattenhaft* (E♭, b. 254), one bright (B from b. 285, but then crushed, bb. 312ff.); one the dark Neapolitan, the other the light (pentatonic) major sixth. They are finally brought together in a single cadential phrase which offers a summary of the whole while rhetorically and motivically imparting the redemptive mode through a chromatically transformed version of the 'symbolic' falling pentatonic melodic line familiar from the preceding examples. The chromatic transformation includes the appoggiatura G♯ (tritone from tonic D), tellingly marked *Schweben* in the score, as a chromatic alternative to the pentatonic added sixth. This is a new chromatic variant of the musical redemptive symbol in which, poignantly, seeds of

[105] Donald Mitchell, *Gustav Mahler III: Songs and Symphonies of Life and Death* (Berkeley: University of California Press, 1985), 577.
[106] Peter Franklin, 'A Soldier's Sweetheart's Mother's Tale? Mahler's Gendered Musical Discourse', in Painter (ed.), *Mahler and his World*, 116.
[107] Cited in Floros, *Gustav Mahler*, 275.

Example 1.15 Mahler, Symphony no. 9, first movement, bb. 409–34; reduction.

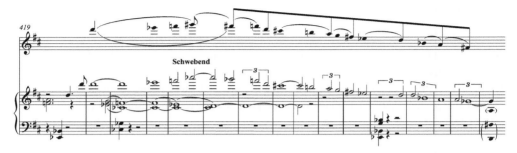

doubt or negation (the shadows) remain. Most poignant of all is the way this gesture approaches silence, as if to conclude that to try to speak of the symbolic is always to fail, and that the most symbolic musical utterance, in romantic terms, is silence; silence that is not empty but replete. This is a fullness of silence approached again at the end of the Ninth's finale. The chorale-like first subject of the last movement builds to a succession of climactic cadences. The first such climax (bb. 23–5) is a straightforward example of the 'salvation' six-four as intensifying dissonances and an upwardly soaring melodic thrust lands on a dominant six-four/five-three which resolves directly to the tonic Db. The second climactic cadence promises the same traditional cadence with bar 72 presenting dissonances and melodic shapes paralleling those of bar 23. But the dominant is omitted and there is a surprise move directly to the tonic. This event – a sort of short-circuiting of the harmonic progression – is then immediately countered by a complete dominant six-four-five to tonic cadence (bb. 76–7). The main central climax of the movement (bb. 117–25) is a move to the return of the tonic Db which begins by stating the dominant six-four/five-three. Chromatic intensifications, however, subvert this diatonic cadential gesture and the harmonic support disappears, leaving the move to the tonic to be achieved by an unaccompanied descent in the upper strings. In the extreme quiet of the movement's closing paragraph, this climactic moment is recalled as a distant echo (bb. 159–61); the diatonic resolution is tentatively sounded (b. 164) but the musical fabric is torn by repeated silences.[108]

Mahler's evocations of the musical symbol in the romantic tradition are part of a crucial reflection, in the post-Nietzschean age of scepticism, of Mahler's relationship to the Wagnerian aesthetics of the 'Beethoven' and

---

[108] On Mahler's 'disappearing' cadences, see Michael P. Steinberg, *Listening to Reason: Culture, Subjectivity, and Nineteenth-Century Music* (Princeton University Press, 2004), 232.

'Religion and Art' essays, and of his investment in the ideas of the early Romantics. Mahler's music presents a series of especially fascinating and diverse examples in the story of the competing claims of allegory and symbol. If the settings of 'Urlicht' and 'Liebst du um Schönheit' move towards affirmations of the redemptive, transcendent symbol, comparison of 'Ich bin der Welt abhanden gekommen' and the Adagietto of the Fifth Symphony suggest that though the condition of *Innigkeit* is highly prized, the symbol actually comes from without. The closing section of the slow movement of the Fourth Symphony can be heard to confirm this external-ity, suggesting new parallels with Adorno's notion of breakthrough. In 'Um Mitternacht' the chromatic and whole-tone negation of the diatonic-pentatonic material which briefly evoke a redemptive mode is so strong that the authenticity of the final cadential affirmation can sound ques-tionably overstated. No such final affirmation ends the Sixth, whose dark close is adumbrated in the opening theme of the Andante by the replacement of an entirely possible salvation dominant six-four harmony by an anguished dissonance which turns the tone from idyllic dream to elegy. If the Eighth Symphony presents Mahler's most monumental explo-ration of how allegorical hierarchies might ascend towards an ultimate affirmation of the romantic symbol, then in the Ninth, by contrast, the cadential figures to which Mahler repeatedly turns as musical evocation of the symbolic are chromatically subverted or peter out into silence. The cadences of the Ninth's closing bars, nonetheless, include tentative, fragile, broken echoes of the redemptive symbol. Hearing the manner in which the symbolic mode is sustained, imperilled, recalled, transformed or silenced in Mahler's music (especially at its cadences) opens up new ways of understanding how it engages with romantic notions of the beautiful and the redemptive. To each of these romantic conceptual and technical variants, the music of Britten, Weill and Henze demonstrates richly com-parable relationships.

2 | Naïve and sentimental: Britten and Mahler

I

For the English 'Romantic Moderns', to use Alexandra Harris's term, the response to the radical experimentalism of international high modernism, and its proclamation of a revolutionary 'year zero' after the apocalyptic experience of the First World War, was a desire once more to seek 'home' through the invocation of tradition, to reinterpret and revalue, rather than brusquely reject, the heritage of the past. In the 1930s this was manifest in a diversity of 'period' reconstructions, including medievalism, Georgianism, baroque, rococo, romanticism, Victorianism. This pageantry of English traditions, Harris argues, went beyond superficial 'dressing up' into a 'sustained commitment to distinct aesthetic values, ways of living, and ways of looking at England'.[1] Out of this wide range of aesthetics and idioms, concepts of neo-romanticism became centrally important in the artistic climate of Second World War England. During these turbulent years, artists such as Graham Sutherland and John Piper re-engaged with the romantic tradition of picturesque images of the English countryside. Such work provoked important debates on the virtues of a retreat from the horrors of conflict into a dream-like alternative world and on the idea that an imaginatively stimulating image of the nation can be generated through invocations of pastoral realms remote from the brutalities of the time. Disputes over neo-romanticism became informed by competing notions of ideals and reality, disconnections and commitment, distance, alienation and immediacy. Britten's *Serenade for Tenor, Horn and Strings*, Op. 31, a work which Tim Barringer argues is 'strongly imbricated' in British neo-romanticism, was premiered in London in October 1943. Barringer argues that the natural harmonics of the French horn in the prologue can be heard to signify a distant, archaic pastoral, the intruding dissonances the contrasting modern world: the triad evokes an 'immemorial peace' while the dissonant fourth and seventh introduce the 'disruptions' and 'discomforts' of the modern predicament opposed to a supposed 'natural'

[1] Alexandra Harris, *Romantic Moderns: English Writers, Artists and the Imagination from Virginia Woolf to John Piper* (London: Thames & Hudson, 2010), 11–12.

order. Within this ambiguity Barringer identifies a strong commitment to tradition:

While gesturing toward a modernist primitivism . . . Britten's prologue is ultimately evocative and, here as elsewhere, the composer's virtuosic powers of invention invert modernist devices, employing them to endorse, even bolster, mainstream musical traditions rather than to subvert or undermine them. This strategy epitomizes neo-Romantic cultural production across all media. The survival of the basic triad – like the survival of a vernacular, but nonetheless indexical, form of representation in the work of Sutherland, Piper and Henry Moore – offers a reassurance that, at least within the work of art or music, the natural order of things remains intact.[2]

That this 'natural order' remains 'intact' is, however, highly questionable, and the status of the musical symbols of nature is more complex than Barringer concludes. Interestingly, however, Barringer continues to note that the 'arcadian implications' of Britten's prologue have stronger resonances with the British romantic tradition in painting than with the English pastoral musical tradition, or of Vaughan Williams's latest version of that tradition, about which, as is well known, Britten held deep reservations. Barringer asserts that Britten selected Samuel Palmer's *Cornfield by Moonlight with the Evening Star* (*c.* 1830) for the front cover illustration of the 1944 Boosey & Hawkes first edition of the vocal score in a 'self-conscious gesture of affiliation'. Palmer's painting was widely reproduced at the time, most importantly in Piper's widely read *British Romantic Artists* (1942). Barringer identifies a tension in the *Serenade* between politically conservative nostalgia and radical critique, one which parallels the contrast between Palmer, the 'conservative ruralist', and the radical William Blake (who was Palmer's early mentor). This tension 'reveals a fault line at the heart of the English pastoral tradition between a high-Tory poetics of vernacular nationalism, and a Radical, critical, self-reflexivity'. Blake's 'The Sick Rose' is the third song in Britten's cycle and the *Serenade* as a whole plays out a 'dialogue' between these two types of pastoral, as it 'blends nostalgic reassurance with existential disquiet, rootedness and alienation, escapism and engagement, just as it navigates a *via media* between musical tradition and modernism'.

Barringer's reading is subtle and in many ways persuasive. He sees the *Serenade* as representing a shift 'far away from the Mahlerian admixture of rage and ironic sentimentality adopted in the *Sinfonia da Requiem*' (composed in 1941 while Britten was in America) and from the 'self-conscious

---

[2] Tim Barringer, '"I am a native, rooted here": Benjamin Britten, Samuel Palmer and the Neo-Romantic Pastoral', *Art History* 34 (2011), 126–65 (at 129–30)

artistry' of the *Seven Sonnets of Michelangelo* (1940, also composed in America), as an artistic return to the landscape of home, which prefigures, in particular, some of the major concerns explored in *Peter Grimes* (1945).[3] This reading of Britten's career in the early 1940s suggests a move into a more directly 'honest' or open-hearted rather than ironically distanced musical idiom, with the key artistic aim being to seek expression of the tensions between comfort and unease, between yearning and peace – or in the German romantic terms which we employed in Mahler – *sehnsucht* and *ruhe*. There are ambiguities of tone, genre and structure in the *Serenade* upon which Barringer is silent, and in this way his reading misses symbolic and technical parallels with Mahler. The generic complexity identified by Arnold Whittall,[4] through which the first song, 'Pastoral', is imbued with the characteristics of a nocturne or a lullaby (possibly designed to create distance from the 'preciousness' and 'heartiness' of Vaughan Williams's musical Englishry), allows the exploration of intricate and often ironic effect. For example, the setting's evocation of a lullaby raises a potent musical icon of innocence, rest and the 'undivided consciousness' of childhood. But these associations are questioned by subtleties in the musical technique, especially through avoidance of root position tonics and dominant harmony and repeated denials of closure. This ambiguity reaches its expressive climax in the final stanza, where the voice and strings are long dissonant over the horn's tonic D♭ pedal which, for Whittall, is 'perhaps the movement's most explicit and ironic pastoral sign', whose 'effect is to prepare a conclusive return to the main tonic'. The effect is ironic, for despite the pedal's persistence in the short coda there remains a tensed coexistence of remnant insecurity within a moment of rest. This can be related to models in German romanticism (a relationship which, as Whittall said in 1993, 'remains to be properly investigated'). But Britten's romanticism is always tinged, balanced or challenged by Classical concerns for simplicity and clarity (and vice versa).

The importance of the coexistent legacies of classicism and German romanticism in Britten's music was noted by Peter Evans, who pointed out how in the *Serenade* 'Britten gave full rein to a gift for simple Nature symbolism, reminiscent of the early German Romantics in the use of instrumental colourings'. Evans also points to Britten's affecting use of triadic arpeggios to 'symbolize rest' at a time when 'the triad's

---

[3] *Ibid.*, 135–8.

[4] Arnold Whittall, 'The Signs of Genre: Britten's Version of Pastoral', in Chris Banks, Arthur Searle and Malcolm Turner (eds.), *Sundry Sorts of Music Books: Essays on the British Library Collections* (London: The British Library, 1993), 363–74.

Example 2.1 Benjamin Britten, 'Pastoral' (Cotton), *Serenade for Tenor, Horn and Strings*, closing bars and diatonic model.

centuries-old hegemony has at last been called into question'.[5] In the final stanza, with the horn tonic pedal reiterated in the syncopated rhythms which informed the oscillating chords in the strings in the first verse, the upper strings take over the role of echoing the falling triadic arpeggio which opens the vocal line (Example 2.1). The technique of switching the role of the instruments is a simple way of varying effect in a strophic setting, but at the final cadence the effect is powerful. The final arpeggiation (of an F♯ minor, enharmonic minor subdominant triad), through its placement in the first violins, is the highest-sounding gesture in the song. In this way it is evocative of a transcendent, heavenly quality. This sense of uplifting to repose is also suggested by the fact that the voice is set a semitone higher

[5] Peter Evans, *The Music of Benjamin Britten* (London: Dent, 1979), 91.

Example 2.1 (cont.)

than in the corresponding moment in the first stanza (reinterpreting, at long range, the song's preoccupation with the conflict between F and G♭). The vocal peak on F♯/G♭ and resolution to F affords allusion to a four-three cadential suspension of hymnic resonance and generates a distant echo of the G♭–F that closes the song's opening vocal phrase. But the harmony adds levels of ambiguity. The minor subdominant suggested by the arpeggiation is a favoured element in romantic cadences where a tone of resignation or melancholy is suggested. This upper triad combines with the pitches darkly clustered in the lower strings to generate an inverted version of what might potentially, given the cadential context, function as a pre-dominant German augmented sixth with added upper F♯. Example 2.1 outlines the potential diatonic model. As Mark notes, there is a sense of harmonic 'disjunction' as the anticipated dominant is absent.[6] The dissonances first between F♯ and G and then G♭ and F sustain the piquant quality of the song's signature accompanimental figure, whose return in the final bars therefore sounds firmly prepared. But the absence of the structural dominant means that the diatonic model is only partially fulfilled; the transcendent potential is implied but unstated; similarly, the 'way to rest', as evoked in Cotton's final poetic line, is subtly destabilized.

The symbolism attaching to Britten's diatonicism is, of course, dependent upon its position in the history of tonality. Carl Dahlhaus famously wrote, in relation to Wagner's diatonicism, that if 'the identity and allegorical or expressive significance of dissonance are due to the fact of its being "determined negation" of, and divergence' from a consonance that itself 'does not need to be heard', then we must contemplate the reverse, that 'chromaticism and dissonance can be sensed as the unheard background to diatonicism and consonance'. This reciprocation can be extended to the relationship of simplicity and complexity: 'if generally speaking, simplicity is the foil to complexity, in Wagner it sometimes seems that complexity provides the background to simplicity'. In this context, overtly 'artificial naivety' is therefore immune to the temptation to be associated with the supposedly natural or instinctive quality of folk music. Also, in this way the diatonicism of *Die Meistersinger* 'makes no attempt to disguise its "sentimentality" – in the Schillerian sense – in that its "archaizing" music is not instinctive but the product of reflection'. The diatonicism is 'not so much restoration as reconstruction. It is a "second" diatonicism, in the sense that Hegel spoke of "second" nature or "second" immediacy, that is, something spontaneous that benefits from stores of awareness and reflection that have been accumulated previously'.[7] To parallel Britten with Wagner may at first seem perverse (though much less so if one recalls Britten's admiration for Wagner, especially in the 1930s), but Dahlhaus's hearing of Wagner's diatonic idiom opens up a way of interpreting diatonicism and simplicity across a range of romantic and post-romantic styles. Whittall has called the diatonicism of Britten's music 'restricted tonality', by contrast with the

---

[6] Christopher Mark, *Early Benjamin Britten: A Study of Stylistic and Technical Evolution* (New York: Garland, 1995), 259. Mark borrows the term 'disjunction' from Kofi Agawu's analysis of the second of Mahler's *Kindertotenlieder*, in whose final bars a potentially anticipated dominant six-four/five-three cadential progression is omitted; 'The Musical Language of *Kindertotenlieder* no. 2', *The Journal of Musicology* 2 (1983), 81–93 (see Agawu's graph on p. 92).

[7] Carl Dahlhaus, *Richard Wagner's Music Dramas*, trans. Mary Whittall (Cambridge University Press, 1979), 74–5, 132–3.

'extended tonality' of post-Wagnerian chromaticism,[8] and has noted how the kind of 'post-atonal tonality' developed by Britten allows traditional procedures of tonal departure and return to be readily sustained or inter-rogated.[9] In particular, Britten's music ascribes high structural and symbolic status to the tonal cadence. In parallel with harmonic 'restriction' there is commonly a sense of compression, an intensification of material and effect at moments of ending, often imbued with an ambiguity between rest and restfulness, fulfilment and denial, and the desire to return. Hans Keller identified what he called the twentieth century's 'melodic crisis' as based upon the impossibility of extended melody necessary because of the 'dia-tonic cadence's loss of potency'. He saw two possible compositional responses. One was to omit cadence and compose open-ended sequences – as in Wagner's 'endless melody'. The alternative was to reinvest in cadence, as found in Britten's 'compression of content'. Keller argues that, 'following his classical tendencies', Britten 'found undreamt-of riches in the cadential phrase', using cadential motifs or phrases 'as receptacles into which looser structures can discharge themselves'.[10] The symbolic and structural weight felt in the final cadential phrase of Britten's 'Pastoral' chimes with Keller's argument. As the examples in the previous chapter demonstrated, cadential discharge as a symbolic moment of potential fulfilment and release is a powerful aspect of the diatonic emphasis in Mahler's music. Cadences in works such as the Rückert settings 'Liebst du um Schönheit' and 'Ich bin der Welt abhanden gekommen' evoke, through the allegorical–symbolic com-plex, a higher, fulfilling repose.[11] The music of Mahler and Britten shares a heightened symbolic and structural investment in diatonic cadence.

At the Snape Maltings on 18 June 1967, as part of that year's Aldeburgh Festival, Britten conducted the New Philharmonia in the first performance of Mahler's 'Blumine' movement following its rediscovery by Donald

---

[8] Arnold Whittall, 'The Study of Britten: Triadic Harmony and Tonal Structure', *Proceedings of the Royal Musical Association* 106 (1979–80), 39.

[9] Arnold Whittall, 'Tonality in Britten's Song Cycles with Piano', *Tempo* 96 (1971), 2–11. Britten's comments on the return to tonality in Schoenberg's Suite for Strings in G in a diary entry of 14 April 1936 are especially interesting here: he called it 'a delightful work … It might be a Hommage to Mahler both in matter and manner – but that doesn't detract from its value – rather adds to it. This seems an unexpected development for Schoenberg – but quite natural.' John Evans (ed.), *Journeying Boy: The Diaries of the Young Benjamin Britten 1928–1938* (London: Faber, 2009), 346.

[10] Hans Keller, 'The Musical Character', in Donald Mitchell and Hans Keller (eds.), *Benjamin Britten: A Commentary on his Works from a Group of Specialists* (London: Rockliff, 1952), 347.

[11] A 'singular feature' of the Rückert songs for Donald Mitchell was 'the memorability of their final cadences … each one an emphatic compositional gesture. These Rückert cadences merit a small study in themselves.' Mitchell, *Gustav Mahler III*, 74.

Mitchell. Mitchell's festival programme note[12] tells the story of the movement's resurfacing and of Mahler's doubts concerning its place in the First Symphony. The movement is a serenade of deliberate pastoral simplicity (Mitchell notes the 'total (if endearing) innocence of its content and its technique') led by a solo trumpet (Mitchell considers the movement to be a foreshadowing of the more complex pastoralism of the posthorn solo in the Third Symphony). Mahler's misgivings about the piece were grounded on what he considered to be its unsymphonic and sentimental character. In recollection, Mahler described it as 'sentimentally indulgent', (*sentimental-schwärmerischer*), as reflecting the 'youthful folly' (*Jugend-Eselei*) of his symphonic Hero.[13] Mitchell suggests that Mahler may have originally felt that 'Blumine' provided an extension of his programme, supplying 'what on the whole is absent elsewhere in the symphony, a note of pure, unalloyed romantic lyricism, neither tinged by irony nor contradicted by ensuing agitation'.[14] Its potential role in the symphony's putative programme becomes clearer through Max Graf's review (of the four-movement version minus 'Blumine') for *Wiener Rundschau* on 1 December 1900. Graf divides the symphony into two parts. The first (movements 1 and 2) is

an idyllic and undesecrated nature, as well as the first joyous play of life's forces. The second shows a corrupted world stripped of peace which must struggle for redemption ... While the first half reflects the world in a flat mirror, the second presents a fragmented and distorted image reflected from the broken pieces of a convex mirror.

In summary, Graf contrasts the 'lyrical–idyllic and the ironic–tragic', that is, a naïve world, with the 'grotesque' and 'grimacing spirit' introduced by the third movement. The finale, in which

redemption is fought out in the battle of the chorales ... explodes with a vehemence that somehow is not able to wreak damage: the tense, naturalistic pathos constricts

---

[12] This is reproduced in Mitchell, *Gustav Mahler: The Wunderhorn Years* (London: Faber, 1975), 218.

[13] Natalie Bauer-Lechner, *Recollections of Gustav Mahler*, trans. Dika Newlin, ed. Peter Franklin (London: Faber, 1980), 158. On the possible autobiographical associations with Mahler's love life as a young man see Mitchell, *Gustav Mahler: The Wunderhorn Years*, 222 and Carl Niekerk, *Reading Mahler: German Musical Culture and Jewish Identity in Fin-de-Siècle Vienna* (Rochester, NY: Camden House, 2010), 49–50.

[14] Mitchell, *Gustav Mahler: The Wunderhorn Years*, 222. Zoltan Roman condemns the movement: 'its symphonic existence is justified neither by the quality of the invention, nor by the treatment of the material'; 'Song and Symphony (I). *Lieder und Gesänge*, Volume 1, *Lieder eines fahrenden Gesellen* and the First Symphony: Compositional Patterns for the Future', in Barham (ed.) *The Cambridge Companion to Mahler*, 84.

rather than stimulates, the listener's imagination. An increase in force is impossible after the first measures, and without an increase . . . coldness always remains . . . In such an atmosphere the final triumph has the effect of sheer force: it shatters rather than elevates . . . This, I think, is the emotional content of Gustav Mahler's First Symphony.[15]

Bruno Walter called 'Blumine' a 'wonderful, idyllic piece',[16] and a reading of the symphony, after Graf, as a move from idyllic naïvety through corruption to redemption reveals the potential expressive function of the simple sentimentalism of 'Blumine' in a five-movement version of the symphony.

The most interesting and problematic aspect of structure and expression in 'Blumine' lies in the handling of cadences. The 'naïve' opening tune begins with a straightforward antecedent of ten bars. The consequent phrase is extended to fifteen bars. This phrase reaches the structural dominant at the beginning of its sixth bar (3 after fig. 2) and its 'sentimental' character can in part be identified with the elongation of the sense of ending, as the dominant six-four/five-three resolution is stretched and sustained, first through rising, ardent, sequences of the tune's chromatic motive and then through five bars of descent from a high violin G (see Example 2.2). If Mahler meant 'sentimental' to be indulgent in unmotivated emoting, then here such a tone seems evident. The cadence returns on two occasions: first, in an only slightly altered variant, as the lead back to the main tune from the contrasting middle section (from 4 bars after fig. 12), and then to form the final structural closure (from 2 after fig. 15). In this last statement, the music on the dominant is condensed to just four bars. The overall move that these cadences project, from initial relative complexity and expansion to simplicity and compression, is an 'anti-developmental' process which may lie behind Mahler's description of the movement as 'unsymphonic'. But, in the light of the examples from the previous chapter, the movement is an early attempt to deploy the dominant six-four cadence as a central symbolic gesture, as well as a perhaps only partially successful attempt to deploy a contrast between expansion and compression of these cadential gestures as a central structural feature.

Britten preceded his 1967 performance of 'Blumine' with the revised (1945) version of his Piano Concerto (with Sviatoslav Richter as soloist). In a coincidental parallel to the compositional and performance history of Mahler's First Symphony, Britten excised a whole movement from the original 1938 version with the third, 'Recitative and Aria', replaced by

[15] Trans. in Painter (ed.), *Mahler and His World*, 284–7.
[16] Mitchell, *Gustav Mahler: The Wunderhorn Years*, 221.

Example 2.2 Mahler, 'Blumine', fig. 2 to 4 after fig. 3.

'Impromptu'. The new movement, though based on material contemporaneous with the composition of the first version of the concerto, offers a rather dark, brittle contrast to the overtly romantic, even sentimental tone, of the big tune of the original aria. It is possible that after the experience of

Example 2.2 (cont.)

the war years Britten felt that there was the danger that the aria would lead to a misunderstanding of his relationship to the more superficially emotional end of romantic style, despite the fact that the movement ends in a collapse or disintegration, suggesting a parallel to those moments of 'negative fulfilment' that Adorno identified in Mahler. These compositional uncertainties of Mahler and Britten share a basis in the task of how to evoke naïve and romantic modes of expression within a broadly ambiguous narrative concerning questions of epiphany (the potential relevance and power of the transcendent moment of resolution and revelation) and of suppression and discharge through fulfilment or breakthrough. They also manifest a shared concern for being misread through the use of conventional or apparently simple materials and allusions to genres of potentially dubious artistic esteem.

Philip Brett noted a characteristic tension in Britten between acknowledgement and concealment as the composer moved on an uncomfortable 'knife-edge between honesty about life's difficulties and a longing for resolution and comfort'.[17] The vibrancy of Brett's critical legacy has meant that this quality has been widely related to Britten's homosexuality. Other aesthetic and expressive aspects have, by contrast, been rather neglected. The music's ambiguity between conflict and integration is in an important sense manifest, as Whittall has noted, in the interaction between social/functional genres and 'primarily aesthetic ones' in which a 'process of transference' from one to the other invokes either an attempt at a new synthesis or overtly subversive tensions. The coexistence of internal and external reference is also manifest in the manner in which these generic manipulations frequently evoke the innocent and hence raise nostalgia, regression, internalization or a certain 'otherness', something exoteric. In themselves, individual generic allusions are often of complex resonance. Of importance, for example, is the 'hymnic', which may be elevated in tone or simply representative of childlike innocence or naivety of faith. The hymnic allusion in the third song of the Hölderlin settings, 'Sokrates und Alcibiades', with its central message on truth and beauty, is for Whittall, 'transcendentally aesthetic rather than religious'. For Whittall this allusion to the hymnic is a rare moment – for Britten – of unambiguous serenity, though we shall turn to consider this song's complexity of tone later in the chapter. More usually, 'Britten the uncertain Christian, walking the knife-edge separating aesthetic self-confidence from social self-doubt, directed his generic allusions towards those moments of purely human self-understanding and illumination that have their own transcendent expressive force.'[18] (Another knife edge!) Britten shared with Mahler a

---

[17] Brett, 'Britten's Dream', *Music and Sexuality in Britten*, 121.
[18] Whittall, 'Along the Knife-Edge: The Topic of Transcendence in Britten's Musical Aesthetic', in Reed (ed.), *On Mahler and Britten*, 290–8.

sustained interest in the transcendent, in the redemptive, and in the search for the clinching symbolic closing moment identified in examples from Mahler's cadences, where the aspiration to the status of the symbol is riven with the scepticism of uncertainty, the artifice of allegory and the ambiguity of suspicion. Processes of concealment, effacement and collapse coexist with the revelatory: processes of unification and resolution, the comforts, if you like, of Classical form, struggle with multifarious and recalcitrant materials. All these are imbricated in the overall search or yearning for a peace, poetically or symbolically associated with some vision of a 'natural' state suggesting the spiritual, but always to be understood as a 'second nature'.

Britten is often figured as a practical, down-to-earth, realistic artist, writing determinedly performable and communicable music, often to commission or for a specific occasion. But this is only one dimension of his artistic personality, for aspects of the Austro-German Idealist and romantic traditions were crucially, if selectively or ambivalently, attractive. Britten's relationship with romantic styles and aesthetics is vital. A useful focus from which to begin examining this neglected area is provided by Schiller's familiar dualism of the naïve and sentimental. Discussion of Mahler in Schillerian terms has a long tradition.[19] In 1914 Guido Adler wrote of Mahler's 'naïve belief in fairy-tales and in a visionary fairy-tale bliss' and how he 'saw with a transfigured artist's view into the heaven that opened itself to him'. Adler continues:

With the childlike spirit of the folk song he was able to raise himself to that point where only imagination and faith, not reason, escort one. A deep longing – for the infinite – runs through almost all of his works, and the finite does not disrupt the seer's view. He performs his devotions in nature and prays in sounds. A yearning for nature stands out here and there, such as that which fills the culture-weary wanderer of the world of our time. Schiller characterizes a poet such as this, who seeks nature, as 'sentimental', and poet who is himself nature, as 'naïve'. In Mahler the naïve and the sentimental alternate – his nature was complex and shows contrasts that were heightened by his temperament. Hence crass contrasts also appear in his art.

In short, Adler notes that in Mahler's music the 'strange mix of the naïve and sentimental creates enigmas that are not easy to unravel'.[20] In 'crass

---

[19] The tradition has a biographical justification: Schiller's work was a topic of debate between Gustav and Alma in 1901; see Alma Mahler, *Gustav Mahler: Memories and Letters*, trans. Basil Creighton, ed. Donald Mitchell and Knud Martner (London: Cardinal, 1990), 20.

[20] Guido Adler, *Gustav Mahler* [1914], trans. in Edward R. Reilly, *Gustav Mahler and Guido Adler: Records of a Friendship* (Cambridge University Press, 1982), 40, 72.

contrasts' between the simple and complex, to use Adler's strident phrase, lie the dangers of misunderstanding. Mahler himself was indeed concerned that by setting the 'simple, naïve style' of the 'Wunderhorn' poems (which, as Susan Youens says, invoke 'the feint that the poems transcribe emotional impulses as they occur') he was too easily open to critical parody, and in the *Lieder eines fahrenden Gesellen* he sought 'to fashion from folk-poetic origins something which is not so simple, not naïve, but modern'. A crucial part of this modernity involved the complex response to a past artistic model (Schubert) which makes the new out of the old.[21] Once again the parallels with Britten's work are strong. This is exemplified especially poignantly by the final song of the Thomas Hardy cycle *Winter Words* (1953; a cycle overtly related to *Winterreisse*), 'Before Life and After', whose opening lines read:

A time there was, as one may guess
And as, indeed, earth's testimonies tell –
Before the birth of consciousness,
When all went well.

And whose last stanza, after the infection of the idyll, expresses the longing for the time when innocence might return:

But the disease of feeling germed
And primal rightness took the tinct of wrong
Ere nescience shall be reaffirmed
How long, how long?

The low register, root position triads moving in parallel motion in the piano accompaniment to these lines may seem to be a primitivistic or 'crass contrast' to the artfulness of Hardy's poetry, or to be naïve in the worse sense of childish or amateurish artlessness, or flirt with over-simplification (Example 2.3).[22] As Evans notes, however, though 'a wilful crudity can be heard in the endless close-position root-triads at the bottom of the texture' this is a 'symbol of a primeval state' which is 'incorporated into a musical scheme that is sophisticated enough'. And the skilful variation of melodic character in the upper piano and voice means that the song 'avoids the pitfalls of neo-primitivism'.[23] The crudely simple, low register triads coexist

---

[21] Susan Youens, 'Words and Music in Germany and France', in Jim Samson (ed.), *The Cambridge History of Nineteenth-Century Music* (Cambridge University Press, 2002), 480. See also Youens, 'Schubert, Mahler and the Weight of the Past: *Lieder eines fahrenden Gesellen* and *Winterreise*', *Music & Letters* 67 (1986), 256–68.

[22] See Whittall, 'The Study of Britten', 28.   [23] Evans, *The Music of Benjamin Britten*, 361.

Example 2.3 Britten, 'Before Life and After' (Hardy), *Winter Words*, closing bars.

with poetic sophistication and melodic expressivity to evoke the yearning for a lost time of innocence. At the cadential return to the home key of D (for Evans, a 'momentous conclusion'), the upper piano line and the vocal line combine in artful counterpoint to create a cycle of descending fourths that alludes to both pentatonic collections (ancient, 'natural') and diatonic dissonances (modern, yearning). The idyllic–elegiac tone thereby evoked by this song is a pervasive aspect of Britten's music, and is an especially productive point of departure for a comparative study of Mahler and Britten.

Schiller's *Naïve and Sentimental Poetry* became a central text for nineteenth-century romanticism. Its tenets are well known, so need only be briefly reviewed at this point. According to Schiller, nature is simple, undivided and spontaneous, and 'so long as man is pure – not, of course crude – nature, he functions as an undivided sensuous unity and as a unifying whole. Sense and reason, passive and active faculties, are not separated in their activities, still less do they stand in conflict with one another.'[24] The naïve poet *is* nature; the sentimental poet, by contrast, *seeks* nature, for the sentimental poet is conscious of the divisive power of artificiality, and yearns for the innocent union with nature that has been lost. The human ideal is a balanced union of nature and culture. But in real life these are in conflict, and in any case, 'pure' nature is a cultural construct, even if it is the product of an art which not only conceals its artifice but also its processes from itself in the working of the mind of the naïve genius, so that it *appears* as a product of nature. The satirical sentimental poet's subject is 'alienation from nature and the contradiction between actuality and the ideal'. The sentimental artist who is more attracted to the ideal tends to the elegiac mode – elegy proper if the ideal is represented as lost, idyll if the ideal is represented as though it was existent. In this mode the sentimental poet reflects on the feelings that the naïve poet describes immediately and directly.[25] For Schiller, the idyll represents the highest mode of sensibility available to the sentimental poet. Crucially, however, the idyllic lies in the future (Elysium) not in the past (Arcadia). This distinction informs Schiller's considerations on the importance of childhood. Childhood is 'the only undisfigured nature that we still encounter in civilized mankind, hence it is no wonder if every trace of the nature outside us leads us back to our childhood'. But Schiller urges that the symbolic allure of the state of childhood must

lead us forward into our maturity in order to permit us to perceive that higher harmony which rewards the combatant and gratifies the conqueror. Let him undertake the task of idyll so as to display that pastoral innocence even in creatures of civilization and under all the conditions of the most active and vigorous life, of expansive thought, of the subtlest art, the highest social refinement which, in a word, leads man who cannot now go back to Arcady forward to Elysium.[26]

Schiller's essay was an important source for the ambivalent romanticists of the twentieth century (it was much admired by Thomas Mann for example).

---

[24] Friedrich von Schiller, '*Naïve and Sentimental Poetry*' and '*On the Sublime*': *Two Essays*, trans, with introduction and notes by Julius A. Elias (New York: Frederick Ungar, 1966), 111.

[25] *Ibid.*, 116–17.   [26] *Ibid.*, 153.

It is a productive point of reference for any consideration of the manner in which romantic ideas are sceptically sustained through the late nineteenth and twentieth centuries. We saw in Chapter 1 how Schiller informed Hirsch's study of romantic *lieder* up to Mahler. Recent scholarship has also explored Mahler and the nineteenth-century symphonic tradition in Schillerian terms. Mahler's Fourth Symphony, for example, has been described as a 'willful distortion' of Beethoven's Ninth with the childhood innocence and violent images in the finale an 'ambivalent Elysium' worlds removed from Schiller's joyful universal vision,[27] and the 'late idyll' of Brahms's Second Symphony has been compared, in passing, with Mahler's nature music.[28] In the previous chapter, we saw how the naïve was evoked, rejected and its return desired in Mahler's setting of 'Urlicht', and Carl Niekerk has talked of how the fourth movement of the Third Symphony, the setting of Nietzsche's 'Midnight Song', is 'surely' sentimental and how it 'points to the problematic nature of all sentimental poetry. The narrator has just woken up, and he desires to return to his previous state of sleep and dream.' This contrasts with the 'naïve, unbroken, unmediated expression' of the *Des Knaben Wunderhorn* text setting in the fifth movement.[29] Ryan R. Kangas's consideration of artificial simplicity and constructed naïvety (noted in Mahler's music by contemporaneous critics such as Ritter and Hirschfeld as well as modern writers such as Johnson) also evokes the spirit of Schiller's naïve and sentimental.[30] And Schiller (after Maynard Solomon's famous reading of Beethoven's Ninth) informs Anthony Newcomb's reading of Mahler's Ninth Symphony as illustrating the paradigm of a 'circular or spiral quest', a spiritual route through evil and suffering, through a fall into conflict and compulsion to move towards a higher integration.[31]

More broadly, Barbara Barry has proposed Mahler as an example of a broadly 'sentimental' composer who highlights the need for 'flexible strategies' in the individual artwork. Barry persuasively argues that Schiller's

[27] Mark Evan Bonds, 'Ambivalent Elysium: Mahler's Fourth Symphony', in *After Beethoven*, 177–8. See Maynard Solomon, 'The Ninth Symphony: A Search for Order', in *Beethoven Essays* (Cambridge, Mass.: Harvard University Press, 1988), 3–32.

[28] Reinhold Brinkmann, *Late Idyll: The Second Symphony of Johannes Brahms*, trans. Peter Palmer (Cambridge, Mass.: Harvard University Press, 1995), 189.

[29] Carl Niekerk, 'Mahler *contra* Wagner: The Philosophical Legacy of Romanticism in Gustav Mahler's Third and Fourth Symphonies', *The German Quarterly* 77 (2004), 196.

[30] Ryan R. Kangas, 'Classical Style, Childhood and Nostalgia in Mahler's Fourth Symphony', *Nineteenth Century Music Review* 8 (2011), 219–36.

[31] Anthony Newcomb, 'Narrative Archetypes and Mahler's Ninth Symphony', in Steven Paul Scher (ed.), *Music and Text: Critical Inquiries* (Cambridge University Press, 1992), 118–36.

terms need to be regarded, even in the work of those composers who seem to fall broadly into one side of the dualism, as 'tendencies'.[32] Keller classes Mahler, in company with Beethoven, as amongst those who are prototypically 'sentimentalic' (to use Keller's idiosyncratic translation) because of Mahler's propensity to focus on 'striving developments'. Keller argues that the basis of Britten's admiration for Mahler lies in the contrast in artistic character,[33] as Britten is identified, in company with Mozart, as a naïve composer of 'front-rank genius'. In support, Keller notes Britten's aversion to Beethovenian development and his preference for a simplicity and clarity which in the modern age may seem anachronistic. But Keller's characterization of Mahler is too one-dimensional (for example, striving development is often seriously questioned or juxtaposed with anti-developmental alternatives – for example, the static, or the breakthrough moment) and as we shall see Britten too is a composer whose music moves between apparent naïvety to an overtly modern sentimental. Barry's proposal of 'tendencies', shifting across a composer's oeuvre and within individual works, is much more persuasive and also a more sophisticated basis for generating hermeneutic reading through comparison of the two composers. Indeed, several recent readings of Mahler's Fourth Symphony have suggested or implied the complexity of naïve and sentimental elements.[34]

II

Britten's Mahlerian awakening is often identified with his hearing the Fourth Symphony while a student at the Royal College of Music in 1930. At first, however, Britten was ambivalent. A diary entry of 23 September 1930 describes the symphony as 'much too long, but beautiful in parts'.[35] A later entry (23 April 1933) is more telling and fulsome in its tribute: 'This

[32] Barbara R. Barry, 'Schiller's (and Berlin's) "Naïve" and "Sentimental": Propensity and Pitfalls in the Philosophical Categorization of Artists', in Christoph Asmuth, Gunter Scholtz and Franz-Bernhard Stammkötter (eds.), *Philosophischer Gedanke und musikalischer Klang: Zum Wechselverhältnis von Musik und Philosophie* (Frankfurt/Main: Campus, 1999), 155–61.

[33] Hans Keller, 'Operatic Music and Britten', in David Herbert (ed.), *The Operas of Benjamin Britten* (London: Hamish Hamilton, 1979), xii–xxxi. See also Keller's essay 'Britten and Mozart' (1946, rev. 1952), in *Music and Psychology*, ed. Christopher Wintle (London: Plumbago, 2003), 164–76.

[34] Raymond Knapp, 'Suffering Children: Perspectives on Innocence and Vulnerability in Mahler's Fourth Symphony', *19th Century Music* 22 (1999), 240. See also parts of Donald Mitchell's reading in 'Swallowing the Programme: Mahler's Fourth Symphony', in Mitchell and Nicholson (eds.), *The Mahler Companion*, 208–10.

[35] Evans, *Journeying Boy*, 53.

work seems a mix up of everything that one has ever heard, but it is definitely Mahler. Like a lovely spring day.'[36] During a visit to Vienna in November 1934, Britten bought the score (the Britten-Pears Library holds a miniature score of the Fourth dated in Britten's hand 'Wien 1934') and the following day he heard it performed under the baton of Mengelberg. Britten's diary entry shows that the symphony's length remained an issue, if less strongly so: 'I enjoyed this work enormously – I know it's long – but not too long (except perhaps the third movement) for me.'[37] His later assessment of the symphony was unequivocally positive: in the 1942 essay 'On Behalf of Gustav Mahler' he wrote, recalling the concert of September 1930, on the striking ambiguity created by the coexistence of apparent spontaneity and complex artifice:

The form was so cunningly contrived; every development surprised one and yet sounded inevitable. Above all, the material was remarkable, and the melodic shapes highly original, with such rhythmic and harmonic tension from beginning to end. After that concert, I made every effort to hear Mahler's music.[38]

In Britten's diaries throughout the 1930s there are many comments on Mahler's music in which he records purchases and reflects on concerts and radio broadcasts. Britten bought the score of *Lieder eines fahrenden Gesellen* in January 1931 and on 6 May that year heard Maria Olszewska perform them at the Queen's Hall, London, where they confirmed his antipathy for Richard Strauss and (especially) Elgar: 'Lovely little pieces, exquisitely scored – a lesson to all the Elgars and Strausses in the world. *Enigma* Variations a terrible contrast to these little wonders.'[39] On hearing a BBC radio broadcast of these songs on 17 December 1935, he called them 'absolute peaches'.[40] Britten mentions several performances of Mahler songs with Sophie Wyss and on 12 April 1936 identified 'Ich ging mit Lust durch einen grünen Wald' as the Britten family's 'great favourite'.[41] He soon began collecting Mahler scores more extensively. The Britten-Pears library holds copies of *Des Knaben Wunderhorn* and the 'Seven Last Songs' ('Revelge', 'Der Tambourg'sell' and the five Rückert songs) dated 1935 in Britten's hand; a score of *Das Lied von der Erde* is dated 1936; a copy of the Sixth Symphony is signed and dated 1937. *Kindertotenlieder* is mentioned especially enthusiastically in a series of diary comments during 1934–6. On hearing Bruno Walter conducting the Fifth Symphony in a radio broadcast

---

[36] *Ibid.*, 138.   [37] *Ibid.*, 231.

[38] 'On Behalf of Gustav Mahler' [1942], in Paul Kildea (ed.), *Britten on Music* (Oxford University Press, 2003), 38–9.

[39] Evans, *Journeying Boy*, 72.   [40] *Ibid.*, 291.   [41] *Ibid.*, 346.

on 4 October 1934 he wrote: 'Enormously long but I was interested and thrilled for the full one hour and ten minutes.'[42] On 11 June 1936 he is reading the scores of the First and Fifth Symphonies and *Das Lied von der Erde* for 'recreation'.[43] Later that year, on 29 October, after attending a concert performance of *Das Lied* he wrote: 'what a work – it moves me more than any other music – certainly of this century. [Mahler] seems to be gaining a large public here – which is almost annoying – one doesn't want to share one's beauty spots!'[44] His teacher, Frank Bridge, gave him the Peters Edition of the Fifth, inscribed 'Benjy. Love from me F.B, Xmas 1936'. On 8 July 1936, Britten notes that he is 'pouring over' the symphonies and comments that 'there is a tremendous amount in common' with later Beethoven Quartets.[45] He heard the Eighth Symphony on 9 February 1938 at a Henry Wood concert: 'execrable performance – but even then the work made a tremendous impression. I was physically exhausted at the end – and furious with the lack of understanding all around.' The next day he noted that the combination of this symphony and a dodgy stomach was 'too much for my health'.[46] Of Mahler's Ninth (27 January 1935) he wrote: 'wonderful . . . I could listen to this for hours. The End is really very moving.'[47] A copy of the 1912 Universal Edition of the Ninth is dedicated 'An meinem liebsten Ben – Weihnacht 1938. Peter'.

Two of Britten's conducting scores of Mahler's Fourth are held in the Britten-Pears Library: the Universal Edition from 1952 (UE 952 L W; the revised edition previously copyright 1943 by Boosey & Hawkes) and the Universal Edition from the Internationalen Gustav Mahler Gesellschaft Kritische Gesamtausgabe Band IV, 1963 with editorial notes by Erwin Ratz (UE 13823). Britten performed and recorded the symphony in Orford in 1961. Both scores are fairly heavily annotated by Britten to note changes in scoring between the two editions. Of greater interest are Britten's interpretative markings, especially in the first movement. In both scores he marks bar 4 'leisurely' and the first cadence of the symphony (b. 6) he writes 'simple'; at fig. 13 he writes 'Easy', and this becomes a very common annotation on the first movement. At fig. 18 he translates 'behaglich' as 'comfortable' in both scores, and at bar 305, again in both, he writes 'casual'. In the third movement both copies have 'very calm' at the cadence of bar 36; at fig. 4, both copies are marked 'charming' (possibly a translation of Anmutig); at bar 147, both have 'gently!' (in 1952 this is emphasized with two exclamations). All these expressive annotations highlight not

---

[42] *Ibid.*, 226.   [43] *Ibid.*, 359.   [44] *Ibid.*, 383.   [45] *Ibid.*, 362.   [46] *Ibid.*, 464.   [47] *Ibid.*, 245.

only the qualities of ease and restfulness, and (perhaps unsurprisingly) the role of cadence in evoking these states, but also the simplicity of the technical means of evocation. The opposing sense of disquiet in the symphony (upon which Mahler once commented to Bauer-Lechner[48]) is highlighted by Britten's annotation of 'passionato', in both of his scores, over the violin part in bars 187–9 of the first movement, a line which is a transformation of the apparent simplicity of the movement's opening and partly sounds like an attempt to return or restart in the face of increasing instability (Example 2.4). But this ardently expressive tone is swiped away by the brassy climax of fig. 16 (bb. 209ff.). In both of his scores, Britten writes 'Broad' here, which, while it may simply be an indication of how he wished the tempo should be felt, is hard to resist interpreting as identifying a vulgarity of tone (especially as, in the BBC recording of Britten conducting the London Symphony Orchestra at Orford Church on 6 July 1961, the tempo does not noticeably slow at this moment, but maintains its rather brisk momentum[49]). This brash climax on a second inversion C major harmony can be heard as a rhetorically emphasized example of 'second tonality'; it has a sort of dominant six-four quality which relates it to the examples from the previous chapter, but epiphany is replaced by cacophony. It reveals the falsity or second-handedness of its diatonicism. On the surface it is uncultured, naïve and direct. Adler would surely cite it as deliberately, constructively 'crass'. It is a mood which is soon dismissed: in Adornian terms its glaring brightness collapses into dark 'negative fulfilment' and the subsequent move into recapitulation is of notable technical subtlety and complex artifice (on which much more in the next chapter). At the risk of reading too much into Britten's markings, they seem to offer illumination as to what he thought to be the important expressive states; in short, the coexistence of restfulness, instability, crudity and sophistication.

Christopher Mark suggests that the 'luminous diatonic passages' of the final movement of Mahler's Fourth 'may well have contributed towards Britten's heavy investment in diatonicism', thus partly fulfilling a 'need to distance himself' from the influence of Frank Bridge.[50] Certainly there

[48] Bauer-Lechner, *Recollections of Gustav Mahler*, 152.
[49] The recording is available on *Britten the Performer 4*: Mahler, Symphony no. 4; *Lieder eines fahrenden Gesellen*; 'Das irlische Leben'; 'Wer hat dies Liedlein erdacht?' (BBCB 80004–2, 1999). Joan Carlyle is the soprano solo in the symphony's last movement; Anna Reynolds sings the *Gesellen* lieder, recorded at the Snape Maltings in 1972, Elly Ameling the two *Wunderhorn* songs, recorded at Blythburgh Church in 1969 (in both the latter with Britten conducting the English Chamber Orchestra).
[50] Christopher Mark, 'Juvenilia (1922–32)' in Mervyn Cooke (ed.), *The Cambridge Companion to Britten* (Cambridge University Press, 1999), 31.

Example 2.4 Mahler, Symphony no. 4, first movement, bb. 184–90.

Example 2.4 (cont.)

appears to have been a difference of opinion between Britten and Bridge on Mahler's significance. Britten noted in his diary on 23 March 1936 that during a conversation with Bridge about his collaborations with Auden: 'in fact we are in complete agreement over all – except Mahler! – though he admits he [Mahler] is a great thinker'.[51] Writing in 1947, Britten noted that Bridge's 'inclination was instinctively towards the French tradition of skill, grace and good workmanship, and away from 19th-century German decadence'.[52] But clarity is something Britten also heard in Mahler: 'I've always inclined to the clear and clean – the "slender" sound of, say, Mozart, or Verdi or Mahler.'[53] (So, Mahler is now grouped with two of the prime candidates as naïve composers!) And Britten's encounter with Mahler's music in the 1930s can be considered a complementary counterpart to his being 'knocked sideways' by Bridge's *The Sea*, a work he heard as a ten year old at a concert conducted by the composer in Norwich in October 1924. A Bridge–Mahler opposition, though easy to hear in many stylistic characteristics, is weakened when recognition is granted to the common ground in their treatments of what, after Thomas Peattie, we might call a 'broken' pastoral.[54] And here lies a key to Britten's development of his own problematically redemptive pastoral moments in which naïve and sentimental relationships to visions of nature mingle in complex ambiguity.

In Bridge's *The Sea*, the seascape's waves become an image of the breakdown of romantic utopian hopes as the circular, regenerative relationship of the naïve and sentimental – Schiller's hope in the regenerative, renewing powers of a cyclic relationship of naïve immediacy and sentimental self-reflection, in a reactivation of innocent play in the face of potentially debilitating self-awareness – collapses.[55] The musical wave, as both picturesque detail and as large-scale structural process, had long held a vital role in generating romantic expressive effect. Such wave processes often suggest Schiller's notion of striving for progression towards Elysium, a voyage towards a higher synthesis of nature and culture envisaged, imagined or desired beyond

[51] Evans, *Journeying Boy*, 342.

[52] Britten, 'Frank Bridge and English Chamber Music' (1947) in Kildea (ed.), *Britten on Music*, 75–6.

[53] 'Conversation with Benjamin Britten' *Tempo* no. 6 (Feb. 1944), 4–5.

[54] Thomas Peattie, 'In Search of Lost Time: Memory and Mahler's Broken Pastoral', in Painter (ed.), *Mahler and his World*, 185–98.

[55] See Jill Berman, 'History can Restore Naivety to the Sentimental: Schiller's Letters on Wallenstein', *The Modern Language Review* 81 (1986), 369–87. For a fuller discussion of Bridge's work, see my essay 'Modern Maritime Pastoral: Wave Deformations in the music of Frank Bridge', in Matthew Riley (ed.), *British Music and Modernism 1895–1960* (Aldershot: Ashgate, 2010), 93–107, from which the following paragraphs are condensed.

the horizon. Though it is infused with nostalgia for the paradise of naïve immediacy and unreflective unity which have been lost in the self-conscious, alienated experience of the modern age, its positive tones suggest that this is a voyage of regeneration not regression. But Schiller's ultimately utopian vision collapses. The notion of a musical wave can move across a divide which Dahlhaus, Adorno (and many others, especially Austro-Germans) have posited between the 'picturesque' – a static, repetitive image of nature – and the 'symphonic' – a dynamic, teleological, developmental, unifying process.[56] It is also, therefore, a potentially powerful notion given modernism's characteristic critique of such polar categories (often heard in Mahler, which in this way exposed and extended tensions immanent in much romantic music). Furthermore, the wave is a close relative to Mahler's *Naturlaut* as part of modernist discourse, as evocative of 'second nature' and deviation from symphonic process, as an exposing of the artificiality of the cultural construction of both musical teleology and the idea of nature.[57]

Britain, by contrast with Mahler's *Mitteleuropa*, is of course a maritime region. In 'maritime' art, Kenneth McConkey writes, 'the sea is not neutral: it is the site for allegory, for fortune, fate and the hand of God. More than any other genre', McConkey continues:

marine and coastal scenes overtly addressed the natural virtues of an island race . . . The sea, like the artist's material, was there to be conquered, and its ubiquity dominated national thinking. It assumed a personality which was unpredictable and which defied interpretation; it was characterized as "she". "Nature", elsewhere a metaphor for growth and decay, was, within these terminologies, a gratuitous and irrational force.[58]

A seascape thus functioned as the backdrop for projecting crucially significant artistic values and subjective, cultural and political apprehensions. It

---

[56] A 'musical depiction of nature is almost always defined negatively, by being excluded from the imperative of organic development, the *Klangflache* conveys a landscape because it is exempted both from the principle of teleological progression and from the textures of thematic-motivic manipulation'. Carl Dahlhaus, *Nineteenth-Century Music*, trans. J Bradford Robinson (Berkeley: University of California Press, 1989), 309. Adorno contrasted Beethovenian teleological, developmental symphonism with Schubert's repetitions of images which, rather than organic transformations or generated by evolution, are apparitions, timelessly the same, though seen in changes of light in the different landscapes viewed by the wandering observer; Adorno, 'Schubert' (1928), trans. Jonathan Dunsby and Beate Perrey, *19th-Century Music* 29 (2005), 7–14. See, amongst the essays collected in response, especially Scott Burnham, 'Landscape as Music, Landscape as Truth: Schubert and the Burden of Repetition', *19th-Century Music* 29 (2005), 31–41.

[57] See Julian Johnson, 'Mahler and the Idea of Nature', in Barham (ed.), *Perspectives on Gustav Mahler*, 23–36.

[58] Kenneth McConkey, *Memory and Desire: Painting in Britain and Ireland at the Turn of the Twentieth Century* (Aldershot: Ashgate, 2002), 107–9.

can therefore invoke the pastoral's ability 'to both contain and appear to evade tensions and contradictions'.[59] It can also sustain and intensify the problematic relationship of man and nature. In particular, the manner in which the pastoral return or retreat contains paradoxes and criticisms, how it approaches the 'anti-pastoral', reveals cultural anxieties of the present.

On its first performance, the critic of *The Times* described Bridge's *The Sea* as 'vividly picturesque and full of fine feeling'.[60] These comments suggest a double quality, both the sensuously immediate particular and a super-sensuous, reflective Idea. Indeed, at crucial moments virtuosic tone painting is displaced by more subjective expression. At the two main climaxes of the first movement, entitled 'Seascape', picturesque, 'surface' melodic wave shapes and the 'tone painting' characteristic of the work's opening disappear. This signals a move from the representational to the subjectively expressive or symbolic – a move from aesthetic contemplation of the seascape to subjective response based on the symbolic resonances of the soundscape. At the high-point of the larger climactic wave form (fig. 3), there is a transformation of a previous birdsong-like *Naturklang* into majestic or celebratory material. This moves into a *Largamente* dynamic climax where the melodic accentuation, rhythmic articulation and dominance of the trumpets alter the topic from depictive sea imagery (or its transformations) to its symbolic association with the heroic, in this context naval and national. The impression is of the monumental – of memorialization through an attempt to create a stable image (see Example 2.5a). There is also an effect of an attempt to 'naturalize' this heroism through the return of an element of melodic pentatonicism. But this change of topic is stated over a move from the tonic major to the minor triad on the submediant, a simple move but one which lends the progression a melancholic hue. This character betrays the truth that the effect at the peak of the wave – whether of the monumental or the 'natural' – is ephemeral, a revelation confirmed by the dissolution of the wave climax over a long sustained supertonic ninth chord.

After a new theme of an idyllic character and chromatic dissolution there is a rather sudden reappearance of the earlier climactic material. Despite repeating the dynamic level, *largamente* broadness and bold, trumpet-led orchestration of the first highpoint, this second statement is deeply prob-lematic. It is not reached by strong, goal-directed, wave-form intensifica-tion – rather, it comes suddenly, as a willed recollection at the movement's

---

[59] Terry Gifford, *Pastoral* (London: Routledge, 1999), 11.
[60] *The Times*, 25 September 1912; cited in Trevor Bray, *Frank Bridge: A Life in Brief*. Online: http://trevor-bray-music-research.co.uk/Bridge.

Example 2.5a Frank Bridge, *The Sea*, 'Seascape', fig. 3.

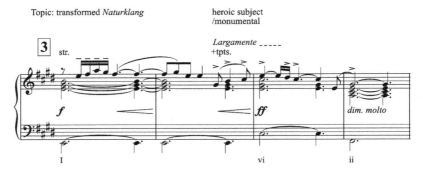

Example 2.5b Bridge, *The Sea*, 'Seascape', fig. 9.

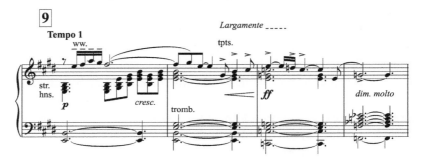

lowest energetic point. In its sudden effect it might suggest the Mahlerian technique of breakthrough, or the Benjaminian rupture of Messianic time. However, at the topical change to the evocation of heroic naval nationalism, the harmony shifts a semitone lower than in the first statement. The transposition replaces the minor triad on the submediant of E (C♯) with a flat submediant C major triad (see Example 2.5b). The effect created is paradoxical. The C *major* triad might suggest a positive transformation, but the darkening of the tone produced by the semitonal lowering is pronounced and this is reinforced by the dissolution now occurring on the Neapolitan F minor ninth. Here lies the crux of the movement. The breakthrough and deformation of wave form evokes the problem of memorializing a vanishing, unrepeatable heroic and idyllic past.

Other important works by Bridge demonstrate similarities with Mahler's interrogations of the structural and expressive function of the romantic, 'salvation' dominant six-four. The Phantasy for Piano, Violin, Viola and Cello (1910) is in the usual Cobbett 'phantasy' arch form. The A section is in F♯ minor, with D major the contrasting second key. In the transition towards the closing paragraph of this first section (3 bars after fig. 3), the D major harmony is turned to an augmented sixth to lead to climactic resolution onto an F♯ minor six-four chord at the return of the main theme. The anticipated resolution to the dominant, however, is absent. The central section is in D minor (♭vi/F♯) with a shift to E♭ at its centre. In the return to the A section (20 after fig. 16), an unstable, attenuated, fragmented return of the work's opening flourish and first theme in D minor moves to a recapitulation of the second theme in its original D major. The A section's original tonic F♯ is so far avoided. Recomposition of this theme is slight and leads to expectation of a climactic move to the dominant six-four of F♯ at the return of the primary theme, as had occurred in the opening section. The build-up to the climax is rewritten and intensified (from fig. 18), but the anticipated climactic six-four is avoided. D minor seventh harmony (D–F–A–C, rather than an augmented sixth) moves directly to F♯ minor root position. (As a kind of short-circuiting of the diatonic model it bears comparison with the cadence in Example 2.1.) Britten seems to be identifying this problematized moment of return, where the preceding exposed romantic model is anticipated but then eschewed or darkened, when he writes:

> there is one moment after a big climax towards the end of the piece when something bigger and more uncomfortable occurs. There comes a kind of nostalgic surge, with a passion outside the scope of the piece and, I think, slightly marring it. It is this tendency which I believe was important in Bridge's early music, if disturbing, and led to his development ... The seed of discontent, or whatever it was, at the end of the *Phantasy*, grew and grew until the horrible protest of his Piano Sonata.[61]

Mahler's music may have confirmed for Britten what the music of Bridge had already suggested, a manner of continuing to hold at a work's centre tensions between naïve and sentimental in a cosmopolitan musical 'dialect' distinguishable from the apparently more parochial pastoralism he heard most prominently exemplified by the music of Vaughan Williams.[62] (Bridge followed a decidedly cosmopolitan path.)

With Bridge's orchestral work in mind, consider Britten's setting of W.H. Auden's poem 'On this Island', titled 'Seascape' in the song cycle which

---

[61] Kildea (ed.), *Britten on Music*, 76. Bridge's Piano Sonata, which Britten identifies as the successor to this moment in the Phantasy, is one of Bridge's most ambitious and darkly hued pieces, written as a work of elegy in the shadow of the First World War. The sonata's slow movement presents material which harks back to Bridge's simpler, more diatonic style of the pre-war years, and builds to an overt statement of the 'salvation' dominant six-four topic (bb. 23–27). The context of this material (it is surrounded by often rather bleakly dissonant music) greatly imperils the nostalgic or utopian desires this moment seems to propose.

[62] See 'The Folk-Art Problem', *Modern Music* 18 (1941), 71–5.

takes this poem's name *On this Island* (1937). (The poem is from Auden's collection *Look, Stranger* of 1936.)

Look, stranger, on this island now
The leaping light for your delight discovers,
Stand stable here
And silent be,
That through the channels of the ear
May wander like a river
The swaying sound of the sea.

Here at the small field's ending pause
When the chalk wall falls to the foam and its tall ledges
Oppose the pluck
And knock of the tide,
And the shingle scrambles after the suck-
-ing surf,
And the gull lodges
A moment on its sheer side.

Far off like floating seeds the ships
Diverge on urgent voluntary errands,
And the full view
Indeed may enter
And move in memory as now these clouds do,
That pass the harbour mirror
And all the summer through the water saunter.

Nathalie Vincent-Arnaud reads the title of Auden's collection as an invitation to a visionary ritual and notes a poetic double reading of the pictorial – one purely referential the other 'metatextual', as it is a product overtly infused by previous artistic representations in the memory of the poet. In Vincent-Arnaud's persuasive reading, the poem begins with the immanence of the physical vision ('Look') and moves to the recreative transcendence of the spirit ('And the full view / Indeed may enter / And move in memory'). The 'trajectory towards destruction in the light' is suggestive of pantheistic romanticism and the last line returns to the sound of the sea in waves of internal rhythms, rhymes and alliteration.[63] In this way, the poem displays,

---

[63] Nathalie Vincent-Arnaud, 'Regards sur un paysage anglais: "Seascape" de W. H. Auden à Benjamin Britten', *LISA e-journal* 4 (2006), 159–69. My thanks to Emilie Capulet for translating this article.

in miniature form, similarities with the ambiguities of Bridge's *The Sea*, which moved from picturesque evocation of naïve, immediate sensation through 'sentimental' reflection.

In a cycle in which many songs overtly display, indeed celebrate, their compositional models and borrowings (and in this way mirror Auden's poetic technique), Britten's setting of this poem is, for Stephen Banfield, the one most independent of any model. Banfield also notes Britten's avoidance of post-Wagnerian harmonic symbolism – the chromatic telling of 'dirty secrets' under vocal declamations – in order to 'bring back the primal nature of song as sung melody'.[64] This suggests the evocation, or desired return to naïve innocence. Mahler famously once declared that he desired 'song not *de-cla-ma-tion*'.[65] Mahler's songs demonstrate how melodic simplicity can combine with harmonic subtleties (as 'telling' as Wagner's erotic harmonies) and poignantly transformed returns, as apparently naïve direct expression turns to sentimental modern tones. In this way, what appears in the modern artwork to evoke the primal will always be revealed as 'second' sense, as mediated and reflective. 'Seascape' suggests similar processes. The song is set in 'innocent' C major, though it opens with a piano motive (G–A–B–B♭) which seems a little more knowingly complicated, a miniature wave rising diatonically to the leading-note, but falling chromatically to deny the expected (desired?) upward resolution of the leading-note, suggesting 'flatness' and implying continued descent to the sixth degree A (Example 2.6, bb. 1–5). The diatonicism in the following vocal melody highlights the leading-note, the sixth (A) and (at its only really dissonant moment) modal mixture. At the end of the first verse, the setting of Auden's line 'That through the channels of the ear', the voice picks up the piano's wave motive in a transposition which emphasizes the A–A♭ chromatic–modal conflict – the 'flatness' of the A♭ triad being heard as departure at the word 'wander'. At the closing line of the first verse ('the swaying sound of the sea'), tonal and motivic return combine, with the voice doubling the piano's G–A–B–B♭–A wave, ending on the 'added' sixth C–E–G–A harmony. The verse moves from depictive motive to inner, psychological relationship of the observer to the seascape (who is urged in the second line of the verse to stand still and silent at the sight). It is set over a bass descent C–B–B♭–A–A♭–G, a traditional figure of lament, related to (or derived from) the melancholic chromatic descent of the opening wave motive.

---

[64] Stephen Banfield, *Sensibility and English Song*, vol. 2 (Cambridge University Press, 1985), 384, 388. For further commentary on the cycle see Donald Mitchell, *Britten and Auden in the Thirties: The Year 1936* (London: Faber, 1981).

[65] Ernst Decsay, 'Stunden mit Mahler', *Die Musik* 40 (1911), 143–4.

Example 2.6a Britten, 'Seascape' (Auden), *On this Island*, bb. 1–17.

In the final verse, set as the return to C following the more tonally mobile middle section, at the key line 'And the full view indeed may enter and move into memory' Britten expands and enriches the potential for 'flatness' heard in the music of the first verse, a move made psychologically potent by the apparently naïve diatonic realm of the opening. This chromatic enrichment is an intensification which leads to the highpoint of the dominant six-four harmony (Example 2.6b). These technical and expressive details allow Britten's music to be precisely compared with Mahler, even when (as through much of this song, excepting perhaps the added sixths) his music

Example 2.6a (cont.)

does not *sound* especially 'Mahlerian'. For Keller, Mahler was the first to develop a 'ruthlessly truthful' music which was 'self-observing'. Britten's music develops similarly: the poetic 'Look!' is musically turned in on itself. The response to the sea view is look inward. And with the caveat that Keller's characterization of Mahler is too one-dimensional, we can agree that if 'the central, interconnected problems of our art are three: the loss of

Example 2.6b Britten, 'Seascape', close.

naivety, how to own up to the pain of it, and how to cope with it', then 'amongst composers without naivety, Mahler ... is the greatest and newest of all time'.[66] In Britten, the more we recognize the conjunction of apparent

---

[66] Hans Keller, 'The Unpopularity of Mahler's Popularity' (1971), in *Essays on Music*, 70.

Example 2.6b (cont.)

naivety and its loss, the stronger are the parallels with Mahler. And through the invocation of memory and the structural procedure of tonal return this 'looking' is not just inward but backwards.

The song ends with the implied pentatonicism of the added sixth chord, with its overt resonances with Mahler, particularly with the ending of *Das Lied von der Erde*. In a letter to Henry Boys of June 1937 (*On this Island* was completed in October that year), Britten described his response to the repetitions of *'ewig'* in Mahler's 'Der Abschied' which he heard in Bruno Walter's pioneering recording: 'It has the beauty of loneliness & of pain: of strength & freedom. The beauty of disappointment & never-satisfied love. The cruel beauty of nature, and everlasting beauty of monotony.'[67] Alongside the echoes of Mahler's harmonic 'earthscape' Britten's 'Seascape' bears fruitful comparison with Mahler's manipulation of formal procedure in conjunction with the preoccupation with looking at beauty, glancing backwards, and the loss of innocence in 'Von der Schönheit', the fourth song of *Das Lied*. Mahler's song demonstrates a combination of strophic and ternary form, of sharply defined contrasts, development and return in the expression of innocence and erotic awakening. The closing section is particularly subtle. For Adorno here the irrecoverable is rediscovered 'the strength to name the forgotten that is concealed in the stuff of experience' is found in 'hope's last dwelling-place'; an idea Mahler 'rescued from childhood'. The youthful maiden casts her lover 'long yearning looks': Adorno argues that 'such is the look of the work itself, absorbing, doubting, turned backwards with precipitous tenderness'.[68] The final poetic lines read:

Und die schönste von den Jungfrau'n sendet
Lange Blicke ihm der Sehnsucht nach.
Ihre stolze Haltung ist nur Verstellung.
In dem Funkeln ihrer grossen Augen,
In dem Dunkel ihres heissen Blicks
Schwingt klagend noch die Erregung ihres Herzens nach.

And the fairest of those lovely maidens
Sends a parting glance of longing love
Her proud demeanour is all pretending.
In the sparkle of her large eyes,
In the darkness of her heated glance,
That melancholy agitation of her heart still vibrates.

The motive associated with the maiden's beauty (first introduced at 2 before fig. 6, returning at 2 before fig. 18) is of more chromatic hue than the diatonic/pentatonicism characterizing much of the song. That which evokes the yearning glance backwards in the vocal part 'restores' pentatonicism (4 after fig. 17). In the instrumental epilogue this conflict between pentatonicism, diatonicism and chromaticism is intensified. The final cadence is especially poignant and complex (see Example 2.7) The chromatic motive of beauty is intensified to turn tonic G major to minor as the first element in an increasing 'flatwards' tonal turn. The pentatonic motive is altered and

[67] Donald Mitchell (ed.), *Letters from a Life: The Selected Letters and Diaries of Benjamin Britten*, vol. 1 (London: Faber, 1991), 493.
[68] Adorno, *Mahler*, 145–6.

Example 2.7 Mahler, 'Von der Schönheit', *Das Lied von der Erde*, close.

employed in chromatic counterpoint whose overt technical cleverness
speaks of cultural know-how rather than natural naïvety. This leads to the
augmented sixth pre-dominant chord on E♭ (fig. 22), whose resolution to
the dominant six-four ushers in the return of pentatonicism and the crucial
top voice chromatic move from D♭/C♯ to D, a reversal of the chromaticism
which underpinned the epilogue's move away from diatonic/pentatonic at 5
bars after fig. 21. The final motivic element is a rising sixth D–B, the major
alternative to the D–B♭ of the chromatic motive. The epilogue's ambiguity,
based on a sense of attempted return to the 'natural' condition of naïvety

which remains culturally coloured is a final reminder of the vocal opening of the song, whose surprise entry on the minor third B♭ clearly signals that this is an idyll that never was. Mahler's use of formal and harmonic return is especially inspired here.[69] Britten's 'Seascape', like 'Von der Schönheit', encapsulates the task of return, an issue which also dominates Bridge's cyclic returns, arch forms and problematic endings (for example, the final cyclic return of the climactic theme in the finale of *The Sea*)[70] and the 'Pastoral' from Britten's *Serenade*, which in this way Barringer hears as prefiguring, in particular, *Peter Grimes*.

Many have commented on the moves from illustrative, depictive music of 'nature' to levels of symbolic and psychological resonance in *Grimes*. For Barringer, *Grimes* explores the 'darker aspects of the neo-Romantic sensibility, allowing Britten to reveal not so much the picturesqueness as the complexity, the incipient violence and intolerance, of the English village and its surrounding land and seascapes'.[71] On the *Grimes* interludes, Desmond Shawe-Taylor, in his review of the first performance, noted a relationship with the apparent simplicity of the *Serenade*: 'It looks so simple, that innate pictorialism of Britten's, which we have already admired in the *Serenade*.'[72] But in a neo-romantic manner, the pastoral image of the uncomplicated life is imbued with psychological turmoil and anxiety. For Harris, Britten's *Grimes* is 'the most passionate of all the period's meteorological art', and reading Crabbe's 'The Borough' while in the United States reignited for Britten the importance of a sense of belonging to place, for it chimed with Britten's ambivalent attraction to the cruel beauty of the Suffolk coast of his home. In this place lie hopes of homely comfort but also threats of violent rejection. The figure of Grimes 'embodies the spirit of disorder and disruption': he is a man who 'yearns for peace', who 'imagines order and then tears it apart'.[73] Such fundamental themes of opposition are paralleled by the tonal structure of the opera. As Brett notes, the 'visionary' Grimes has music characteristically in D, E or A, keys which conflict with the tonal worlds used in music related to the 'reality' of the Borough (for example, E♭ in the pub or storm scene, B♭ in the courtroom and during the manhunt).

---

[69] In a study of Britten's *Night-Piece* (another piece in C where, as in 'Seascape', the pentatonic added sixth plays a vital role), Christopher Wintle writes: 'ternary form is central to tonal music; yet it is easy to forget that the form distils many kinds of feeling – the return of the known, the joy and relief of a child at a parent's return'. Christopher Wintle, *All the Gods: Benjamin Britten's 'Night-Piece' in Context* (London: Plumbago, 2006), 82.

[70] Bridge pursued the potential of 'arch forms' throughout his career; see Trevor Bray, 'Bridge's *Novelletten* and *Idylls*', *The Musical Times* 117, no. 1605 (1976), 905–6.

[71] Barringer, '"I am a native, rooted here"', 154.   [72] Cited in Brett, *Peter Grimes*, 153.

[73] Harris, *Romantic Moderns*, 164.

The musical restoration of order in the ternary design of Grimes's aria which ends Act 1 scene 1 (from fig. 41) begins with Grimes recalling the stormy weather on the fateful day when his apprentice died, with rising E–F ninths as a melodic encapsulation of the human effort to survive against a hostile nature, emphasizing the traditionally mournful ♭6–5 motive in A minor, but also, through its subsequent descent, outlining a melodic wave. There are four varied statements of this melodic idea, each of which begins in A minor, but on the fourth statement ('And the boy's silent reproach') the tonality shifts flatwards, emphasizing the melancholic motive as A♭–G in a fleeting C minor before a wrenching return to A minor (achieved by enharmonically inverting the sinking A♭–G to leading-note rising to tonic G♯–A). Two further varied restatements of the melodic arch or wave in A minor complete the first section. Balstrode interrupts Grimes to provide the transition to the contrasting middle section ('This storm is useful; you can speak your mind ... There is more grandeur in a gale of wind to free confession'). The middle section is a vivace dialogue between Balstrode and Grimes set in a D major with Lydian and chromatic inflections. When Balstrode leaves Grimes to rejoin the community that is drinking in the pub, the return to A minor and Grimes's soliloquy is marked by one of the opera's most famous musical moments. The mode turns to major and a new largamente variant of the wave-like melody carries the poignant line 'What harbour shelters peace' (see Example 2.8). Brett writes:

This passage is one of the most powerfully symbolic in the work, because it juxtaposes Grimes's grandest sweep of melody, signifying his visionary side, with an inversion of a motive associated with the Borough in the inquest scene at the beginning, hinting again at the process of 'internalization' and the seeds of destruction that it inevitably sows. The longing for peace, for resolution, is a theme that returns often in Britten's works. In *Grimes* it is not available. The protagonist goes silently to his death, a death, moreover, with no resonance, since society ignores the suicide of its victim as the daily round is resumed at the end of the opera.[74]

Ludmilla Kovnatskaya notes that on the appearance of this theme 'external movement and action is replaced by inward contemplation'. The theme 'floats high above all day-to-day cares and worries' (note again, the parallel with Bridge's moves from picturesque to inner subjectivity). She identifies the theme's semantically significant elements as including

---

[74] Philip Brett, 'Grimes and Lucretia', in *Music and Sexuality in Britten*, 61.

Example 2.8 Britten, *Peter Grimes*, Act 1, 5 before fig. 49.

the key of A major, which for Britten represented 'the realm of the purest feelings and thoughts, the most passionate romantic lyricism, an Apollonian perfection'.[75] But the harmony is in fact functioning not as a tonic A, but as an unresolved dominant of D. The middle section (from fig. 44) had been based on a chromatically and modally conflicted D in which Grimes insists to Balstrode that he can win over the Borough and marry Ellen Orford through commercial success ('They listen to money'). The vision theme's chromatic brass chords suggest that harmonically we are on an altered dominant of D, pulling back to the key of the middle section, so that there is conflict between Grimes's idealized vision of a peaceful home and his belief, confided to Balstrode, in the potential to acquire this through worldly industry. Harmonic complexity is paralleled by motivic subtlety. As Evans

[75] Ludmilla Kovnatskaya, 'Notes on a Theme from *Peter Grimes*', in Reed (ed). *On Mahler and Britten*, 172–85.

Example 2.9 Britten, *Peter Grimes*, first interlude, 8 after fig. 12.

has outlined, stages in thematic transformation and motivic derivations can be plotted from 'We strained into the wind' where Grimes 'looks back on a past traumatic experience', whose E–F–E is an adumbration of the motive symbolizing the coming storm (A–B♭–A) which will follow Grimes's 'aria', in whose 'ternary shape' at the return of the A section the 'beatific' dream is on a 'pedal that is ominously motivic (its E–F natural shake is part of the storm's Phrygian figure)'.[76] But the process can be traced further back. The first orchestral interlude builds to a portentous climactic moment whose structural placement and harmonic treatment is crucial (8 after fig. 12; see Example 2.9). Harmonic, textural and rhetorical intensifications are generated by extensions of the chordal motive and the move from E♭ to A (the crucial tritone opposition of two worlds); the melodic peak F–E picks up the first high notes of the interlude, and the bass A♭ enharmonic suggests the leading-note of A but also the subtonic (in this way adumbrating the end

[76] Evans, *The Music of Benjamin Britten*, 107–9.

of the opera). The passage (suggestive of an Adornian negative fulfilment) offers the promised but denied restoration of order through intensification towards musical resolution. At the end of Grimes's aria, as Evans notes, 'there is no cadence, or rather cadence becomes a mockery of the singer's vision, when his reiterated E–F♯ ("Where night is turned to day") is seized on by the orchestra and turned to a G♭–F♭ (by implication) preparation for the E♭ Phrygian of the storm [interlude II]'. At the end of the scene, therefore, there is a failure of the desired or imagined restoration of order and peace which was prefigured in the musical character of the moment of return in the aria's ternary design (fig. 49).

Grimes's vision theme, presented over a dominant, possesses a pentatonic (anhemitonic) descent which can be heard as a relative to the Mahler cadential patterns discussed in the previous chapter, with their evocations of redemptive resolution.[77] But the transformations noted above sound as dystopian twists to the utopian model. The music of Grimes's aria also demonstrates the move between picturesque and inner subjectivity as the storm becomes the overt symbol of Grimes's psychological turmoil. This has, of course, long been recognized. Keller commented on it in the early 1950s and also suggested that Grimes's visionary theme 'derives' from a motive in the second movement of Mahler's Fifth. A footnote by the editors here reads: 'Britten, one gathers, had heard the Symphony only once.'[78] But, as noted above, Britten's diaries record his enjoyment of the Fifth Symphony in 1934 and that he was studying it in the summer of 1936, the year he was to receive a miniature score of the symphony as a Christmas gift from Bridge. And Keller's identification has wider resonances. The major transformation of the aria's opening motive at the moment of 'return' in Grimes's aria compares with an important moment in Mahler's movement. As is well known, the second movement includes towards its end the apparently unprepared 'breakthrough' of a redemptive chorale in D major (Floros calls it a 'vision of paradise'[79]), but there is a short adumbration of this redemptive moment in the bars immediately preceding the recapitulation of the main first section, signalled by a rising ninth/falling second E–F♯–E (bb. 315–17; Example 2.10).[80] Mahler's movement is, of course, in the same key as Grimes's aria and also includes the tritonally related E♭

[77] For Kovnatskaya, the 'anhemitonic scale links the theme to Mahler's poetics of the inner world of contemplation and the external world of Nature'. 'Notes on a Theme from *Peter Grimes*'.

[78] Hans Keller, '*Peter Grimes* II: The Story; the Music not Excluded', in Mitchell and Keller (eds.), *Benjamin Britten*, 115.

[79] Floros, *Gustav Mahler*, 146.   [80] This is noted by Floros, *Gustav Mahler*, 148.

Example 2.10 Mahler, Symphony no. 5, second movement, bb. 314–21.

minor (the key of Britten's storm) as one of the main contrasting secondary keys in its developmental middle section. As a storm piece in A minor, it is clearly also suggestive of subjective inner turmoil (the movement is described 'Stürmisch bewegt. Mit grösser Vehemenz'; in other words, the picturesque depiction of the movement of the storm is a parallel to the emotional quality of vehemence) and with a denied redemptive vision the parallels are so close as to suggest the possibility of a degree of direct modelling on Britten's part.

In the storm interlude, Grimes's visionary theme twice returns untransformed, if on second appearance truncated (figs. 60 and 62). It appears again, now suggestively transformed, in Act 1 scene 2. On three occasions in this scene the pub door opens and the storm music bursts in; when the door opens for a fourth time Grimes is revealed, 'looking wild', and the intruding music is his visionary theme in new guise (fig. 74, Example 2.11). The theme is now presented in a strange alteration of the original line suggesting an alternative pentatonic on A♭. This semitone shift down from the original moment adumbrates the final return of the theme in the opera's fog-shrouded denouement (Act 3 scene 3; Example 2.12). When Ellen and Balstrode come into view, Grimes's agitated repetitions of his name in response to the cries of the searching crowd slow to a melismatic rendering which alludes, in its opening pitches, to the augmented/perfect fourths of the Vision theme's harmony and, in its fall, to a chromatic distortion of the theme's pentatonic descent. This ends on the crucial E–E♭ semitone. Under the A♭ statement of the vision theme the chorus sustains the F♭–E♭ dyad against Grimes's *dolcissimo* F♮–E♭. Most poignantly and beautifully crafted of all, Grimes's homage to Ellen ('Her breast is harbour too. Where night is turned to day, to day') is an elaboration of the vision theme whose chromatic enrichment combines seven successive transposed statements of the semitonal dyad to generate an enharmonic allusion to the dominant seventh of Britten's heavenly key of A, chiming momentarily with the F♭s in the chorus. The technical and symbolic materials of this transformation are remarkably comparable with the final paragraph of the first movement of Mahler's Ninth (recall Example 1.15). A vision of peaceful beauty remains just out of reach. Tragically, Grimes asks what and where is home in the very place which is, or should be, his home. When Grimes dies at sea, the people of the Borough go about routine tasks of daily order and tidiness. 'Britten asks whether the restoration of order that traditionally completes a tragedy has, in this case, been achieved at too high a price. The wild weather has been banished and the damage repaired, but has something of immense value been lost?'

Example 2.11 Britten, *Peter Grimes*, Act 1, fig. 74.

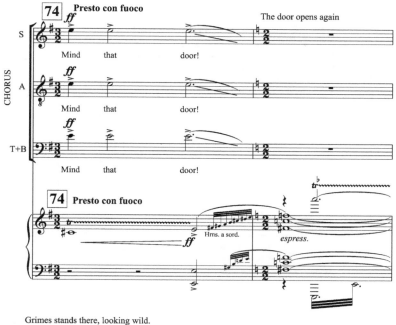

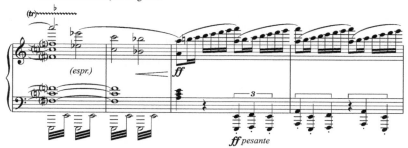

Britten wanted the opera to be 'a reconciliation of art and place', but he 'would never be complacent about the meaning of "home"'.[81]

III

Thomas Mann's son, Golo, reported that his father felt that Britten would be the ideal composer of an opera based on *Doktor Faustus*.[82] The final sections

[81] Harris, *Romantic Moderns*, 164, 168.
[82] Humphrey Carpenter, *Benjamin Britten: A Biography* (London: Faber, 1992), 515.

Example 2.12 Britten, *Peter Grimes*, Act 3, 4 before fig. 52.

Example 2.12 (cont.)

Example 2.12 (cont.)

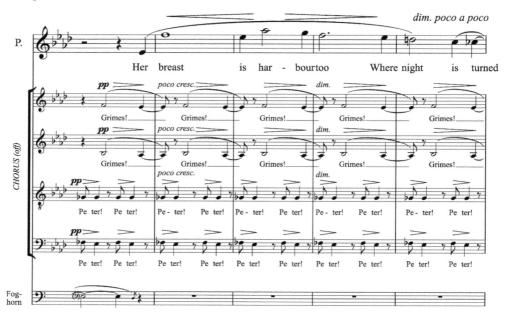

of Mann's book tell of the death of the composer Adrian Leverkühn's beloved five-year-old nephew Nepomuk (nicknamed 'Echo'), whom the narrator Zeitblom describes as 'seraphic', pure and precious, a manifestation – in 'extraordinary completeness' – of 'the child'. The tragic loss leads Leverkühn to declare that he will 'take back' Beethoven's 'Ode to Joy' from the Ninth Symphony in a giant 'lamento', in music 'very certainly non-dynamic, lacking in development'. 'The echo', he continues, is 'the giving back of the human voice as nature-sound, and the revelation of it as nature-sound is essentially a lament.' Of the work's conclusion, Leverkühn states: 'Purely orchestral is the end: a symphonic adagio ... it is, as it were, the reverse of the "Ode to Joy", the negative, equally a work of genius, of that transition of the symphony into vocal jubilation. It is the revocation.'[83] Pertinent here to the theme of this chapter are notions of the return of the human voice to 'nature' and the elegy that accompanies it. Britten's D-obsessed *Sinfonia da Requiem*, Op. 20, is, in part, a comparable revocation of Beethoven's Schillerian Elysium, and in this aspect Britten's work again shares expressive and technical space with a 'revenant' Mahler (to recall Kramer's term). To indulge in the game of allusion-spotting, the last movement, 'Requiem Aeternam', in its tempo Andante molto tranquillo and especially the indication 'Comodo' following the climax, recalls the Andante comodo of the first movement of Mahler's Ninth. Britten evokes the 3–2 '*Ewig*' motive in the horns, and further echoes of Mahler can be heard in aspects of theme, orchestration (flutes, horns, harp, timpani), harmony (modal mixture on D) and the melodic shape of the D major string theme at fig. 40, a cyclic transformation of motives from the first movement which, in its declining phrase, recalls similarly shaped and structurally placed 'grief' motives in the main theme of the Andante movement of Mahler's Sixth. If we accept these allusions as significant, they suggest that if, after the fashion of Mann's Leverkühn, this movement is a taking back of Beethoven's developmental, teleological Ninth, it can be understandable as such through comparison with the first movement of Mahler's Ninth and, through this, offers a potential reinterpretation of the relationship between the naïve and sentimental.

In a comparison of Leverkühn's *Lamentations* with the finale of Mahler's Ninth, Berthold Hoeckner hears Mahler's use of the flute towards the close as encapsulating the naïve and heavenly (Nepomuk) versus the horns'

---

[83] Thomas Mann, *Doctor Faustus: The Life of the German Composer Adrian Leverkühn as Told by a Friend*, [1947], trans. H. T. Lowe-Porter (Harmondsworth: Penguin, 1968), 447, 459, 466–7, 470.

chromatically darkened '*Ewig*' motive to generate the moment's core ambiguity, with its well-known allusion to the *Kindertotenlieder*.[84] In Britten's finale, the tranquil (Stravinskian?) flute trio[85] contrasts with the string theme in what Whittall calls the 'occlusion of serenity' in the move towards a tone of 'post-Mahlerian lament that was an especially important element in the large-scale works of Britten's earlier years'.[86] For devotees of the allusion game, the final bars might appear especially replete with Mahlerian elements and techniques – most powerfully when the 3–2 '*Ewig*' horn motive is counterpointed with an impassioned falling line where, for the only time, flute and strings (previously bearers of oppositional thematic types, one we might call naïve, the other sentimental) combine melodically (bb. 93ff; Example 2.13). The dissonances and intervallic shapes are closely comparable with the flute descent towards the close of the first movement of Mahler's Ninth Symphony (bb. 423ff.). After fig. 44 there is a strong harmonic sense of an augmented sixth on B♭ and the D major triad in the following bar sounds like a possible dominant six-four. But the implied resolution of B♭ to A in the bass is absent (B♭ versus B♮, the minor and major sixth, is a key opposition in the tonal expressive content of the movement). The cadential descent in upper strings and woodwind further negates the diatonic dominant implications in D by suggesting instead an elaborated A♭ (♭V, the symmetrical tritone from D) and then, in complete descending arpeggiation, D♭ (♭I or perhaps, enharmonically, a 'dominant function' VII).[87] The momentary deflection from expectations of transcendent resolution in D major to D♭ is a miniature echo of the D–D♭ of the first and last movements of Mahler's Ninth where, as we saw in the previous chapter, the transcendent, salvation dominant six-four-five is first problematized and then ultimately rejected for a chromatic alternative (recall Example 1.15). The tensed cadential coexistence of D and D♭ also adumbrates the similarly elegiac coexistence of tonalities a semitone apart in the final statement of Grimes's vision theme (as previously shown in Example 2.12).

Mark describes the ending of the *Sinfonia da Requiem* as one of 'beguiling simplicity' offered 'after music of palpable tonal and textural complexity' to make a 'genuinely simple statement ... that attains complexity from its

[84] Hoeckner, *Programming the Absolute*, 252–4.
[85] For Mitchell, the 'Mahlerian', established in the *Sinfonia* by the opening funeral march, coexists with an 'equal assimilation of the influential Stravinsky', heard overtly in the last movement's flute trio; 'The Musical Atmosphere', in Mitchell and Keller (eds.), *Benjamin Britten*, 37–8.
[86] Arnold Whittall, *Exploring Twentieth-Century Music: Tradition and Innovation* (Cambridge University Press, 2003), 91.
[87] For an alternative analytical reading of this passage see Mark, *Early Benjamin Britten*, 203.

Example 2.13 Britten, *Sinfonia da Requiem*, close.

Example 2.13 (cont.)

context'. Mark also notes how this quality is also found in the ending of the *Variations on a Theme of Frank Bridge* Op. 10.[88] Wilfrid Mellers reads the *Variations* as pervasively 'Mahlerian', but fails to progress beyond passing use of the word as an adjective to describe individual elements of striking and allusive character.[89] A series of parodic variations are enclosed by slow music of contrasting subjective eloquence which demonstrates contrasted handling of departure from and return to Bridge's theme, suggestively drawn from the second of the *Idylls* for String Quartet (1906). The first variation, Adagio, the initial move away from the Bridge source, is set in the 'simple', symbolic key of C. Bridge's original melodic falling fifth E–A is altered to the tritone E–A♯, harmonized as two root position C and F♯ major triads. Thus a rising bass C–F♯ symmetrically balances the viola melody. This single and apparently simple gesture encapsulates the questioning of the basis of Bridge's tonal language through anti-tonal symmetrical division harmonized in major triads with no adornment (by contrast, nearly all of Bridge's chords are adorned or chromatically altered). On their immediate restatement, however, the triads are chromatically inflected to generate two augmented triads (C–E–G♯ followed by D–F♯–A♯) which together complete a whole-tone collection. Symmetrical systems of organization continue as the second set of chords is then transposed up three semitones, to complete a 0369 intervallic structure (see Example 2.14). All these features can be shown to derive from implications in Bridge's harmony, but only in order to offer an ambiguous leave-taking. In a sound world characteristic of Britten's music, the triads, which through their simplicity and directness suggest a naïve level of expression, are placed in modern, symmetrical structures. It is at once more and less chromatic than Bridge's *Idyll*. Its surface chords are initially the simplest elements of the diatonic system, but they no longer function diatonically. In Bridge, the diatonic was not imperiled but enriched by the chromatic; in Britten, by contrast, the simplest elements of the diatonic are reorganized into chromatic relationships which propose an alternative, non-diatonic tonal world.

The concluding Lento e solenne (fig. 40) has been described as a 'consummatory D major', an 'incandescent' Adagio in which the influence of Mahler's 'slow symphonic perorations' may be discerned.[90] It possesses an emotional quality once more generated by the questioning of the possibility of closure by recapitulation. It marks the return of Bridge's *Idyll* theme in

---

[88] Christopher Mark, 'Simplicity in Early Britten', *Tempo* 147 (1983), 8–14.

[89] Wilfrid Mellers, 'Paradise, Panic and Parody in Britten's Frank Bridge Variations', *Tempo* 217 (2001), 26–36.

[90] Eric Roseberry, 'The Concertos and early orchestral scores: aspects of style and aesthetic', Cooke (ed.), *The Cambridge Companion to Britten*, 236.

Example 2.14 Britten, *Variations on a Theme of Frank Bridge*, first variation, opening.

Example 2.15 Britten, *Variations on a Theme of Frank Bridge*, final variation, opening.

complete, if rhythmically recast, form at the original pitch. But the accompaniment is shifted down from the original E minor to D major. The result is dissonant, expressive melodic emphasis on E (Bridge's tonic) as the second scale degree which persistently fails to fall to the new keynote. More significantly, the reharmonization of the melody over a D major triad means that its opening E–A motive generates a pentatonic collection, diatonically heard as D with added second and sixth. Bridge's original is thereby changed from diatonic–chromatic to diatonic–pentatonic and alternative redemptive qualities from the post-romantic pastoral world are potentially evoked. But the second motive of Bridge's theme now outlines an A♭ triad over the D major triad in the lower strings (see Example 2.15). The chromatic, tritonal symmetry thereby generated recalls the opening of variation 1 and this chromatic–symmetrical tonality dominates the rest of the section. These tonal superimpositions undermine the hope for resolution through return. They also weaken the promise of ending on a single, unambiguous tonal home, suggesting instead the likelihood of sustained tonal dualism of the kind found in Examples 2.12 and 2.13. Britten's melody only once expands beyond the pitch structure of Bridge's original theme. As the closing cadence is approached (1 before fig. 42), joined variants of Bridge's chromatic closing motive (at the pitch level of both his antecedent and consequent phrases) ascend to stratospheric registers as the bass moves to the final D pedal via E♭. The diatonic perfect cadence is avoided (there is no dominant A in the bass). The transcendent realm promised by the pentatonic–diatonic opening is here evoked by the cadential melodic descent from 'heavenly' heights. But the pentatonic prospects of the opening have long been left behind for the chromatic alternative and do not now return. After this moment of tonal complexity, the *fff* close on unison Ds in the final bar can sound like a rather unexpected gesture of clarity, one which too firmly resolves the preceding ambiguity.

Britten's investment in the expressive potential of reinterpreting triadic functions at cadence points in a highly simplified disposition is further exemplified by the third of his *Six Hölderlin Fragments*, Op. 61 (1958), 'Sokrates und Alcibiades'.

Warum huldigest du, heiliger Sokrates,
Diesem Jünglinge stets? kennest du Grössers nicht?
   Warum siehet mit Liebe,
   Wie auf Götter, dein Aug' auf ihn?

Wer das Tiefste gedacht, liebt das Lebendigste,
Hohe Tugend versteht, wer in die Welt geblickt,
   Und es neigen die Weisen
   Oft am Ende zu Schönem sich.

And why favourest thou, holy Socrates,
Such a stripling as this? Know'st thou no higher things?
   And why gazest upon him
   Like an immortal, with eyes of love?

Who most deeply enquires, loves what is liveliest,
And true Virtue perceives, who has observed the world,
   And at moments the sages
   Must be yielding to Beauty itself.[91]

Britten's musical setting reinforces the poetic sense of question and answer. The interrogating, puzzled first stanza is laid out in two-part counterpoint in Britten's sparest, most ascetic manner. The vocal part is couched in rather

[91] Trans. Elizabeth Mayer and Peter Pears from the Boosey & Hawkes edition, reproduced with permission. Recent scholarship has revealed that the text that Britten set erroneously has 'Tugend' instead of 'Jugend' (line 6). A perhaps more precise and poetically preferable translation is: 'Holy Socrates, why always with deference / Do you treat this young man? Don't you know greater things? / Why, so lovingly, raptly, / As on gods, do you gaze on him?' / Who the deepest has thought, loves what is most alive, / Wide experience may well turn to what's best in youth, / And the wise in the end will / Often bow to the beautiful'. In Friedrich Hölderlin, *Poems and Fragments*, trans. Michael Hamburger (London: Anvil Press, 2004), 105. Hamburger's is also preferable, given the interpretative emphasis on musical cadence in Britten's setting, for retaining the sense of ending in the final poetic couplet.

Example 2.16 Britten, *Six Hölderlin Fragments*, 'Sokrates und Alcibiades', bb. 22–8.

recitative style, its free rhythmic declamation entwining around the single piano line, sometimes approaching unison with the instrumental part, sometimes in dissonant conflict, sometimes elaborating it or more simply echoing it (compare 'heiliger Sokrates' with the following line). The piano lines are clearly based on a sequence of triads, which are sometimes fused (for example, the implied opening D–F♯ triads), embellished (the second line can be heard as neighbour notes to D♯ before a descending B triad) or smoothly linked (C moves to E♭ via passing/leading-note D, or is this a *note échapée?*). In the crucial final line of the first stanza, all adornment or ambiguity is removed in 'pure' descending D♭ and then E triads on the piano. The voice strengthens the sense of clarification and 'arrival' through C–D♭ and E♭–E dyads which sound as leading-note to tonic moves over the D♭ and E triads in the piano (Example 2.16). In combination, these elements project a strong sense of cadence, and of transcendence, illumination, or epiphany. (Whittall, recall, noted how allusion to the 'hymnic' in this setting is 'transcendentally aesthetic rather than religious', offering a rare moment of 'unambiguous serenity' in which beauty and truth are revealed to coincide.) The enharmonic treatment of the A♭–G♯ across the D♭ and E triads is particularly effective, and this G♯ then resolves to A at the move to the tonic D.

In the answering second stanza, the piano exposes in root position the triads on all twelve notes in the same sequence which underpinned, in unheard or latent fashion, the two-part counterpoint of the first: D–F♯–B–A–C–B♭–A♭–G–E♭–F–D♭–E. The spare counterpoint of the preceding stanza moves to full harmony. This change is suggestive of a number of possible readings, of the cerebral moving to the sensuous, of two voices moving into one, or of completion or revelation. The opening of the second poetic stanza proposes a synthesis of depth of thought and surface attractions of physical vitality. The setting also suggests an element of identity-switching as the vocal line reproduces the pitch succession of the piano line of the first half, in rhythmically simplified form. The final descending arpeggiation of Db is coincident with the word 'Schönem' and suggests a concluding transcendence of physical beauty. If, as Evans suggests, the song's 'structural transparency' eschews 'nineteenth-century textural ideals',[92] this cadence nonetheless sustains an engagement with the romantic ideal of a clinching, synoptic and epiphanic cadence. In this way the song encapsulates what Harry E. Seelig calls Britten's 'post-romantic approach to Hölderlin':[93] 'post'-romantic in that though the song's harmonic syntax and textural dispositions are clearly distant from romantic practice, the cadential gesture evokes, through its melodic profile and expressive effect, the transfigurative ambition characteristic of romantic thought.[94]

IV

The entry of Alcibiades towards the end of Plato's *Symposium* held great attraction for Mahler. In a letter to Alma of June 1910, Mahler recalls reading *Symposium* as a boy:

I remember being delighted most of all by the sudden irruption of Alcibiades, crowned with vine-leaves and pulsing with young blood – and then, in a delightful contrast as a dying echo of it all, by the way Socrates, the only one of the company who has not fallen into a drunken sleep, gets up thoughtfully and goes out on to the market place to philosophize. It is only when youth is past that one arrives at a pleasure in the various themes, and finally at the discovery that it all draws to a head, by cunningly contrived gradations, in the wonderful discussion between Diotima and Socrates, which gives the core of Plato's thought, his whole outlook on the world. In all Plato's writings Socrates is the cask into which he pours his wine. What a man must Socrates have been to have left such a pupil with such an imperishable memory and love! The comparison between him and Christ is an obvious one and has arisen spontaneously in all ages. – The contrasts are due to their respective times and circumstances. There, you have the light of the highest culture, young men, and a 'reporter' of the highest intellectual attainments; here, the darkness of a childish and ingenuous age, and children as the vessels for the most wonderful practical wisdom, which is the product of moral personality, of a direct and intensive

---

[92] Evans, *The Music of Benjamin Britten*, 366.

[93] Harry E. Seelig, '"Wozu [lieder] in dürftiger Zeit" : Britten's *Sechs Hölderlin-Fragmente* as a "Literary Song Cycle"', in Suzanne M. Lodato, Suzanne Aspden and Walter Bernhart (eds.), *Word and Music Studies IV: Essays in Honor of Steven Paul Scher on Cultural Identity and the Musical Stage* (Amsterdam: Rodopi, 2002), 101–22.

[94] Hugh Wood wrote that 'the musical character of the settings reflects a deep awareness that the composer is now dealing with a language used by Schubert and Wolf and Mahler'. 'Britten's Hölderlin Songs', *The Musical Times* 104, no. 1449 (1963), 781–3.

contemplation and grasp of facts. In each case, Eros as Creator of the world! No more for today, my dear, except my love – and do write! (Your Gustav[95])

In the section of *Symposium* highlighted by Mahler, Diotima is reported by Socrates as saying:

This is the right way of approaching or being initiated into the mysteries of love, to begin with examples of beauty in this world, and using them as steps to ascend continually with that absolute beauty as one's aim, from one instance of physical beauty to two and from two to all, then from physical beauty to moral beauty, and from moral beauty to the beauty of knowledge, until from knowledge of various kinds one arrives at the supreme knowledge whose sole object is that absolute beauty, and knows at last what absolute beauty is.[96]

The passage strongly suggests the ascending ladder of allegories to the symbolic level of absolute beauty that, as we saw in Chapter 1, was so important to how Mahler interpreted Goethe's *Faust* in the second part of the Eighth Symphony. The essential relationship is that between the contemplated earthly beauty and Platonic ideal beauty, between the sensuous and the metaphysical. But this relationship can inform a diversity of views and lead to different outcomes. Affirmation, ironic detachment, pessimistic negation, psychological confusion or denial – all these are potential conclusions. These ambiguities were famously explored in Mann's *Death in Venice*.

Mann reflected on the content of his short story in a letter of 4 July 1920 to Carl Maria Weber in which he quoted from both his *Reflections of a Non-political Man* and Hölderlin's 'Sokrates und Alcibiades':

But what else have we here if not the translation of one of the world's most beautiful love poems into the language of criticism and prose, the poem whose final stanza begins: 'Wer das Tiefste *gedacht*, liebt das *Lebendigste*'. This wonderful poem contains the whole justification of the emotional tendency in question, and the whole explanation of it, which is mine also.[97]

Britten's decision to set Hölderlin's poem, where the gaze can be posed as confirming the 'decadent trope . . . that knowledge comes through scopic contemplation, through the sensual appreciation of beauty, as readily as through the pure exercise of intellect',[98] offers much potential for

[95] Mahler, *Memories and Letters*, 332.
[96] Plato, *The Symposium*, trans. Walter Hamilton (Harmondsworth: Penguin, 1951), 94.
[97] Cited by Christopher Palmer, 'Towards a Genealogy of *Death in Venice*', in Reed (ed.), *On Mahler and Britten*, 224.
[98] Paul Harper-Scott, 'Made you Look! Children in *Salome* and *Death in Venice*', in Lucy Walker (ed.), *Benjamin Britten: New Perspectives on His Life and Work* (Woodbridge: Boydell, 2009), 120.

post-Brettian interpretation. But Britten's subsequent decision to compose an opera based on *Death in Venice* opened an opportunity to explore not only its homoerotic subject matter (which has recently received voluminous critical comment) but also its rich, vivid and ambiguous investigation of key dualisms in romantic thought, such as physical and ideal beauty, sensuality and spirituality, and Nietzsche's Apollonian and Dionysian.[99] Mann's story also allowed Britten to explore another symbolic seascape as a site for a potent and personal example of the search for a redemptive synthesis of these dualisms. In this latter regard, Britten's music and Myfanwy Piper's libretto can, in part, be heard and read as affirmative adaptations of Mann's ultimately more ironic and pessimistic text. Clifford Hindley proposes that

> Britten saw in Mann's story not only a tale of pathological disintegration but the elements of a positive synthesis along the route from which Aschenbach turned aside – a potentiality which had eluded, or had perhaps been repressed by, Mann . . . what in Mann is represented, almost unquestioningly, as progressive self-abandonment to an obsession is transformed in the opera into a double movement, towards and away from a positive realization of the Platonic ideal – that of a 'sublimated love of youthful beauty'.[100]

Hindley has also compared the opera to Britten's setting of 'Sokrates und Alcibiades'. In Britten's song, the triad, as Palmer and Evans both note, functions as 'symbol of beauty'. By contrast, there is a notably spare use of 'pure' triads in *Death in Venice*. A key theme, however, is based on second inversion triads, which in the wider context of the opera's pervasive levels of dissonance is highly marked. It is first heard when the hotel manager shows Aschenbach the view of the sea from the window of his room (Act 1, Fig 59; Example 2.17.) In another symbolic seascape, the beauty of the sea is a 'symbol of infinity or the ultimate spiritual reality', what Mann called, the sea's 'immeasurable . . . form of perfection'.[101] A series of six-four major

---

[99] See Ruth Sara Longobardi. 'Reading Between the Lines: An Approach to the Musical and Sexual Ambiguities of *Death in Venice*', *The Journal of Musicology* 22 (2005), 327–64; 'Multivalence and Collaboration in *Death in Venice*', *twentieth-century music* 2 (2005), 53–78.

[100] Clifford Hindley, 'Contemplation and Reality: A Study in Britten's *Death in Venice*', *Music & Letters* 71 (1990), 511–23 (at 511–12). Hindley elsewhere demonstrates how Britten's thematic and motivic manipulations serve to convey, to quote David Matthews, 'Aschenbach's quest for transcendence' in which visible beauty is a manifestation of the 'eternal essence of Beauty'; 'Platonic Elements in Britten's *Death in Venice*', *Music & Letters* 73 (1992), 407–29.

[101] The sea of beauty is described in Plato's *Symposium* as symbol of the ultimate reality to which all aspire.

Example 2.17 Britten, *Death in Venice*, Act 1, 2 before fig. 59.

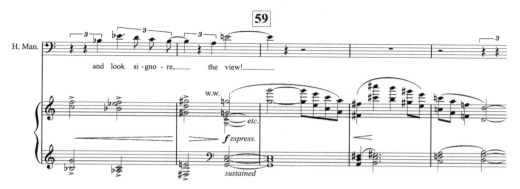

triads rises in counterpoint with two statements of a wave-shaped theme. An initial melodic ascent is succeeded by falling arpeggiations of pentatonic collections: it bursts open, *'espress.'* and *forte*, evoking at once a sense of both immediacy and deep import. The series of six-fours, with their move from a C major to a G major triad, suggests a dominant six-four/five-three progression in Britten's favoured idyllic key of C, though this sense of progression is weakened by the parallel triadic motions. The theme's second statement, with its mildly dissonant peak note sounding as an appoggiatura followed by descending pentatonicism, confirms that it is also a late relative of Grimes's 'vision' theme (compare with Example 2.8).

Upon the manager's exit, Aschenbach reasserts his artistic commitment to 'simplicity, beauty, form', but only for his mood to change to doubt: 'Was I wrong to come here, what is there in store for me here?' Now (fig. 65, Example 2.18) the 'view' theme returns *pianissimo*, underpinned by parallel minor six-four triads beginning on C minor. The sequence begins as a minor mode parallel to the first statement, but it does not reach the G triad that suggested potential resolution in the theme's first appearance. Instead, a long descending sequence falls from an F minor six-four triad to a return to the C minor six-four coincident with the close of Aschenbach's vocal phrase in which he seeks solace in the sea and 'Serenissma' (7 after fig. 65). The orchestral phrase which follows continues the descent as Aschenbach's mood darkens: he notes that 'the sky is still grey, the air heavy with a hint of sirocco' – the disease-bearing wind at which the harmony returns again to C minor. This melancholic version of the theme is then extended and when Aschenbach sings 'How I love the sound of the long low waves, rhythmic upon the sand', the overlapping statements of the theme over static harmony (subtly suggestive, perhaps, through the

Example **2.18** Britten, *Death in Venice*, Act 1, fig. 65.

sustained A♭ and 'half-diminished' harmony of the second act of *Tristan*)
confirm that the music has moved from a visionary to a primarily representational mode evoking wave forms. The association of variants of this
motive with picturesque detail is furthered in scene 5. After Aschenbach's
first eulogy on Tadzio's beauty ('What mysterious harmony between the
individual and the universal law produces such perfection of form?'), the
scene shifts from the hotel to the beach and a slow ornamented version of
the vision theme (fig. 77) leads to Aschenbach's line 'The wind is from the

West' expressed in a further decorated, melismatic melody clearly repre-senting the movement of the wind and the 'lazy sea'. A further variant provides a parallel melismatic statement of 'Serenissima'. It is Aschenbach's plea for calm harbour after the vision of beauty embodied by Tadzio. In a fine example of motivic linkage these ornamented lines prefigure the descending arabesques which follow the first enunciation of the boy's name 'Adziu!' (fig. 91). In short, Aschenbach's original commit-ment to beauty based on simplicity and form is challenged by a vision of beauty which (explicitly orientalized and queered) is evoked by ornament and excess. Aschenbach's artistic challenge is how to respond and inte-grate or formalize this beauty.

Hindley concludes that when Aschenbach first sees the view from the hotel window 'he feels touched by a sense of Absolute Beauty which (in true Platonic fashion) may be mediated by innumerable beautiful things in the world: of particular significance is the sea; of greater value is the perfect human form; but greater than either is that Absolute Beauty to which all beautiful things point. In other words the theme may be taken to suggest a vision of the Transcendent.'[102] (It is perhaps, to evoke the dualism of Chapter 1, a 'symbol' which lapses in its melancholy *Abgesang* into allegory.) Aschenbach will come to see Tadzio as the humanly beautiful symbol of the transcendent (as well as the object of sexual desire). The Schillerian dimension is also overt, as Hindley continues: 'The sea, the limitless void, the nothingness which is a form of perfection, forms the backdrop against which the Games of Apollo will be played out. That symbol of Absolute Beauty is, mythologically, the "Elysium" to which Aschenbach is now transported.' In the vision of Elysium that is Apollo's games towards the end of Act 1, the chorus leads to a climactic dominant version of Tadzio's motive. Aschenbach declares Tadzio as his source of inspiration with the famous, oft-quoted line 'Eros is in the word' – but destabilizing desire motives here confirm that Elysium is an impossible fantasy. After the games conclude, Aschenbach sings (fig. 175) 'The boy, Tadzio, shall inspire me' to a line based around an ascending A major triad. The line at fig. 178, 'when thought becomes feeling, feeling thought', is sung to an expanded variant of this melodic line for his declaration of the physically beautiful source of his inspiration, the sort of union of opposites which seemed to be offered by the romantic symbol, over the stable quasi-tonic sonority (which is, of course, Tadzio's motive presented as a simultaneity) (Example 2.19, fig. 178). The orchestra soon

---

[102] Hindley, 'Platonic Elements', 409.

Example 2.19 Britten, *Death in Venice*, Act 1, 4 before fig. 178 to 5 after fig. 183.

Example 2.19 (cont.)

Example 2.19 (cont.)

becomes more eloquent (the music imagined by Aschenbach?) during which the move away from that 'tonic sonority' supports rising then falling pentatonic lines (rising A–C♯–E–F♯–A–B; falling C–[D]–C–A–G–E), to return to a falling A triad (confirming that this whole orchestral line is a developed expansion of Aschenbach's preceding vocal line). A return to the tonic sonority (fig. 179) marks the beginning of an intensified repeat of this process. Aschenbach's 'when the mind bows low before beauty' is a variant of the falling section of the line from fig. 178, and there is a second climactic build in the orchestra which leads to a descending chromatic variant of Tadzio's motive (2 before fig. 180). This suggests that the balance between thought and feeling is destabilizing, tipping in favour of sensuality and *Sehnsucht*. Another return to the tonic sonority at 'When nature perceives the ecstatic moment', sung to a further elaboration of Aschenbach's original vocal phrase from fig. 178, initiates another intensification, this time to an unaccompanied, even more chromatic melodic variant of the Tadzio collection. At fig. 181 a third and final variant of this process begins ('When genius leaves contemplation for one moment of reality'). The build-up this time leads to the melodic climax coincident with the return of the tonic sonority as Aschenbach sings one of the opera's (and Mann's) most famous lines, 'Then Eros is in the word', where the vocal line states the Tadzio motive form in expansive transfiguration, free from the chromaticisms of the preceding climaxes (fig. 183). This may be heard as a symbolic moment of transcendent unity. But in the preceding pentatonic and chromatic adumbrations of this climactic moment, in which melody and harmony are unified, there were intensifying tensions. The transformed version of the Tadzio motive is revealed to be another variant of Grimes's vision motive, as an 'imagined' or desired moment of fulfilment. In the echo of this passage towards the very end of Act 1, just before Tadzio's mother comes to collect her son and he smiles at Aschenbach as he passes him ('So longing passes back and forth between life and the mind'; fig. 186), the music is unstable, expressive of *Sehnsucht* but a strong harmonic allusion to the fifth progression F♯–B–E–A offers an unusually clear sense of tonal closure. The final bar is a second inversion E major triad, an echo or transformation of the defining harmonic character of the view theme (Example 2.20), now tentative, registrally displaced and spare in texture.[103]

---

[103] The setting of 'I love you' has received several detailed critical readings. See, for example, Longobardi 'Reading Between the Lines'.

Example 2.20 Britten, *Death in Venice*, Act 1, closing bars.

With the failure of this visionary ideal of potential unity, Act 2 presents the theme of 'Sehnsucht'. The Phaedrus monologue which follows the Dionysian dream (the polar parallel of the Apollo games towards the end of Act 1) ends with a passage of powerfully constructed polyphony based on a statement of vision theme (2 before 131), notably in its minor form from Act 1, fig 65. Hindley writes:

What originally burst upon Aschenbach so unexpectedly when he first opened that window looking upon the sea now no longer comes as a gift. It is something to be worked for, affirmed in a struggle of faith and life: no longer a lyrical outpouring, but a severe, assertive and, even if noble, somewhat academically flavoured piece of counterpoint. One might even be forgiven for surmizing that, however moving, its assertiveness is also a cover for doubt.[104]

It confirms the tone of the Schillerian sentimental artist, but also suggests the allegorical, for the symbolic theme is recalled in highly constructed artifice, rather than the instantaneous revelatory moment of its first appearance. Nonetheless, for Hindley, the close of the opera proposes a 'kind of affirmation', ambiguous but not totally despairing, in which Aschenbach 'recalls his moment of vision and, despite all that has happened, seems to affirm its abiding truth'.[105] The twelve bars beginning

[104] Hindley, 'Platonic Elements', 427.   [105] *Ibid.*, 428.

at bar after fig. 325 allude to the form given to Aschenbach's creed 'When thought becomes' and the A–G♯–F♯ of the closing bars is a final partial echo of the 'Eros is in the word' line. It is a condensed fragment of memory: one of profound, questioning ambiguity. Is the visionary moment of transcendent Beauty ultimately deceptive, illusory? What are the claims of beauty as Tadzio walks out to sea? For Hindley, these final bars evoke a 'quasi-religious aspiration which again and again in Britten's work had striven to redress the suffering and injustice of this life. Yet the musical symbol of that attainment – the Vision theme – is conspicuously lacking from this last page, a sign, surely, of agnosticism rather than affirmation.' In a musical parallel to the physical image of the sea lapping up against Tadzio's body, the last bars of the opera superimpose Oriental arabesques and aspiring melodic shapes, echoes of the differing visions of beauty previously proffered by the view theme and the ornamental figures.[106]

In Mann's *Doctor Faustus* amongst the first of Leverkühn's compositions after making his pact with the devil are settings of Paul Verlaine's 'Chanson d'Automne' and Blake's 'The Sick Rose'. The coincidences with Britten are striking (the Verlaine poem is set in Britten's *Quatre Chansons Françaises* and the Blake is of course the third song of the *Serenade*, composed, Palmer notes, 'uncannily' just as Mann began sketching his novel in 1943). For Palmer, Blake's poem is 'a virtual distillation of "ambiguity" of the kind that Mann saw in Venice':

O Rose, thou art sick!
The invisible worm
That flies in the night,
In the howling storm,

Has found out thy bed
Of crimson joy,
And his dark secret love
Does thy life destroy.

Palmer notes how Mann and Britten were both preoccupied with themes of a lost, unrecoverable paradise and the associated notions of *Sehnsucht*, nostalgia, and childhood (embodied, for example, by 'Echo' in *Doctor*

---

[106] Eric Roseberry hears echoes of the ending of the first movement of Mahler's Ninth Symphony, and beyond this, that the overall 'tonal effect' of the opera closely parallels the structural and expressive ambiguity underpinning Mahler's movement; 'Tonal Ambiguity in *Death in Venice*: a symphonic view', in Donald Mitchell (ed.), *Benjamin Britten: 'Death in Venice'* (Cambridge University Press, 1987), 93–4.

Faustus). For Palmer, this accounts for 'the appeal of the thoroughly "sentimentalic" Mann to the "naïve" Britten'.[107] Palmer's designation of Britten as a 'naïve' artist follows Keller (he explicitly borrows Keller's rather idiosyncratic 'sentimentalic'). But as we have seen, Britten's simplicity evokes a complex, ambiguous negotiation with Schiller's dualism. Mann wrote that the 'evil simplicity' of Blake's poem was 'completely reproduced' in Leverkühn's music.[108] Mann's description of a malign or perverted simplicity is strikingly appropriate for the tone of Britten's setting, indeed for much of the music discussed in this chapter, and of its relationship to a characteristic tone in Mahler. Palmer hears a strong connection between Britten's settings of Blake and Mann in their symbolic use of major–minor antitheses. Indeed, comparison of the vocal line of the setting of Blake's elegy with Aschenbach's final line at the end of Act 1 of *Death in Venice* reveals some tellingly shared characteristics. In the opera, the broken emotional quality which imbues the declaration 'I love you' is generated by the false relation of C and E major triads, with the vocal line emphasizing the G natural–G♯ contradiction, separating out 'I' and 'you' by a poignant rest and a shift from arioso-like melisma to 'almost spoken' slow declamation (Example 2.20). The 'recitativo' delivery of the text in the Blake setting aspires to an arioso character as the harmony shifts from E to C, on which harmony it climaxes before returning to the modally mixed E at its close (Example 2.21). Blake's verse, titled 'Elegy' in Britten's *Serenade*, confirms the Schillerian mode of the sentimental poet who tends towards sympathy for the ideal as an elegy proper if the ideal is represented as lost (the mode is that of the idyll if the ideal is represented as though it were existent). The final bars of this elegy, which offer another example of a tritone harmonic movement (here B♭–E) as replacement for the V–I cadence, sound as a transformed – or perhaps, better, in Mannian terms, malignly deformed – version of the ending of the setting of 'Pastoral'. Compare Example 2.22 with Example 2.1: the horn's high F–E recalls the resolution of G♭–F in the vocal line at the close of 'Pastoral'; the syncopated strings parallel the earlier song's syncopated horn pedal; the *forte*, *pizzicato*, rapidly descending B♭ arpeggio in the bass is a bleak transformation of the *pianissimo*, *legato*, leisurely F♯ minor arpeggio in the upper strings at the close of 'Pastoral'. The two cadences articulate what Barringer identified as the 'double pastoral' character of the *Serenade* in which dissonances are explored between 'nostalgic reassurance' and 'existential disquiet', between 'rootedness'

---

[107] Palmer, 'Towards a genealogy', 224–5.   [108] Mann, *Doctor Faustus*, 161.

Example 2.21 Britten, 'Elegy' (Blake), *Serenade*, figs. 11–12.

Example 2.22 Britten, 'Elegy', close.

and 'alienation'.[109] The horn's final major–minor motive echoes and encapsulates the dark tonal and timbral shift at the denial of a redemptive major tonality in the closing section of the first movement of Mahler's Second Symphony (see in particular the trumpet and oboe parts in bars 439–40). It sounds the sentimental elegy as the song of experience and lost innocence.

---

[109] Barringer, "'I am a native, rooted here'", 135.

3 | Real and surreal: shocks, dreams and temporality in the music of Weill and Mahler

I

In his first surrealist manifesto, André Breton famously proclaimed: 'I believe in the future resolution of these two states, dream and reality, which are seemingly so contradictory, into a kind of absolute reality, a *surreality*, if one may so speak.'[1] As David Cunningham notes, Breton's declaration, in which he envisages the tension between two opposing states being resolved in higher unity, has strong Hegelian resonances. There are echoes, too, of Schiller, for Hegel credited Schiller with identifying and articulating the desire for wholeness and reconciliation in the modern age. Thus in Breton's surrealist vision there lies a legacy of the romantic notion of a higher wholeness. In the influential writings of Walter Benjamin and Maurice Blanchot on surrealism, however, through their emphasis on the self-consciousness of the failure to achieve completion (figured by irony, contradiction and disintegration), such wholeness is less easy or even impossible to envisage.[2] This negative turn is also apparent in the contrasting characteristics assigned to the romantic fragment and the surrealist shard. While the material of the former is characteristically pregnant, vital, exceptional, poetic, incomplete yet suggestive of a longed-for fulfilment,[3] the latter is characteristically barren, old, commonplace, prosaic yet provocatively suggestive of unanticipated moments of fresh insight. In the romantic fragment a whole, while unrealized, is always imagined, anticipated or desired; in the surrealist montage or collage, aesthetic reconciliation in wholeness or synthesis no longer appears to be an aspiration, and the symbols of this unity are often dismissed as illusory, parodied, or

---

[1] 'Manifesto of Surrealism' (1924), in André Breton, *Manifestoes of Surrealism*, trans. Richard Seaver and Helen R. Lane (Ann Arbor: University of Michigan Press, 1972), 14.

[2] See David Cunningham, 'The Futures of Surrealism: Hegelianism, Romanticism, and the Avant-Garde', *SubStance* 34 (2005), 47–65; Maurice Blanchot, 'Reflections on Surrealism', in *The Work of Fire*, trans. Charlotte Mandell (Stanford University Press, 1995), 85–97; Walter Benjamin, 'Surrealism: The Last Snapshot of the European Intelligentsia', in *One-Way Street and Other Writings*, trans. Edmund Jephcott and Kingsley Shorter (London: New Left Books, 1979), 225–39.

[3] Schlegel, in his 'Athenäum Fragmente' (1798), is the most seminal source. For discussion and illustration with examples from Schubert, see Richard Kramer, 'The Hedgehog: Of Fragments Finished and Unfinished', *19th-Century Music* 21 (1997), 134–48.

iconoclastically smashed into pieces. If a new type of wholeness *is* encountered or conjured, it is unanticipated. The material of the romantic fragment suggests a redemptive, conciliatory beauty that lies beyond sensuous material; the shards of surrealism can suggest, to use Breton's term, a 'convulsive' beauty beyond the realms of expectation.

Blanchot realized, however, that the juxtapositions manifestly central to surrealism were in many ways extensions of German romantic practice. Suddenness, understood as 'an expression and a sign of discontinuity and non-identity, as whatever resists aesthetic integration' can be traced from the early Romantics (for example, Friedrich Schlegel's *Über die Unverständlichkeit* (On incomprehensibility), 1800), through Nietzsche to Benjamin, Breton and the twentieth-century avant-garde. As Karl Heinz Bohrer puts it, at a 'historically advanced moment of the romantic process of secularization', Kierkegaard and Nietzsche 'diagnosed the sudden as a central perceptual category of modern consciousness', with the 'mythic' dimension which characterizes the romantic moment being replaced by a 'psychological' dimension.[4] As we shall see, Adorno retained, by contrast with Benjamin, investment in dialectical reconciliation and utopian closure. Two different ways arise of glimpsing future states: one in the spontaneous, sudden instant, the leap into the unknown, the other achieved through development, process and progressivism. Cunningham's view is that surrealism proposes 'neither an immanent end nor a utopianist projection', but a need or desire for an unknown future that comes from the 'unexpected' itself. Furthermore, 'this complex (Romantic) experience of the infinitely configured "plurality" of fragmentation' is 'one akin to the "negativity" of the allegorical rather than the symbolic'.[5] The symbolic unity of particular and universal is destroyed. As we saw in Chapter 1, the allegorical was raised by Benjamin in his *Trauerspiel* study as the mode which informed fragmented or ruined artistic forms, by contrast with Classical notions of formal totality and teleological process which, for Benjamin, were no longer authentically available. We also saw, however, that Benjamin's notion of Messianic breakthrough betrayed his debt to the notion of the romantic symbol as instantaneous revelation, an unforeseen glimpse of redemptive wholeness. Competing modes of temporality appear to be at play. Futures might be glimpsed in shards of material which seem to promise new unities of mundane reality and other-worldly dreams; through

---

[4] Karl Heinz Bohrer, *Suddenness: On the Moment of Aesthetic Appearance*, trans. Ruth Crowley (New York: Columbia University Press, 1994), vii, 45.

[5] Cunningham, 'The Futures of Surrealism', 65.

unexpected combinations, inert material might be suddenly awoken to new life to generate a transcendent, redemptive effect redolent of the seemingly discredited romantic symbol; post-Hegelian notions of dialectical resolution in a higher synthesis might exist in conflict with the shock of irreconcilable juxtaposition and *Sehnsucht* generated, in romantic fashion, out of unfulfilled yearning for reconciliation.

In a 1941 essay, Ernst Křenek identified Mahler's music as anticipating the techniques and temporality of musical surrealism. Of the post horn interlude in the Third Symphony, he wrote that its material is

neither novel nor original. The striking boldness of this and many similar passages lies in the fact that such apparently commonplace associations are used with the will to give voice to deep emotion and profound philosophical thought. The result is obtained by choosing first an obviously outworn, obsolete symbol, so that it appears as a quotation from another age and style, and by then placing it in a surprising context of grandeur and monumentality. Seen from this angle, Mahler's style anticipates the basic principle of surrealism to an amazing extent.[6]

Křenek notes the 'alarming context into which the familiar material is brought, by virtue of disconcerting contrapuntal combinations and over-sized dimensions. The shock reaction produced is akin to that caused by certain surrealistic devices which show the familiar living-room through a distorting magnifying glass, as it were, and thus reveal it as a horror chamber.' Everyday materials, the stuff of custom and comfort, are reshaped and displaced. Articles well worn or borrowed, on the cusp of discard, are joined in disturbing combination. Mahler's achievement, according to Křenek, lay in his developing techniques through which these combinations (cheek by jowl, or polyphonic) generate a special type of new music. He writes that Mahler 'remained faithful to his *montage* of "quotations". However, it is probably just this fixation on obsolete thematic material that induced him to elaborate his new contrapuntal methods, and these methods were precisely the factor which determined the direction of the most progressive trend in music to the present day' (he is thinking of Schoenberg).[7] Thus Křenek points to a tendency in Mahler towards musical montages which, through their technical construction, create novel temporal process and contrapuntal connection. The effect of such combinations for Křenek can range from the grandiose to the grotesque.

---

[6] Ernst Křenek, 'Gustav Mahler', in Bruno Walter, *Gustav Mahler*, trans. James Galton, with a biographical note by Ernst Křenek (New York: The Greystone Press, 1941), 163.

[7] *Ibid.*, 207, 214–15.

Mahler's music proposes a new kind of polyphony. Karen Painter has argued that the sonic world of modern orchestral polyphony 'rarely imparts the kind of solidity typical of more rigorous practitioners of older methods. The result was to abandon the ethos of struggling and striving associated with counterpoint since the eighteenth century and Beethoven's symphonies in particular.' Mahler's modern musical counterpoint, with its extreme contrasts and materials recovered from childhood, is an especially interesting example for Painter. This kind of 'modern polyphony did not project the sense of control that came through traditional counterpoint, with its tightly wrought structure of thematic lines proceeding at a similar or identical rhythmic pace'. It was a polyphony that 'defied' subjective unity and formal synthesis, one characterized by clashing simultaneity rather than organic connection.[8] In Mahler's music, however, there is frequently an ambiguous temporal character in which adumbrations of a surrealist counterpoint based on juxtaposition and simultaneity coexist or compete with the 'old' counterpoint of connected relationship based on tension and release, a polyphony which generates large-scale, teleological progression to synthesis or resolution rather than static mosaic. In this way a future state can be dimly intimated or more brightly revealed either by the shock instant of an unmediated particular juxtaposition or through long-range processes of development and relationship. It is this double quality, an ambiguity between moment and montage, between the implicitly progressive and the arrestingly provocative, latent in the forms of surrealism itself, which is most interesting when we consider Weill's music of the 1920s and early 1930s.

II

As a student, Weill declared Mahler to be an 'exemplification' of the 'thoroughly modern person'[9] and Mahler's music to be a manifestation of the 'ultimate in modernism'. He held Mahler to be a crucial example to help 'understand what it means to be "new"'.[10] Recent critics are agreed that the significance of Mahler's music was sustained throughout Weill's

---

[8] Painter, *Symphonic Aspirations*, 58–62.

[9] Letter to Hanns Weill, 21 February 1919; trans. in David Farneth, Elmar Juchem and Dave Stein (eds.), *Kurt Weill: A Life in Pictures and Documents* (Woodstock, NY: The Overlook Press, 2000), 22.

[10] Letter to Hanns Weill, 27 June 1919; trans *ibid.*, 24. Here Weill contrasts Mahler with 'false, trivial, whitewashed and far-fetched' elements in the music of Richard Strauss.

compositional career. Alexander Ringer, for example, identifies Mahler as a 'life-long model' for Weill.[11] Similarly, Douglas Jarman states that in Weill's music the influence of Mahler 'never disappeared'.[12] Consider a specific example of a critic comparing Weill's music with that of Mahler. Donald Mitchell's opinion is that the fourth interlude of Mahler's setting of the *Wunderhorn* text 'Revelge' 'prepares the entrance into the kingdom of the dead', and that 'not until the 1920s, in particular with Weill's settings for Brecht's plays, does one encounter music as hard, cruelly realistic, and violently plebeian, in fact as anti-romantic, as this'. Mitchell considers the conflicting temporalities at play in Mahler's music to be a vital example for Weill: 'it is exactly this dramatic tension between expectation and contradiction that we find in the orchestral songs of Kurt Weill, who was surely much influenced by this aspect of Mahler's highly original treatment of his materials, above all when deliberately "popular" invention was involved. One feels that for Weill, the *Wunderhorn* songs must have had a special technical significance.'[13] Mitchell continues to note Mahler's contradictions of romantic expectations, some of which he highlights as generating a 'traumatic realism'. It is this deployment of unmediated, occasionally violent oppositions and the turn to the shocking and the banal within a musical tone which is often pervasively deathly that are so crucial to Weill's works from the mid 1920s. Mitchell's comments chime with Adorno's characterization of Mahler's music as an authentically modern, critical engagement with romantic notions of teleology and organic wholeness, partially but powerfully based on the provocative employment of shock juxtapositions of borrowed fragments of vulgar materials. Adorno's reading of the move towards recapitulation in the first movement of Mahler's Fourth Symphony is closely comparable with the ideas highlighted by Mitchell as of particular significance in 'Revelge' (composed in July 1899, this song was creatively entwined with the Fourth Symphony). Stylistic, structural, aesthetic and political aspects of Adorno's reading open up features which are especially promising for the interpretation of Weill's music of the mid 1920s, exemplified by *Der neue Orpheus* – which also resonates with the 'Schattenhaft' scherzo of Mahler's Seventh – and the Violin Concerto.

---

[11] Alexander L. Ringer, '*Kleinkunst* and *Küchenlied* in the Socio-Musical World of Kurt Weill', in Kim Kowalke (ed.), *A New Orpheus: Essays on Kurt Weill* (New Haven: Yale University Press, 1986), 39.

[12] Douglas Jarman, *Kurt Weill: An Illustrated Biography* (London: Orbis, 1982), 90. For a discussion of Mahler's influence on Weill's two symphonies, see Robert Bailey, 'Musical Language and Formal Design in Weill's Symphonies', in Kim H. Kowalke and Horst Edler (eds.), '*A Stranger Here Myself': Kurt Weill-Studien* (Hildesheim: Georg Olms Verlag, 1993), 206–15.

[13] Mitchell, *Gustav Mahler: The Wunderhorn Years*, 146, 261.

The passage from the climax of the development to the beginning of the recapitulation in the first movement of the Fourth Symphony is one of the most widely discussed in all of Mahler's output (see Example 3.1). A sustained, cacophonous C major six-four moves to a highly dissonant chord over the pedal G, possibly suggesting a dominant harmonic function. Over this almost bitonal sonority, with its striking G–D♭ tritone and grinding G–A♭ ninth, the brass enunciate what Constantin Floros calls a 'distorted paradise motif'.[14] It is a plunge from the promise or hope of heaven to the threat or fear of Hades. From this moment of unexpectedly violent collapse chromatic harmony emerges which is uncertain of its orientation or destination. Out of the depths of these deathly, dark wanderings sounds a trumpeted triadic summons, which, as is well known, will reappear as the opening of the funeral march of the Fifth Symphony. The recapitulation which follows, the artistry of which Mahler considered particularly well concealed, is at first splintered and insidious, and thematic recall is continued only after a complete halt and silence.[15] Adorno's description of this passage characterizes the C major climax as an 'intentionally infantile, noisily cheerful field' whose brashness grows 'increasingly uncomfortable'. This is followed by the trumpet's 'solemn fanfare' announcing a 'call to order'. The development, 'at the dictate of the fanfare', which 'cannot be further developed, only repeated', 'dwindles', leading to the 'masked' recapitulation, whose resumption after a general pause brings childlike relief at the release from dark of the 'forest' to brightness of 'market place' as 'the destructive urge, which malevolently lurks behind all triumphal music and shames it, is absolved as unrationalized play'.[16] Adorno's description points up the passage's semantic and structural paradoxes, formed by the conjunction of innocent yet discomforting noise, developmental growth cut short, triumphalism and sudden destructiveness, the infantile, funereal and mercantile. Amidst all these impulses and conflicts the moment of thematic return is questioned and then rescued, and the trumpet signal rising up from the abysmal plunge

[14] Floros, *Gustav Mahler*, 120–1.

[15] This moment has been described by Robert Samuels as 'formally, and at the level of textual discourse . . . the outcome of aporia'; *Mahler's Sixth Symphony: A Study in Musical Semiotics* (Cambridge University Press, 1995), 141–3.

[16] Adorno, *Mahler*, 54–5. For Mitchell, who is critical of Adorno here, the development explores an expression of 'Experience' far removed from 'Innocence' (which he equates with Adorno's image-world of childhood); 'the music withdraws from this encounter with foreboding and agitation, and unequivocally reasserts its "optimism". But for a significant stretch of musical time we have, so to say, been suspended over an abyss.' Mitchell, 'Swallowing the Programme: Mahler's Fourth Symphony', in Mitchell and Nicholson (eds.), *The Mahler Companion*, 208–10.

Example 3.1 Mahler, Symphony no. 4, first movement, bb. 209–39.

Example 3.1 (cont.)

Example 3.1 (cont.)

Example 3.1 (cont.)

Example 3.1 (cont.)

Example 3.1 (cont.)

Example 3.1 (cont.)

Example 3.1 (cont.)

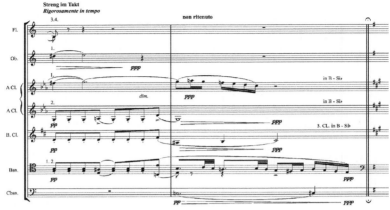

leads Adorno to state that 'Like Euridice, Mahler's music has been abducted from the realm of the dead.'[17]

The call to order in the Fourth Symphony, the trumpet's *'kleiner Appell'*, a command to reassemble in the 'old formation' sounded amongst 'confusion and crowding', was the spur for a famous Natalie Bauer-Lechner recollection. Overhearing the 'musical pandemonium' of the musics of two barrel-organs and a distant military band, or fairground distractions, bands and choral groups, Mahler cried 'that's polyphony, and that's where I get it from! . . . The only difference is that the artist orders and unites them all into one concordant and harmonious whole.'[18] But how commanding is the unifying Orphic call in the first movement of Mahler's Fourth, where Carl

[17] Adorno, *Mahler*, 56. Carolyn Abbate observes that by the nineteenth century the authority of Orpheus's voice, 'his power to command obedience, raising the dead, all these gifts, settled down into the brass section of the orchestra' and especially into the apocalyptic trumpets of the Requiem. *In Search of Opera* (Princeton University Press, 2001), 53.

[18] Bauer-Lechner, *Recollections of Gustav Mahler*, 154–6.

Krebs, the critic of *Der Tag*, for example, could only hear musical 'bric-a-brac' amongst which the composer 'glued a few instrumental effects, such as a squealing flute, a howling trumpet and a clinking harp, to hold the whole thing together'?[19] The music seems precariously poised on the edge of disorder.

Adorno's recourse to the myth of Orpheus and Euridice, in reaction to the potentially cataclysmic crisis at the climax and the momentarily imperilled thematic return which follows, recalls the use of Orphic mythic allegories in his 1938 essay 'On the Fetish-Character in Music and the Regression of Listening'. Adorno writes:

> music represents at once the immediate manifestation of impulse and the locus of its taming. It stirs up the dance of the Maenads and sounds from Pan's bewitching flute, but it also rings out from the Orphic lyre, around which the visions of violence range themselves, pacified.[20]

Adorno observed that this combination in music of the 'Panic' and 'Orphic' leads to an 'unstable balance' between 'momentary stimulus and totality'. Thus, the succession of disparate yet familiar gestures, the precarious yet productive conjunction of sensory disorientation and appeasing order in Example 3.1 might be taken to confirm Adorno's conclusion that Mahler's symphonies 'do not express a discipline which triumphantly subdues all particulars and individuals', 'instead they assemble them in a procession of the liberated, which in the midst of unfreedom necessarily sounds like a procession of ghosts. To use the term for an awakening . . . all his music is a reveille.'[21] The diatonicism of both the C major six-four and the trumpet's triadic summons, for all their noisiness and assertiveness, turn out to be precursors of ghostly shadows, especially minatory when found amongst the sunny, pastoral naïvety of the Fourth. The resolutions they seem to promise are far from certain. In this way they can represent the pervading 'inauthenticity' which was the Fourth's crucial aspect for Adorno, a quality which allows Mahler to use 'plain, unadorned' tonal chords as 'cryptograms of modernism' expressing alienation, screaming of pain, panic and horror, and (as he notes in the Fifth but is also suggested by this moment in the Fourth) an intercutting with 'inhuman voices of command'.[22]

---

[19] Trans. in La Grange, *Gustav Mahler Vol. 2*, 413.

[20] 'On the Fetish-Character in Music and the Regression of Listening' (1938), trans. in Theodor W. Adorno, *Essays on Music*, selected with introduction commentary and notes by Richard Leppert (Berkeley: University of California Press, 2002), 288.

[21] Adorno, 'Mahler' (1960), in *Quasi una Fantasia*, 85–6, 97.   [22] *Ibid.*, 85–6.

Mahler once described the 'basic tone' of the Fourth Symphony in terms of a shadowless, 'undifferentiated blue of the sky'. 'Only once', he continued, 'does it become overcast and uncannily awesome [*spukhaft schauerlich*] – but it is not the sky itself which grows dark, for it shines eternally blue. It is only that it seems suddenly sinister to us – just as on the most beautiful day, in a forest flooded with sunshine, one is often overcome by a shudder of Panic dread.'[23] The happiest of circumstances may be darkened by psychic obnubilation. After the Panic of the moment of disarray at the end of the development, the Orphic rescue from fearful disorder is required for formal and expressive security. But after the opening up of a portal to pandemonium, to the horrific and spooky spirits of Adorno's dark forest, the light and bright commodities of the marketplace which emerge in the light of thematic return are for a while scant and tawdry consolation. At the recapitulation, Mahler's proud moment of concealed technique, there is a disorientating complexity of tone and allusion. Adorno urged that the 'authentic', 'modern' artwork demands an aesthetics and hermeneutics which will not explain away the 'moment of unintelligibility' (*das Moment des Unverstandlichen*) or dismiss the moment of strangeness (*das Moment des Befremden*).[24] As Hoeckner explains, the 'moment' is both a temporal and a material category, it is both the 'instant' (*Augenblick*) and the 'part' (*Bestandteil*), which is founded on a dialectic between the instant and process, and the part and the whole.[25] In the symphonism of Beethoven's 'heroic' middle period works, Adorno heard a dynamic, developmental (and Hegelian) process in which the particular is meaningful only in the whole, but this whole is also immanent in the moment.[26] At the moment of structural and semantic crisis in Mahler's music, the instability between Panic momentary stimulus and redemptive Orphic totality is heightened. At Mahler's 'moment' in the history of Austro-German music from Beethoven to Schoenberg, however, the lost whole may be 'momentarily recuperated', for 'at the moment of crisis, the modern subject reconstitutes itself through moments of intense experience that may be triggered by the trivial'.[27] The six-four C major chord in Example 3.1 is an attempt to rescue what Hatten describes as a 'sense of transformation to an "elevated" major tonic triad' and the closural stability of the 'arrival' or 'salvation' six-fours

[23] Bauer-Lechner, *Recollections of Gustav Mahler*, 152.
[24] See Max Paddison, 'Adorno's *Aesthetic Theory*', *Music Analysis* 6 (1987), 358.
[25] Hoeckner, *Programming the Absolute*, 9.
[26] See Colin Sample, 'Adorno on the Musical Language of Beethoven', *The Musical Quarterly*, 78 (1994), 378–93.
[27] Hoeckner, *Programming the Absolute*, 257–8.

(with thematic statement presented over the dominant pedal to suggest apotheosis).[28] Adorno insists, however, that in the modern age 'Beethoven – his language, his substance and tonality in general, that is, the whole system of bourgeois music – is irrecoverably lost to us, and is perceived only as something vanishing from sight. As Eurydice was seen.'[29] As one of Adorno's principal advocates, Rose Subotnik, observed, Mahler invokes Beethovenian totality negatively, 'as if', by 'constructing enormous symphonic patterns out of elements too discontinuous to effect any large-scale unity'. The condition of 'post-totality' is heard in Mahler's 'self-contained moments' which 'resist the traditional push to develop'. Though he 'may seem momentarily to resuscitate the illusion of necessary development in time', 'the sense of progress between Mahler's variants . . . turns out only to be part of a "ghost-pull", a negative image of a progressive development that can no longer occur'.[30] The returning, redeeming thematic figure of the opening movement of the Fourth is a ghostly intruder, a phantom whose shadow-play leads to a breaking of the tone.[31]

Nonetheless, Adorno's aesthetics crucially continued to place value on notions of directedness and wholeness, a commitment which, as Hoeckner highlights, ran parallel with a commitment to 'truth'. In Adorno's familiar diagnosis, a fatal weakness for momentary delights disastrously distracts the listener from properly apprehending the whole. Thus, the critique of whole by partial moments, a source of artistic truth, is suspended as such events are debased to a merely diversionary function. Adorno argued that this descent into a memorability of disconnected parts has a precursor in great

---

[28] Hatten, *Musical Meaning in Beethoven*, 15, 97.

[29] Theodor W. Adorno, *Beethoven. The Philosophy of Music*, ed. Rolf Tiedemann, trans. Edmund Jephcott (Stanford University Press, 1998), 6.

[30] Rose Rosengard Subotnik, 'The Historical Structure: Adorno's "French" Model for the Criticism of Nineteenth-Century Music', in *Developing Variations: Style and Ideology in Western Music* (Minneapolis: University of Minnesota Press, 1991), 208, 215, 219, 223. Vera Micznik's comparative analysis of Mahler's Ninth with Beethoven's 'Pastoral' Symphony is based on the contrast between the plethora of individuated materials (with 'gestural semantic connotations') in the former and 'Classical' developmental procedures in the latter. 'Music and Narrative Revisited: Degrees of Narrativity in Beethoven and Mahler', *Journal of the Royal Musicological Society* 126 (2001), 193–249.

[31] Raymond Knapp hears a pervasive 'dreamlike sense of unreality' in the movement, which is sustained by the coexistence of 'normality' – the 'organic' motivic processes and formal designs of 'symphonic discourse' – 'with a fragmented presentation of "naïve" material, in which individual gestures and phrases sharply contrast with their neighbors in tone and instrumentation even as they clearly recycle a relative handful of basic motives'. There is, then, both 'sophisticated organicism' and 'unsophisticated cobbling of material' and this creates a 'discursive context in which the hierarchy of intruder and intruded on seems constantly in jeopardy of being overturned'. 'Suffering Children', 240.

music itself, thanks to the emphasis on climaxes and repetitions in the technique of late romantic compositions, especially those of Wagner.[32] In the Fourth Symphony, Adorno believed that Mahler 'takes on himself precipitously the historical process of the regression of hearing. Consolingly he hastens to succor an ego-enfeebled humanity incapable of autonomy or synthesis. He simulates disintegrating language in order to lay bare the potential of what would be better than the proud values of culture.'[33] Max Kalbeck, who preferred the organic symphonism he heard in Brahms, wrote in 1902 that in Mahler's Fourth 'the many episodes, interruptions, incidents, outbreaks and evolutions thwarting the formal development of music periods make the listener restless and distracted'.[34] In the conflicting responses manifest in distraction and concentration lies a central challenge in the aesthetics and reception of modern art. Walter Benjamin saw positive possibilities in the distracting shock effects of film, through which this art may mobilize the masses.[35] Adorno was suspicious (at best) that this was a dead end in art. He heard in Mahler, however, a model for the possibility of 'the improvisatory displacement of things, as the sort of radical beginning':

It is not for nothing that Mahler is the scandal of all bourgeois musical aesthetics. They call him uncreative because he suspends their concept of creation itself. Everything with which he occupies himself is already there. He accepts it in its state of deprivation; his themes are expropriated ones. Nevertheless, nothing sounds as it was wont to; all things are diverted as if by a magnet. What is worn out yields pliantly to the improvising hand; the used parts win a second life as variants.

The crucial dimension for Adorno is that such 'music really crystallizes the whole, into which it has incorporated the vulgarized fragments, into something new, yet it takes its material from regressive listening. Indeed,

[32] See Adorno, *In Search of Wagner* (London: Verso, 1984), 48, 109. On Wagner's role, as decadent miniaturist in the Nietzschean sense, in the cultural process of regressive listening, see Karen Bauer, *Adorno's Nietzschean Narratives: Critiques of Ideology, Readings of Wagner* (New York: State University of New York Press, 1999), 147–51. For a critique of Adorno's 'structural listening' which has already become something of a classic, see Rose Rosengard Subotnik, 'Toward a Deconstruction of Structural Listening: A Critique of Schoenberg, Adorno, and Stravinsky', in *Deconstructive Variations: Music and Reason in Western Society* (Minneapolis: University of Minnesota Press,1996), 148–76.
[33] Adorno, *Mahler*, 56.
[34] Max Kalbeck, *Neues Wiener Tagblatt*, 16 January 1902; trans. in Karen Painter, 'The Sensuality of Timbre: Responses to Mahler and Modernity at the *Fin de siècle*', *19th-Century Music* 18/3 (Spring 1995), 255.
[35] Walter Benjamin, 'The Work of Art in the Age of Mechanical Reproduction' (1936), in *Illuminations*, ed. Hannah Arendt, trans. Harry Zohn (London: Fontana, 1973), 232–3.

one can almost think that in Mahler's music this experience was seismo-graphically recorded forty years before it permeated society.'[36] The geo-logical image is striking. Mahler's music sings as that of an Orphic prophet in the underworld of a crisis before it catastrophically reaches the surface and irrevocably shatters apparently solid structures. This is prophecy in the spirit of the new mythology of Friedrich Schlegel, whose new organicism, 'fissured' or 'cracked', is 'more than naïve restoration', but ordered chaos amongst the multiplicitous and disruptive.[37]

The 'consistently fractured' musical language exemplified for Adorno by Mahler's Fourth 'challenges the conventional view that music is a pure, unmediated art, a belief which people cling to despite the fact that relations between people have undeniably become more complex and that the world they inhabit is increasingly bureacratized'.[38] Disenchanting, desensitizing and alienating, the result is eruptive and heterogeneous, registering the seismic shocks at which the hierarchical, rational order of society quakes and crumbles.[39] Mahler's music, heard as heralding the imminent end of the 'moment' of Austro-German music and of the romantic fragment, is a vulgar and rude awakening from the blissful dream of bourgeois culture. According to the reviewer in the *Frankfurter Zeitung*, in the Fourth Symphony 'worldly tumult smothers the melody of the heart, the coarse noises of this lower world drown out the serene beauty and destroy the contemplative dreaming of the idealistic artist'. The *Bayrische Kurier* called the symphony a 'restless and nervous' work of 'incredible cacophony' which tells of the visions of a 'man so haunted by painful and disagreeable hallucinations that he cannot sleep'.[40] Adorno's notion of Mahler's music as 'reveille' can be heard in the interaction of topic and structure in the first movement of the Fourth. As Knapp says, the close of the exposition suggests a 'lullaby leading to an uneasy sleep besieged by nightmare', and the 'devastating' 'collapse' and funereal call is a 'nightmare experience too extreme to be tolerated. As in a nightmare, which according to common wisdom must end before the dreamer's dreamt demise, we are allowed a respite from this extremity of devastation: we simply wake up, safely in

---

[36] Adorno, 'On the Fetish-Character in Music', 314–15.

[37] See Daverio, *Nineteenth-Century Music and the German Romantic Ideology*, 185–7.

[38] Adorno, 'Mahler', 83. For further discussion see Franklin, "'. . . his fractures are the script of truth'", 271–94.

[39] Alastair Williams writes, 'in Adorno's Mahler, the self-legitimising bourgeois subject is shattered not only by its own contradictions and uncertainties, but also by an openness to experiences beyond its normal boundaries'. 'Torn Halves: Structure and Subjectivity in Analysis', *Music Analysis* 17 (1998), 286.

[40] La Grange, *Mahler Vol. 2*, 401, 405.

G major, just in time to hear the conclusion of the G-major theme (b. 239).'
For Knapp, therefore, the 'disorientation of the remainder of the first
group in the recapitulation may, in extension, be seen as corresponding to
the disorientation that follows an awakening from a disturbing dream,
in which nightmare and reality must be firmly separated'.[41] However, the
returning theme's potentially charming and elegant melodic turn and
chromatic appoggiatura, both familiar figures of sentimental yet seductive
beauty, are instructed to be played 'ohne Ausdruck' and 'streng im Takt'
(bb. 236–7). The repetitions of low woodwind dissonances in its accompaniment, which recall the high woodwind tritone and fifth chirpings which
are insistently and uncannily repeated after the collapse into the abyss (and
hence also allude to the sleigh-bells of the symphony's very opening),
reinforce the mechanical and grotesque, the empty, expressionless and
vulgar. The Eurydice rescued here is a fragile phantom, without feeling,
possibly even frigid, a figure which momentarily counters all hopes of
regression to, or nostalgia for, neoclassical restoration. The renewal of
symphonic form, the return to developmental life, is under serious threat
of fatal disintegration. It is in conditions such as this that, as Calvin Thomas
argues, Adorno hears a nostalgia which is 'not for a lost object but rather for
a lost possibility', it is 'not a conservation of the past but a move to redeem
the hopes of the past', to 'reactivate' rather than 'regress'. Nostalgia arises for
the rapidly vanishing 'historical moment' in which the capacity to listen
properly involves being able to hear the pain of the suffering subject.[42]

The abducted Euridice represented by this music is part of a sensual play
of colours and figures rather than an organic structure; she is a trinket in the
marketplace. The thematic splintering which emerges from the moment of
chaotic disarray is the kind of 'anti-symphonic' indulgence that spurred
critics to eroticize and feminize Mahler's music, which is heard as degraded
and fallen as the sexually licentious woman.[43] The theme portrays the
rescued character as a childlike, fetishized dancing doll in a worn-out
eighteenth-century dress. Clothed in familiar but tawdry garments,
Eurydice appears at first irredeemable; Orpheus is momentarily neutered,
emasculated by modern culture, atrophied after the efforts of the call to
order. Both figures peer into a deathly abyss, a nightmare in necropolis,
which is also a move towards the subterranean world of the dreamwork,
where forms are splintered and figures dismembered. Recapitulation begins

---

[41] Knapp, 'Suffering Children', 248–9.
[42] Calvin Thomas, 'A Knowledge That Would Not Be Power: Adorno, Nostalgia and the Historicity of the Musical Subject', *New German Critique* 48 (1989), 155–75.
[43] For examples of this reception see Painter, 'The Sensuality of Timbre'.

with a decapitation: the head of the theme is on the wrong side of the divide. Eurydice is headless, as Orpheus is ultimately fated to be.[44]

Writing in 1930, Adorno stated that in Mahler's music 'the depraved essence underneath the form is the only place where the true images are stored . . . it is not a romantic return to lost simplicity that is occurring in Mahler's work when it inclines toward lower things. Rather, he is searching for the higher contents in their downward plunge.' Crucially, however, 'utopia ceases to be romantic as soon as it actually takes the productive forces of the lower [elements] into its power'. Nonetheless, Adorno cautioned that Mahler should not be 'summarily severed' from romanticism; rather he 'remains dialectically linked to it' and its 'archaically corroded material'.[45] This ambiguous position has perhaps inevitably led to a varied response from recent critics. The recapitulation in Example 3.1 has been described by Raymond Monelle as a 'nostalgic, neurotic return', one which occurs amidst a passage in which the 'tissue of Romantic expression is ruptured', as a succession of musical 'topics', which here 'seem to possess a rawness', create an 'effect of montage'.[46] Kofi Agawu has argued that Mahler's characteristic oppositions of 'organic connectedness' versus 'disjunction' and 'discontinuity' place him at a 'halfway stage between Beethoven and Stravinsky'.[47] By contrast, David Schiff, after discussing the Fourth Symphony, dismisses the

misleading . . . account of Mahler's music which sees him primarily as a precursor. Today Mahler is often praised as a proto-collagist, forerunner of Ives, Stockhausen and Berio, a label which sanitizes the music into an acceptable modernist aesthetic, but one which is belied by the music. For Mahler's intertextual, metalinguistic themes do not appear in the guise of disjunct quotations, but rather in the seamless, unifying developmental web of the ripest late romanticism.[48]

---

[44] Ritter wrote that the first movement 'could be Daniel in the lion's den, Orpheus slaughtered by the Maenads, genius delivered to the beasts!' The 'subconscious and almost surrealist approach' to interpreting the symphony which La Grange attributes to Ritter, 'gave him a much deeper understanding of Mahler than did the sterile didacticism of most music professionals of the time'. La Grange, *Mahler*, 397, 404.

[45] Adorno, 'Mahler Today' (1930), trans. Susan H. Gillespie, in *Essays*, 603–10.

[46] Monelle, *The Sense of Music*, 181, 184.

[47] Kofi Agawu, 'The Narrative Impulse in the Second *Nachtmusik* from Mahler's Seventh Symphony', in Craig Ayrey and Mark Everist (eds.), *Analytical Strategies and Musical Interpretation* (Cambridge University Press, 1996), 226–41 (at 232). In the Fourth's coexistence of the 'comforting and terrifying', of the 'conventional and the bizarre', Mark Evan Bonds notes that 'there is ample thematic dialectic, but no true synthesis'; and despite Mahler's proclamations of 'organic development' in the first movement there is 'virtually no mediation', but rather an effect approaching the 'surreal'. Bonds, *After Beethoven*, 182, 186.

[48] David Schiff, 'Jewish and Musical Tradition in the Music of Mahler and Schoenberg', *Journal of the Arnold Schoenberg Institute* 9 (1986), 223–4.

That the readings of Monelle, Agawu and Schiff all possess persuasive elements confirms that the closing section of the development and the start of the recapitulation of the first movement of the Fourth is music ambiguously poised on the cusp between an apparently lost image of post-Beethovenian romantic symphonism and the new language of surrealist montage.[49] The Orphic trumpets prophesy a further 'epochal boundary' or 'threshold', an aporia that suggests an opening towards a modern ironic realm and the avant-garde of surrealism, where 'advanced' material is no longer the authentic 'indicator of the historical moment'.[50] It is an impulse towards the shift from moment to montage, and thus raises a future of new aesthetic and hermeneutic challenges and a demand for a philosophy of the new Orpheus.

III

Der neue Orpheus (completed in September 1925) is one of Weill's most important yet problematic works from the early stages of his career. Stephen Hinton describes it as 'one of the most curious and elusive in Weill's output', lying 'stylistically between highly charged expressionism and bitter parody, aesthetically between concert and cabaret'.[51] Hinton elsewhere states that in *Der neue Orpheus* Weill tackles the Orpheus myth 'with essentially surrealistic means. The classical, even pastoral allusions are there, but they are placed firmly in the urban "now" of the 1920s.' For Hinton, the piece is 'seminal in Weill's development'.[52] Weill was aware of the work's importance. In a letter of the winter of 1925–6 he wrote: 'gradually I'm forging ahead toward "myself", that my music is becoming much more confident, much freer, lighter – and simpler'.[53] The work is a

---

[49] In the apparently 'lost' first part of the first subject, on the 'wrong side' of the recapitulation, Mitchell hears both 'nervy compulsion to refer constantly to the past, if only, eventually to abandon it' and an expression steeped in the 'modern mode' of irony; 'The Modernity of Gustav Mahler', in Günther Weiss (ed.), *Neue Mahleriana* (Berne: Peter Lang, 1997), 175–90.

[50] Peter Bürger, 'The Decline of the Modern Age', trans. David J. Parent, *Telos* 62 (1984–5), 117–30.

[51] Stephen Hinton, 'Weill: *Neue Sachlichkeit*, Surrealism, and *Gebrauchmusik*', in Kowalke (ed.) *A New Orpheus*, 82.

[52] Hinton, *Weill's Musical Theatre: Stages of Reform* (Berkeley: University of California Press, 2012), 78, 80.

[53] Kim Kowalke, 'Looking Back: Toward a New Orpheus', in Kowalke (ed.), *A New Orpheus*, 1. For a different translation of the same passage see Hinton, *Weill's Musical Theatre*, 78. In 1952 a BBC panel considered the work 'distasteful' and 'unhealthy', and that it represented 'that diseased part of the European mentality which helped to bring about the catastrophe of Hitler and the War'; cited in Erik Levi, 'The Rehabilitation of Kurt Weill', *Kurt Weill Newsletter* vol. 18 nos. 1–2 (2000), 17.

setting of a poem by Iwan Goll, who met Weill in Berlin at the house of Georg Kaiser.[54]

Goll is a fascinating artistic figure. He rejected both romantic symbolism and nostalgia for a Classical world and had an ambiguous attitude towards Expressionism.[55] Working in Germany and Paris, Goll uncovered and explored the 'cracks in the petrified city', the experience of the loss of centre and play of sensual surfaces in the post-Baudelaire metropolis.[56] By the end of the First World War, the 'revolutionary impulse of early Expressionists – the destruction and rebirth of the city through Eros – had degenerated into misplaced idealism'.[57] In 1921 Goll wrote: 'If one wanted to be critical, it could certainly be proved that Expressionism is at its last gasp ... yes, my dear brother Expressionist: taking life too seriously is the great danger today.'[58] He thus followed Jarry and Apollinaire into explorations of the absurd and surreal. He was drawn to the 'grotesque potential of mass-produced artefacts' as he developed both an 'interest' in and an 'apprehension' with 'banal mechanical objects' – 'machines, automata, puppets and mannequins'. For Goll the 'image' was the 'unmediated juxtaposition of distant realities'.[59] In this he shared much with the idea of Pierre Reverdy (1918), quoted by Breton in his 1924 *Manifesto of Surrealism*, that creation in the mind of the artist is not born of comparison, but 'from juxtaposition of two more or less distant realities. The more the relationship between the two juxtaposed realities is distant and true, the stronger the image will be' and 'the greater its emotional power and poetic reality'.[60]

In the preface to his play *Methusalem, or the Eternal Bourgeois* (premiered in Berlin in 1924), Goll argued that the 'modern satirist' rejects 'realism' and finds 'new stimuli' in 'surrealism and alogic'. 'Surface reality is stripped away to reveal the Truth of Being' as 'alogic' – 'the most intellectual

---

[54] Jurgen Schebera, *Kurt Weill: An Illustrated Life*, trans. Caroline Murphy (New Haven: Yale University Press, 1995), 71.

[55] Robert Vilain and Geoffrey Chew, 'Iwan Goll and Kurt Weill: *Der neue Orpheus* and *Royal Palace*', in Eric Robertson and Robert Vilain (eds.), *Yvan Goll–Claire Goll: Texts and Contexts* (Amsterdam: Rodopi, 1997), 97–126, esp. 98–103.

[56] Richard Sheppard, 'The Crisis of Language', in Malcolm Bradbury and James McFarlane (eds.), *Modernism 1890–1930* (Harmondsworth: Penguin, 1976), 323.

[57] Richard Sheppard, 'German Expressionist Poetry', in Bradbury and McFarlane (eds.), *Modernism 1890–1930*, 389.

[58] Quoted in Wolf-Dieter Dube, *The Expressionists*, trans. Mary Whittall (London: Thames and Hudson, 1972), 206.

[59] Jeremy Stubbs, 'Goll versus Breton: The Battle for Surrealism', in Robertson and Vilain (eds.), *Yvan Goll–Claire Goll*, 77, 79, 81.

[60] Breton, *Manifestoes of Surrealism*, 20–1.

form of humour' which 'ridicules banalities of language, exposing the basic sophistry of mathematical logic and even dialectics'. Alogic for Goll was a new psychology which 'will serve to demonstrate the multi-hued spectrum of the human brain, which can think one thing and say another and leap with mercurial speed from one idea to another without the slightest ostensibly logical connection'.[61] Goll's central poetic themes include transience yet continuity, organic decay, death, fear, anxiety, identity, boredom and suffering, and the poet's role as social outcast. He was also fascinated by love's power, and the nature of the beloved. These themes he explored through shifting topics and characters from classical mythology into modern life. 'Eurydice' in *Métro de la Mort* (1936), for example, explores the urban underworld and the poet's predicament of loneliness and failure.[62]

Goll's poem *Der neue Orpheus* had a complex genesis in two languages (French and German). Its writing was spread over six years (1918–24), during a period of shifting artistic allegiances in his career.[63] The German context and precedent for the topic and imagery of the poem is provided, for example, by Rilke's poetic versions of Orpheus and Kokoschka's expressionist identification with Orpheus's plight in his play *Orpheus und Eurydike* (1917–18). Goll's poetic work has aspects in common with Rilke,[64] but he rejects the message of transfiguration, self-transcendence, unity of life and death, and existential salvation in Rilke's *Sonnets to Orpheus* (1922).[65] Kokoschka's play, a *cri de coer* written in the wake of the wounds of war and his disastrous affair with Alma Mahler, tells of a vulnerable male artist who is dominated and destroyed by woman. This leads to clashing expressions of love and hate, in pain and hallucinations, sexual conflict and suicidal tendencies. (In 1919 he created a life-sized doll of Alma, an effigy he ripped apart, decapitated and tossed in the garbage, the 'dustcart, in the grey light of dawn, carried away the dream of Eurydice's

---

[61] Goll, preface to 'Methusalem, or the Eternal Bourgeois' (1922), in *Seven Expressionist Plays*, trans. J.M. Ritchie and H.F. Garten (London: Calder, 1968), 79–80.

[62] On these topics see Margaret A. Parmée, *Ivan Goll: The Development of His Poetic Themes and their Imagery* (Bonn: Bouvier Verlag, 1981).

[63] In addition to Vilain and Chew's account, see also that by Ricarda Wackers, 'Eurydike folgt nicht mehr oder Auf der Suche nach dem neuen Orpheus', in Heinz-Klaus Metzger and Rainer Riehn (eds.), *Kurt Weill: Die frühen Werke 1916-1928* (Munich: edition text+kritik, 1998), 107–12.

[64] See Vilain and Chew, 'Iwan Goll and Kurt Weill', 101–3.

[65] See Judith E. Bernstock, *Under the Spell of Orpheus: The Persistence of a Myth in Twentieth-Century Art* (Carbondale: Southern Illinois University Press, 1991), 64–69 and 151–3 on Kokoschka, 25–29 and 135–8 on Rilke. See also Walter A. Strauss, *Descent and Return: The Orphic Theme in Modern Literature* (Cambridge, Mass.: Harvard University Press, 1971).

return'.[66]) As Susan Cook says, Goll's 'hero, in true expressionist fashion, struggles against his society, which is responsible for the ruination of his beloved'. 'Much of the text's poetic images and its free-verse form', however, 'are more characteristic of the surrealist movement.'[67] Goll writes against both the possibility of romantic affirmation and the tormented breast-beating of the expressionist. In Peter Bürger's terms, this is a signal of the end of the modern and a breaking into the avant-garde. The new Orpheus, an ironized bourgeois professional figure in a 'stiff hat', is found in the modern metropolis. He has left the Greek hills, and 'has come to you, down into the everyday street of the daily grind', where 'mankind is miserable and imprisoned in the dark underworld, in cities full of mortar, tin and paper'. He seeks to free the trogladytic metropolis by spreading his message through a diverse array of musical media: domestic piano lessons, the circus, the military band, pseudo-Bachian organ counterpoint, the concert hall, movie-house music, the phonograph, player-piano and the radio. His Eurydice is found at the railway station, in shabby old clothes and excessive make-up, but she is irretrievably lost in the crowd. Left alone in the waiting room, Orpheus shoots himself. After this suicidal act there is no afterlife, no postlude offered by the god's singing head.[68]

At one point Goll's Orpheus, 'In all season-ticket concerts, cruelly pierces the hearts with Gustav Mahler'.[69] Geoffrey Chew notes that in Weill's music for this section a 'Mahlerian' scherzo type is detectable.[70] It is part teleological development, part unmediated juxtaposition, part linear counterpoint, part incongruous simultaneities (Example 3.2). It is struck up by a virtuoso soloist leading a demonic orchestral machine. Dance allusions and violin figures shift in a rapidly moving montage which reeks of estrangement and alienation behind the masks of the last ball. For Ricarda Wackers the variation, through its materials and the key of A minor, evokes Mahler's Sixth Symphony, with the 3/8 metre being an overt 'allusion' (*Anspielung*) to Mahler.[71] At the start, the bass pedal A

---

[66] Oskar Kokoschka, *My Life*, trans. David Britt (New York: Macmillan, 1974), 118. For a full and richly illustrated account of this relationship, see Alfred Weidinger, *Kokoschka and Alma Mahler* (Munich: Prestel, 1996).

[67] Susan C. Cook, *Opera for a New Republic: The 'Zeitopern' of Křenek, Weill, and Hindemith* (Ann Arbor: UMI, 1988) 118.

[68] For a full, comparative discussion of the form and content of Goll's poem and Weill's setting, see Ricarda Wackers, *Dialog der Künste: Die Zusammenarbeit von Kurt Weill und Yvan Goll* (Münster: Waxmann, 2004), 159–204.

[69] This was a function allotted to the music of Berlioz in the French version of the poem; Vilain and Chew, 'Iwan Goll and Kurt Weill', 106.

[70] *Ibid.*, 109.   [71] Wackers, *Dialog der Künste*, 197.

Example 3.2 Kurt Weill, *Der neue Orpheus* (Goll), 'Mahler' variation, 2 before fig. 24 to fig. 26 (piano reduction).

Example 3.2 (cont.)

provides some tonal foundation to juxtapositions of white note and black pentatonic collections in the semiquaver–quaver–quaver chordal motive and a sinuous, five-note inner motive, whose chromatic moves suggest shifts between whole-tone fragments (F♯–D–C; F–E♭). Upon the entry of the singer, the harmony abruptly shifts between C and E triads (both with dissonant superimpositions) but a degree of controlling A minor tonality remains in play. From 7 bars after fig. 24 the music becomes more dynamic in a goal-directed sense as a chromatic rising line (C–C♯–D–D♯–E) gives contrapuntal direction towards the climactic moment of tonal clarity in A minor (fig. 25) where the voice now (romantically?) stretches the first syllable of 'Herzen'. This dynamic, teleological, cadential thrust is then further intensified as the bass moves from tonic A to dominant E and the inner line reverses the preceding ascent into E–E♭–D–C♯ (4 after fig. 25). The climactic dominant is elaborated by superimposed interval cycles: ascending E–G♯–C–E in the bass; descending G♯–F–D–B in the upper part; descending E–C♯–A♯–G in the inner part. The violin's high trilled C♯ suggests modal mixture in A and also Mahler's favoured pentatonically inflected symbolic dominant (recall the examples in Chapter 1). Weill's 'Mahler' variation therefore encapsulates a dual temporal character with juxtaposition and superimposition in conflicting coexistence with teleological progressivism. It is the latter which tends to become the more dominant character as the music builds to a climactic cadence which alludes to the redemptive aspirations of Mahler's music through hints of tonic major and pentatonic elements.

In the following variation, Orpheus becomes a movie-house pianist, playing an allusion to the tune of the Pilgrims' Chorus from Wagner's *Tannhäuser* as a lament for the virgin's cinematic death. There is a smooth harmonic-cadential link from the preceding variation, and melodic and gestural aspects of the 'Mahler' scherzo return, but these mediating elements only serve to emphasize the stylistic juxtaposition. Goll's poem continues: 'Gramophones, pianolas, steam-organs spread Orpheus's music. Up the Eiffel Tower on 11 September he gives a radio concert.' Orpheus now becomes a 'genius', travelling across lands from Athens to Berlin, to the underworld of the city to seek to redeem his Eurydice. No longer the romantic genius peering yearningly towards the distant horizon, he turns to the technologies of the mechanical age (already perhaps adumbrated by the machine-like rhythmic character of the Mahler parody) in an attempt to overcome distance, to call to the lost beloved. The New Orpheus has adopted the recorded voice of a 'Caruso' which, through recent developments in transmission at the Berlin Technical University, 'could be transmitted in all its purity to our ears through the roaring metropolis'.[72] He thus seeks to throw his voice 'undiminished across great distances', a reproduction or modern version of the Wagnerian singer's 'overwhelming sound', a 'miraculous transmission' to produce the hallucination of the return of the image of the distant beloved.[73] Caruso–Orpheus becomes an 'icon of phonography', attempting to assume a 'personality so powerful that he seems to be present when he isn't'.[74] But the effect for the listener in the encounter with the technologically disembodied voice is as likely to be one of panic as of joy. Orpheus's voice becomes a sirenic song which attempts to raise the dead.[75] Uncanny and spectral, his organic body is already broken. The gramophone is the mechanical instrument of his decapitated singing head. As Kittler writes, 'our media technology can retrieve all gods', as it

[72] Adolf Slaby, *Voyages of Discovery into the Electric Ocean* (1911), cited in Friedrich Kittler, *Gramophone, Film, Typewriter*, trans., with an introduction, by Geoffrey Winthrop-Young and Michael Wutz (Stanford University Press, 1999), 95.

[73] See Abbate, *In Search of Opera*, 28–31. As Kittler says, Wagner's invisible orchestra 'has the exact function of an amplifier' so that sound overwhelms motive, theme, counterpoint, provoking Elsa or Isolde's 'acoustic hallucination' of the presence of the distant beloved. 'World-Breath: On Wagner's Media Technology', in David J. Levin (ed.), *Opera Through Other Eyes* (Stanford University Press, 1994), 224–5.

[74] Evan Eisenberg, *The Recording Angel: Music, Recordings and Culture from Aristotle to Zappa* (London: Pan, 1988), 120–1.

[75] Barbara Engh, 'Adorno and the Sirens: Tele-phono-graphic Bodies', in Leslie C. Dunn and Nancy A. Jones (eds.), *Embodied Voices: Representing Female Vocality in Western Culture* (Cambridge University Press, 1995), 120–35.

stores and transmits from the 'realm of the dead'.[76] Orpheus is the com-
mercially reconstituted, inorganic hero; we have the technology, we can
rebuild him.

What is the phonographic future for the post-Mahlerian musical god?
After the effect of the concert performance of Mahler has subsided, leaving
the bourgeois concert audience shattered, what type of music must follow
for the broadcasting Orpheus? For Adorno, it would certainly not be
Beethoven. 'Beethoven defies the gramophone',[77] and when listening to
Beethoven's Fifth broadcast on the radio 'the individual elements of symphony acquire the character of quotation'. The symphony degenerates into
a 'medley' of alienated atoms assembled 'in a kind of montage', and the
'sententious' character of the symphonic theme, 'detached from the immediacy of the dramatic action and structure, is easily reified, trivialized'.[78] In
Weill's hammering motives and long cadenza on the dominant of C minor
resolving into a turbulent Allegro (fig. 29), the Beethovenian heroic style
might be heard as being evoked negatively, just as Subotnik hears in
Mahler's symphonism. The old assurances of the possibility of a redemptive
rising seem irrecoverably lost. Vanished is the 'liminal experience' offered
by Beethoven's Fifth, which Lawrence Kramer identifies in the 'intensity
with which it turns the presence of a motive into an assault on the listener's
nerves' involving a process towards a move to C major, a passage out of
Hades.[79] Orpheus's technological resurrection is an illusion of mechanical
reproduction, with as much a sense of loss as of recovery, for the intensity of
momentary experience which the Romantics privileged in music is undermined.[80] With the repeatable accessibility of recordings, an occasion such as
a performance of a Beethoven (or Mahler) symphony loses its 'festive' and
'sacrificial' character.[81] Adorno's concession is that the recording does,
however, rescue the ephemeral and perishing art in the deathly modern
world – technologically capturing the sounds of 'creation' to leave an
inscription in a 'trace'. It becomes, in Thomas Levin's words, 'an allegory

[76] Kittler, *Gramophone, Film, Typewriter*, 13.
[77] Theodor W. Adorno, 'The Curves of the Needle', (1927), trans. Thomas Y. Levin, in *Essays*, 272.
[78] Theodor W. Adorno, 'The Radio Symphony' (1941), in *Essays*, 251–69.
[79] Lawrence Kramer, *Music and Poetry: The Nineteenth Century and After* (Berkeley: University of California Press, 1984), 234–41. Kramer compares this with Rilke's 'Orpheus. Eurydice. Hermes' – on Rilke see pp. 230–4.
[80] Christopher Hailey, 'Rethinking Sound: Music and Radio in Weimar Germany', in Bryan Gilliam (ed.), *Music and Performance during the Weimar Republic* (Cambridge University Press, 1994), 22.
[81] Jacques Attali, *Noise*, trans. Brian Massumi (Minneapolis: University of Minnesota Press, 1985), 99.

of a phenomenal moment . . . that is, a present marker of a past event which is radically past: determinate yet irrevocable'.[82] Orpheus has deserted the concert hall for the radio broadcast. His Eurydice is not, it seems, to be sought amongst the moneyed bourgeois in expensively reserved seats (they are irredeemable?), but in the mass audience. If the 'symphonic' is threatened with obsolescence, he must speak also in the tones of the popular idiom. Orpheus has to become a musical polyglot. He can change his musical language as easily as he changes his hat; his new modern 'symphony' must, as Mahler famously believed, contain the whole world.

Weill's work opens with a substantial instrumental introduction based upon the juxtaposition of hyper-expressive gestures with material evoking the mechanical (Example 3.3). A shimmering string pedal – cliché of creation–developmental symphonic openings, now uncannily doubled and modernized by the dissonant major second – underpins chromatic voice-leading which, in the manner of early Schoenberg, ensures coherence and progression as the tonality 'wanders'. The opening chromatic motif on the solo clarinet, expressively emphasizing appoggiatura figures and alluding to an ambiguous and conflicting tonal background, is followed by a complex outburst of expressionistic character. The melodic character suggests a process of developing, intensely subjective expression based on motivic evolution in the 'organic' manner. The repeated F–A♭ third, however, which seems to force the metrical change from duple to triple time, is an insistent, unchanging, and increasingly incongruous element. This dyad is a resistant, obstinate object, highlighted by its hard-edged instrumentation. It is sometimes 'in place' harmonically, at other times strikingly alien as the organically developmental process to which it does not belong leads to a climactic return of the opening theme. It is a recalcitrant, mechanical sound amidst an expression of subjective self-creation. The threat of annihilation is clear as the introduction then moves into a funereal codetta, with a descending marching bass recalling the final pages of the first movement of Mahler's Second Symphony. In its tendency to juxtapose screams and brutal, deathly musical objects, Weill's music is redolent of Goll's 'alogical' expression of 'the multi-hued spectrum of the human brain' and the dark dreams of surrealism. Orpheus is introduced as trapped in the psychic shadows of a modern urban nightmare, in the alogical machinery of dream montages.

---

[82] Thomas Y. Levin, 'For the Record: Adorno on Music in the Age of Its Technological Reproducibility', *October* 55 (1990), 33, 39–41. Franklin makes the point, without pursuing its implications, that Adorno's 'later intensive reexamination of Mahler's output took place at a time when score-reading and the concert experience could be supplemented by long-playing records'. "'. . . his fractures are the script of truth'", 289.

Example 3.3 Weill, *Der neue Orpheus*, bb. 1–9.

But the introduction's closing bars evoke a lamenting, melancholic quality which, as we will see, adumbrates the rather different tone and temporality of the work's ending.

The 'alogical' aspect of Weill's introductory section can be compared with features in the *'Schattenhaft'* scherzo from Mahler's Seventh. Adorno designated the movement as a 'development-scherzo' in which the Trio 'literally becomes the victim of symphonic development, brutally distorted … only to recover its beauty in a consequent phrase of dignified composure'.[83] The 'Wild' passage (from 2 bars after fig. 163, Example 3.4) is an example of

[83] Adorno, *Mahler*, 104.

Example 3.3 (cont.)

a theme subjected to shocking dislocation followed by a regaining of
formal expressive beauty; it is in this way a miniature Orphic redemptive
journey. But does this, as Adorno asserts, also form part of a 'symphonic
development'? Floros questions Adorno's 'development-scherzo' label
for the movement, and points to the use of 'montage'[84] in which two
themes are superimposed and the antecedent is interrupted by a *più*

[84] Floros, *Gustav Mahler*, 201, 203.

Example 3.4 Mahler, Symphony no. 7, third movement, 2 after fig. 163 to 3 after fig. 166.

Example 3.4 (cont.)

Example 3.4 (cont.)

Example 3.4 (cont.)

Example 3.4 (cont.)

mosso woodwind shriek. The harmonic progression is suddenly arrested and turned to minor: this is not a developmental extension of the antecedent phrase. The shock, intrusive event halts the music's progress on a bass dominant, which is only granted its progressive function, rehabilitated in familiar rhetorical and tonal circumstances, by the consequent (as Adorno observes, this begins at fig 165) which is then allowed to run its course through climax and closure. The rest of the movement, however, increasingly sounds like a montage of independent musical figures. Half-remembered fragments and banal accompanimental chords (with no fluent melody or regular dance structure to fulfil their function) persist and become increasingly isolated as piercing screams (*'grell'*), which ignore mechanical reiteration of chords, cut across the rigidly asserted basic tempo. This undermines the sense of symphonic development and teleological musical time. It is, furthermore, no merely quirky ending. Floros describes the opening of the movement as having a 'grotesque, eerie effect' which 'leads to a *perpetuum mobile'*. The grotesque quality lies partly in the distorted, clumsy articulation of the dominant pedal which characteristically underpins many romantic examples of such 'creation' openings. But the movement's supposed germination of musical ideas and generation of a perpetual motion is twice brutally halted (the second occasion by a harrowing screech, *'kreischend'*) and the resumption is each time more grotesque, as it mechanically, even manically attempts to go through the creation process once more.

In its early reception Mahler's movement was heard as an extension of romantic or occultic delight in the grotesque. After the first performance, Richard Batka wrote in *Prager Tagblatt* (20 September 1908) that in the 'truly demonic scherzo' 'much of what seems to sound so trite at the outset later takes on the character of a grotesque, eerie humour, reminiscent of E.T.A. Hoffmann'. On the same day, Richard Specht wrote in the Vienna *Neue Freie Presse* that the Scherzo is 'full of darting mischief', with 'a grotesque duet between the kettledrum and bassoon', the 'whole thing being a fleeting spectre in strange twilight colours'.[85] In the following year, Kalbeck compared the symphony unfavourably with Beethoven. His criticism focused on how the 'attention of the listeners is distracted from the chief matter by dazzling superficialities. Innumerable nuances and combinations of timbres keep the senses awake and put the mind to sleep.' He continued:

---

[85] Translations from Donald Mitchell, 'Reception', in *Gustav Mahler: Facsimile Edition of the Seventh Symphony* (Amsterdam: Rosbeek, 1995), 47–8.

The blasé and the hysterics – they constitute today the scatty majority with which the modern artist must reckon – are grateful when they get first the whip and then the sugar loaf. In parts of the work it is possible to think of flagellantism. But that is a sign of the age, which shuns nothing so much as intellectual exertion the moment it is intent in entertainment, and does not shrink from a painful procedure which promises its nerves a new emotion.[86]

Kalbeck's striking images of listening as debased stimulation recalls Adorno's positive characterization of Mahler's play with the expectations of the bourgeois listener and the unrecoverability of Beethovenian teleological synthesis. After the First World War, however, it is not difficult to anticipate that the '*Schattenhaft*' scherzo might have suggested a protosurreal, even Freudian reading. As Peter Revers has noted, the motives are 'whirled about' 'as in some surreal scene', as 'whole segments of more complex thematic unities are often suddenly cut off' in an 'assembly of disconnected fragments' suggesting 'total disintegration'.[87] The image is no longer Hoffmannesque; this is no midsummer night's dream. It is now more like the cruel, nightmare comedy of the Bergsonian mechanical encrusted upon the living. In the descent into dream, suggested by the play of the scherzo's whirling shadows, linear continuities collapse. Temporal relations and rational order are questioned. Mahler's music, an awakening from a parade of grotesque but familiar ghosts, exposes the psychological and social 'truth' of the dream in a parallel to the Freudian translation of the dream underworld, through interpretation, into the language of waking life. In *The Interpretation of Dreams*, the guiding metaphor for this process is a journey, and the Surrealists delighted in the 'Gradiva' theme, with Freud's analysis of the power of its dreams and delusions, of an archaeologist's dream journey from the modern metropolis to an ancient underworld of fetishisms and fantasies.[88] In Mahler, the resurrection of dead forms is, similarly, no neoclassical restoration: the rubble and ruins from ruptured layers form a conglomerate of detritus, in which the archaeological unearths the 'alogical'.

[86] Kalbeck, *Neues Wiener Tagblatt*, 5 November 1909; trans. in Sandra McColl, 'Max Kalbeck and Gustav Mahler', *19th-Century Music* 20 (1996), 182–3.

[87] Peter Revers, 'The Seventh Symphony', in Mitchell and Nicholson (eds.), *The Mahler Companion*, 389.

[88] See Ritchie Robertson, 'Introduction' to Sigmund Freud, *The Interpretation of Dreams*, trans. Joyce Crick (Oxford University Press, 1999), xi; James Hillman, *The Dream and the Underworld* (New York: Harper & Row, 1979); Sigmund Freud, 'Delusions and Dreams in Jensen's *Gradiva*' (1907), trans. James Strachey, *The Penguin Freud Library vol. 14 'Art and Literature'* (Harmondsworth: Penguin, 1985), 27–118.

IV

It has often been observed that the formal layout of the five movements and the character of the central movements of Mahler's Seventh Symphony were a probable model for Weill's Violin Concerto (1924), a work closely related to *Der neue Orpheus*.[89] It was noted after the concerto's performance at the ISCM Festival held in Zurich during June 1926. Hans Schnoor in the *Dresdner Anzeiger* (29 June 1926) wrote: 'Weill's imagination seems to be especially creative only when it comes to form ... As in Mahler's Symphony no. 7, the individual movements are interconnected in concept and mood. A compulsive rhythm, which characterizes the entire work, also ensures symphonic unity.' Walther Jacobs in the *Kölnische Zeitung* (26 June 1926) wrote: 'the two night musics of the central movements, notturno and serenata, which continue to savour Mahleresque moods, are really compelling in their peculiar form of orchestration'.[90] The three middle movements of the concerto – Nocturne, Cadenza and Serenade – are each examples of *Nachtmusik*. They are preceded by a larger-scale first movement that descends into darkness and are succeeded by a wake-up call finale. In a review of a performance of the concerto in Frankfurt, Adorno noted the influence of Stravinsky and a Busonian lucidity, 'but most of all' he discerned 'a highly curious, shrilly expressive and painfully laughing Mahler, who calls into question all the play taken for granted and thereby pushes off from matter-of-factness into the dangerous surreal realm of today's Weill'.[91] In the concerto's second movement, the nocturne's waltz, the xylophone's playful hooks and the secure, regular triple metre strike a light comic tone, but the skeletal effect and tritonal relationships between G♯ and D suggest the shadows of a *danse macabre*. The violin's subsequent attempts at sleazy, slinky erotic moves (for example, fig. 8) are dislocated by changes of metre which disrupt the imagined scene of dance-floor seduction. The overriding effect is of mechanisms which may go awry, or, as in the movement's closing bars, ones which merely peter out or wind down exhausted. The melodic charm and lyrical, stratospheric realm of the high violin is brought down to earth (or even below), broken by angular bass figures and fanfare versions of introductory material (fig. 29). Even at its entrance, the sweetly singing violin seems incompatibly superimposed on brittle, mocking accompaniment figures.

---

[89] See, for example, Kim Kowalke, *Kurt Weill in Europe* (Ann Arbor: UMI, 1979), 260.

[90] Trans. Andreas Eichhorn, 'Introduction', Kurt Weill, *Music with Solo Violin* (*The Kurt Weill Edition Series II, volume 2*) (New York: Kurt Weill Foundation for Music, 2010), 18.

[91] *Die Musik* 27 (February 1930); trans. Eichhorn, 'Introduction', 20.

Mahler's nocturnal, nightmarish '*Schattenhaft*' movement was closely related by Adorno to the second movement of the Ninth Symphony. This he termed another 'development-scherzo', but the Ländler section he considered to be 'probably the first exemplary case of musical montage'. Mahler's music here is heard to be 'anticipating Stravinsky', but with a tone not of parody, rather of a 'dance of death', a tone which had been 'more serenely struck in the Fourth'. Furthermore, Adorno insists that in Mahler's montage there is a kind of resurrection to authentic life-forms as 'fragments of themes reassemble themselves into a damaged afterlife', as the 'collage picture made from deformed clichés' which constitutes the Ländler main theme 'pillories reified, petrified forms'. The result, crucially for Adorno, is that the scherzo of the Ninth 'remains dynamic, does not take delight in the mere montage of senselessly ossified, immobile elements, but carries these with it in symphonic time, thereby making them again commensurate with the subject'. The 'frisson' created by this coexistence of montage and dynamism was, by contrast, 'repressed by the Surrealist Stravinsky'.[92] Adorno's readings of Mahler's scherzos as anticipations of surrealism which nonetheless demonstrate crucial differences from Stravinsky require further contextualization if Weill's early music is to be positioned with careful regard to Adorno's characterizations of the 'dialectical' and 'socially aware composer'. In the 1932 essay 'On the Social Situation of Music', Adorno divided contemporary music into the affirmative (that with a passive, commodifying, non-dialectical character) and that which is a negation of bourgeois categories. The latter is further subdivided into several types, one of which is the 'socially aware' composer who 'denies himself the positive solution and contents himself with permitting social flaws to manifest themselves by means of a flawed invoice which defines itself as illusory with no attempt at camouflage through attempts at an aesthetic totality'. Such a composer's 'surrealistic music', Adorno argues, was developed out of Stravinsky's *L'Histoire du soldat* and draws upon materials from outworn nineteenth-century bourgeois musical style and contemporary consumer music. Adorno explains that Weill's music stands close to *Histoire* because it explores

---

[92] Adorno, *Mahler*, 161–2. For a reading of this movement as the 'internal interaction of forces within a protagonist's psyche', 'the curruption of the individual by modern urban society' through 'banalization and brutalization' see Anthony Newcomb, 'Action and Agency in Mahler's Ninth Symphony, Second Movement', in Jenefer Robinson (ed.), *Music and Meaning* (Ithaca: Cornell University Press, 1997), 131–53.

a style based upon montage, which abrogates the 'organic' surface structure of neoclassicism and moves together rubble and fragment or constructs actual compositions out of falsehood and illusion, as which the harmony of the nineteenth century has today been revealed, through the addition of intentionally false notes. The shock with which Weill's compositional practices overexpose common compositional means, unmasking them as ghosts, expresses alarm about the society within which they have their origin.[93]

Although Adorno mentions Weill's collaborations with Brecht as examples of this category, he could equally have cited *Der neue Orpheus* in this context, with its distanced references to nineteenth-century and contemporary popular styles and techniques of shock functioning as musical elements in a social seismograph, raising the dead from the past in a montage-based challenge to organic connection.

Stravinsky's *Histoire* was enormously important for Weill. At its German premiere in Berlin in 1923, Weill's String Quartet Op. 8 was also performed. The scherzo of the quartet has some similarities with the 'Mahler' scherzo of *Der neue Orpheus*, but it lacks the surrealist extremes of juxtaposition and the paradox or conflict between developmental and mechanical processes found in the Goll setting. These are things which Weill may well have picked up from hearing Stravinsky's piece,[94] supplementing or further realizing Weill's development of techniques found in Mahler's *Schattenhaft* scherzo and the other *danses macabre* in the Fourth and Ninth Symphonies. The Stravinsky 'debt' was acknowledged. In his essay 'Die neue Oper' (1926), Weill extolled *Histoire* for its mix of play, pantomime and opera, as 'the intermediary genre with the most certain future'.[95] In 1932 Adorno praised *Histoire* as an example of Stravinsky's best work, in which 'artistic logical consistence becomes socially dialectical'. 'Despair' is 'driven to the boundary of schizophrenia', it is the 'expression of a subjectivity achieved only

[93] Theodor W. Adorno, 'On the Social Situation of Music' (1932), trans. in *Essays*, 396–7 and 409. For another discussion of this passage see Max Paddison, *Adorno, Modernism and Mass Culture* (London: Kahn & Averill, 1996), 100–1.

[94] See Hugo Leichtentritt's review: 'Weill has taken this cabaret number rather too seriously and has made of it a complicated piece of *symphonic* writing, with an orchestra à la Stravinsky, a toilsome and not very amusing affair.' *Musical Courier* 94 (24 March 1927); trans in Kowalke, *Kurt Weill in Europe*, 46.

[95] 'Die neue Oper', *Der neue Weg* 55 (16 January 1926), trans. in Kowalke, *Kurt Weill in Europe*, 465. Weill's enthusiasm for the grotesque and the parodic in this generic juxtaposition was shared by his teacher Busoni, who admired Stravinsky's *Histoire* on its German premiere. Busoni retained, however, a concern for dialectical contradictions moving towards unity, and a neoplatonic idea of beauty and love, which he heard in Mozart. See Tamara Levitz, *Teaching New Classicality: Ferruccio Busoni's Master Class in Composition* (Frankfurt: Peter Lang, 1996), 113, 262.

through fragments and ghosts of past objective musical language'.[96] Two years earlier Adorno asserted, with apparent enthusiasm, that musical surrealism recognizes that 'original meaning cannot be restored', the '"surrealist" technique is capable of producing constructive unity, consistent precisely in its enlightened and abruptly expounded inconsistency – a montage of the débris of that which once was'.[97] The secret of this authenticity lies in the dialectic between 'enlightened inconsistencies' and 'constructive unity', which ensures against the dangers of regression to reification and illusions of 'natural' unity.

As Max Paddison states, Adorno's early critique of Stravinsky is 'very much in keeping with the diversity and tolerance of the experimental cultural and political milieu of Weimar Germany at this point'.[98] At least by 1934, however, Adorno's enthusiasm for the possibilities of surrealism was waning, and the essay identifying Schoenberg as an example of the 'dialectical composer' was written to air his misgiving.[99] In this essay, Adorno describes Schoenberg's music as 'shocking' and a 'cause for alarm' because of its apparent paradoxes, 'wealth of harmonic relations' and 'unbridgeable gulf between self-empowered, baldly signifying sounds'. 'What is difficult', Adorno continues, 'is the movement between the extremes itself', the radical refusal to submit unreflectively to categories of organicism and development, but to face up to the challenges of profound 'contrasts' and 'catastrophes'. The 'dialectical' composer is characterized as one involved in solving a riddle. The Moment of Truth, realized through attempts at mediation rather than the play of montage, emerges as an awakening, as a return from the depths of the unconscious underworld. 'This consciousness struggled free of the abyss of the subconscious, of dream and desire, fed itself on its material like a flame, until the light of a true day transformed all the contours of music. This is its greatest success between the extremes, no longer play, but truth itself'.[100]

By the *Philosophie der neuen Musik* (1949), Adorno's condemnation of *Histoire* as undialectical becomes notoriously scalding. The subjectivity it expresses is now described as having regressed to primitive, childish unselfconsciousness, expressed in a mélange of 'jazz pastiches' and 'scraps of

---

[96] Adorno, 'On the Social Situation of Music', in *Essays*, 407.
[97] Adorno, 'Reaktion und Fortschritt' (1930), trans. in Max Paddison, *Adorno's Aesthetics of Music* (Cambridge University Press, 1993), 90.
[98] Max Paddison, 'Stravinsky as Devil: Adorno's Three Critiques', in Jonathan Cross (ed.), *The Cambridge Companion to Stravinsky* (Cambridge University Press, 2003), 195.
[99] See Susan Buck-Morss, *The Origin of Negative Dialectics* (Hassocks: Harvester Press, 1977), 124–35.
[100] Adorno, 'The Dialectical Composer' (1934), in *Essays*, 203–7.

commercial goods'. Stravinsky 'performs a *danse macabre* around its fetish
character', the 'organic-aesthetic unity is dissociated', there is a disconnec-
tion of thought and action, an alienation of body from subject. Adorno
considers Stravinsky's 'thoroughly disjunct compositional procedure' as
still related to Mahler, but 'is in many respects [his] opposite pole'.[101]
Stravinsky's music is condemned because it

continually directs its gaze towards other materials, which it then 'consumes'
through the over-exposure of its rigid and mechanical characteristics. Out of the
externalized language of music, which has been reduced to rubble, *L'Histoire*
constructs a second language of dream-like regression … comparable to the
dream montages which the Surrealists constructed out of the residue of the wakeful
day. It might be in this way that the interior monologue is constructed which music,
deluged upon city dwellers from radio and juke boxes, carries in its relaxed
consciousness. This second language of music is synthetic and primitive; it bears
the markings of technology.[102]

Such comments recall that in the Preface to *Philosophie der neuen Musik*
Adorno proclaims the 1938 essay 'On the Fetish-Character in Music' as the
book's crucial forebear. The listener in the age of the musical broadcast
succumbs to the technologically amplified particular, and is thus distracted
from appreciating the life of the whole. In a footnote Adorno declares that
the surrealist montage, this 'primitive', 'second language', is 'anti-organic'
and lifeless. This represented a serious decline in modern music, in particular because of the effect on musical temporality. Time, for Adorno, is
music's 'problem', it must 'create temporal relationship' yet must 'not lose
itself' to time. Disastrously, Stravinsky's 'spatial', block constructions and
juxtapositions are 'a convergence of music and painting' which leads to
'crass infantilism'.[103] This contrasts with the montage effects in the scherzo
of Mahler's Ninth, which, as we have seen, Adorno heard as 'dynamic', as its

[101] Theodor W. Adorno, *Philosophy of Modern Music*, trans. Anne G. Mitchell and Wesley
V. Blomster (London: Sheed & Ward, 1973), 171n, 174, 195n; on 'jazz' in *Histoire*, see
Richard Taruskin, *Stravinsky and the Russian Tradition* (Oxford University Press, 1996), 1301–
18. For an insightful and concise discussion of Adorno's Schoenberg–Stravinsky polarization
see Paddison, *Adorno's Aesthetics of Music*, 266–70.
[102] Adorno, *Philosophy of Modern Music*, 183.
[103] Theodor W. Adorno, 'On Some Relationships between Music and Painting' (1965), trans.
Susan Gillespie, *The Musical Quarterly*, 79 (1998), 66–8. On the contrast between Schoenberg's
sense of continuity with tradition, the moment of Austro-German absolute music and
Stravinsky's discontinuities as 'emblems' of exile and alienation, as disjunction from history, see
J. Peter Burkholder, 'Musical Time and Continuity as a Reflection of the Historical Situation of
Modern Composers', *Journal of Musicology* 9/4 (Fall 1991), 412–29. For further discussion of
the issue of symphonic time see Cross, *The Stravinsky Legacy*, 227–41.

objects are carried forward in 'symphonic time', 'thereby making them again commensurate with the subject'. Stravinsky's repetitions are a negation of temporal form through empty clowning and mimicry. Here lies music's fatal condition. Sources appear as individuated pieces of 'bric-a-brac', so that 'style' is destroyed, 'rendered *impotent* by dreams hastily cobbled together and arranged'.[104] There is no damaged afterlife. The resurrecting force of stylistic authenticity is disempowered. Symphonic time is thus identified with subjective survival, and montage therefore becomes an imperilling experience for the subject. To survive this threat the subject must somehow anticipate the shock. The problem of how to sustain subjective expression in the face of the experience of the shock of the new becomes a central issue of 'modern' music. This is exemplifed by turning to the tactic, a favourite of Goll's, of placing old allegorical or mythical characters in shocking or anachronistic circumstance.

In a fine analysis of central aspects of the Weill–Schoenberg relationship, Alexander Ringer concludes with the view that both the *Mahagonny Songspiel* and Stravinsky's *Histoire* could not have been written without the example of *Pierrot lunaire*.[105] The new Orpheus's other predecessor, from the other side of Adorno's modernist divide, is clearly Stravinsky's *Petrushka*. For Adorno, of course, Stravinsky's clown, by contrast with Schoenberg's Pierrot, is pitilessly sacrificed and the music does not identify with the suffering subject. In Schoenberg, by contrast, 'pathos' arises in the 'expression of shelter and security in desolation', 'hope beyond hopelessness' in an 'identification with the victim', all of which is 'alien to Stravinsky' and his empty clowning. In Schoenberg the subject is 'saved by his anticipation of anxiety', 'self control' is retained in the experience of shock. In Stravinsky 'there is neither the anticipation of anxiety nor the resisting ego',[106] and this is central to the 'regressive sado-masochism' of Stravinsky's music.[107] The 'damaged afterlife' which Adorno heard in Mahler seems

---

[104] Adorno, 'Stravinsky. A Dialectical Portrait' (1962), in *Quasi una fantasia*, 152, 156.

[105] Alexander L. Ringer, 'Schoenberg, Weill and Epic Theatre', *Journal of the Arnold Schoenberg Institute* vol. 4 no. 1 (1986), 77–98. Geoffrey Chew hears Weill's *Orpheus* partially as a parody of *Pierrot*, Vilain and Chew, 'Iwan Goll and Kurt Weill', 109; and for Susan Cook the seven variations of *Der neue Orpheus* suggest 'skits' in a *Kabarettrevue*; Cook, *Opera for a New Republic*, 118. See also her discussion of *Kabaret* and *Kabarettrevuen*, 33–6.

[106] Adorno, *Philosophy of Modern Music*, 141–3, 156. See also Paddison, 'Stravinsky as Devil', 197.

[107] For discussion see Thomas, 'A Knowledge That Would Not Be Power', 170–1. See also the letter from Adorno to Benjamin of 29 February 1940; Theodor W. Adorno and Walter Benjamin, *The Complete Correspondence 1928–1940*, ed. Henri Lonitz, trans. Nicholas Walker (Cambridge: Polity Press, 1999), 319–24.

denied by inane Stravinskian clowning.[108] Is the voice of Goll and Weill's new Orpheus vacuous or vatic? The central part of the work is cast as a set of variations, in a controlling formal sign of the survival of identity in difference, of masks overlying a single theme or subject. The apparently random musical juxtapositions of the revue, the shocks of stylistic inconsistency, are countered by the traditional belief that underneath there lies a unifying figure. But the mechanically recorded voice which concludes this set of variations and signals the beginning of Orpheus's grubby demise suggests that beneath the diverse masks there is only a deathly, uncanny absence. Crucially, this is a dual character which is sustained right through to the end of the work.

Although the bases of Adorno's Stravinsky–Schoenberg polarity have been widely challenged, they serve as useful polemical ideas to refine the positioning of Weill's early music within the aesthetics and styles of expressionism and surrealism.[109] Weill's music of the mid 1920s seems to underline the fact that the gulf Adorno set out in *Philosophie der neuen Musik* is far from unbridgeable, and that examples from Mahler's music already made this possibility apparent. The coexistence of expressive and mechanical process in the opening section of *Der neue Orpheus* can be compared, for example, with the explosive version of the same duality in the first two of Schoenberg's Op. 16 Orchestral Pieces ('classics' of musical expressionism). The opening of Variations for Orchestra Op. 31 (1926–8), mechanically winds up to an expressionistic outburst. This is answered by a B–A–C–H 'call to order' on trombones before the statement of the theme, in which as Peter Franklin says, 'elements of the dialectic remain active in almost literally Mahlerian fashion'.[110] As David Drew says of Weill's Violin Concerto, 'although from a strictly musical point of view no Schoenberg influence is audible ... the sense of Schoenberg's spiritual leadership to which Weill's radio notes of Feb. 1926 pay tribute is perhaps implicit in

---

[108]   This reveals Adorno's debt to Freud's theories of trauma and the necessary protection against stimuli as found in *Beyond the Pleasure Principle*. See Sigmund Freud, *Beyond the Pleasure Principle* (1920), in *The Penguin Freud Library, vol. 11 'On Metapsychology'* (Harmondsworth: Penguin, 1991), especially part IV, 295–305 for shock, and part VI, 316–35 for Eros and the death instinct. On the 'shock experience', of sex, dreams and city life, which Benjamin saw as the very centre of the artistic work of Baudelaire see 'On Some Motifs in Baudelaire' (1939), in *Illuminations*, 152–96, esp. 156–66.

[109]   In the final phase of Adorno's critical engagement with Stravinsky, in the essay 'Stravinsky: a Dialectical Portrait' (1961), there is an admission that his bald opposition of Stravinsky's 'static' music with Schoenberg's developmental idiom was in need, at least, of some refining.

[110]   Peter Franklin, *The Idea of Music: Schoenberg and Others* (London: Macmillan, 1985), 101.

some of the Concerto's characteristic attitudes'.[111] Weill's music bestrides the divide between the despair of expressionistic outbursts and shock juxtapositions expressed in the temporalities of the surrealist dream-machine. To 'cruelly pierces the hearts' of the bourgeois audience Weill's clowning Orpheus moves from circus clown to become Mahlerian conductor and then a techno-wizard. And if he has picked up and learnt to play the Soldier's violin, then there is little love recovered between this fiddler Orpheus and his 'Doll', as he then moves from concert hall to movie house, broadcasting studio, and beyond.

This Orpheus's tale is of lost love in the city streets and institutional spaces of the modern technological world, whose most meticulous observer was Adorno's sparring partner, Walter Benjamin. Adorno's essay on fetishism and regressive listening was a formalization of his response to Benjamin's ideas on art in the age of mechanical reproduction, explored more informally in the famous correspondence of 1935–8. As Adorno recognized, Benjamin's aim was 'to make philosophy surrealistic'. This aim emerged from Benjamin's fascination with the 'shock-like flashes of obsolete elements from the nineteenth century', and constructions in which 'meanings emerge solely through a shocking montage of the material', all of which led to 'dialectics at a standstill'.[112] As is well known, Benjamin's reading of Louis Aragon's *Le Paysan de Paris* led him to declare that Surrealism was 'born in an arcade', where products of the ruins of the bourgeoisie, the shattered 'wish symbols' of the nineteenth century, are 'on the point of entering the market as commodities'. But they 'linger on the threshhold' of the magical and the mercantile. The 'true fairies of the arcades' are the dolls, 'playthings' garbed in 'fashionable dress', and the street 'gutter' is a portal to the underworld. Under the acquisitive collector's gaze the interpretation of the detritus of the urban marketplace gives it an 'afterlife' in the 'now of the moment'.[113]

Three central terms have become familiar from Benjamin's writing: aura, allegory and constellation. While it is not the purpose to offer here a full

---

[111] David Drew, 'Weill and Schoenberg', *Kurt Weill Newsletter* vol. 12 no. 1 (Spring 1994), 11. Weill's article on Schoenberg appeared in *Der deutsche Rundfunk* IV/9 (28 February 1926), 581–4. Schoenberg is an 'irrelevance to Weill criticism' according to Richard Taruskin, 'Review of Kowalke, ed., A New Orpheus', *Kurt Weill Newsletter*, vol. 4 (1986), 12–15.

[112] Adorno, 'A Portrait of Walter Benjamin', in *Prisms*, trans. Samuel and Shierry Weber (London: Spearman, 1967), 230, 237, 239. See Benjamin's 'One-Way Street' (1925–6) and 'Surrealism: The Last Snapshot of the European Intelligentsia' (1929), in *One-Way Street and Other Writings*, 45–104 and 225–39.

[113] Walter Benjamin, *The Arcades Project*, trans. Howard Eiland and Kevin McLaughlin (Cambridge, Mass.: Harvard University Press, 1999), xii, 13, 82, 693.

attempt to define or critique these terms, they assume importance in the development of an analytic–hermeneutic response to musical works which lie precariously on the cusp of moment and montage, on the magical–mercantile threshold. Benjamin's concept of aura is dependent upon the work of art's 'unique existence at the place where it happens to be'. This authenticity requires the presence of the original and is therefore jeopardized by 'mechanical reproduction' which 'reactivates the object' in new contexts and shatters tradition.[114] In 'Some motifs in Baudelaire' (1939), Benjamin defines 'allegorical' art (in a manner redolent of Goll's post-Baudelaire urban alogic) as that fashioned out of the loss of this aura, where 'the ruins of the bourgeoisie' are juxtaposed in 'elements of dream, memory and fantasy stimulated by shock but recalling or anticipating a different, collective character of experience'.[115] Adorno, as we have seen, sought a more dynamic dialectic. He thus rejected techniques of reproducing obsolete objects in shocking montages, unless they are integrated in an advanced aesthetic totality, a dynamic whole which deprives the fetishized objects of their self-evidence.[116] Adorno's adherence to dynamic temporality contrasts with Benjamin's delight in a new experience of time in surrealism's shock of the now, in an awakening and remembering at the privileged moment on the edge of the dream world.[117] For musical correlatives, reconsider Adorno's description of the 'moment of rupture', the 'physical jolt' of the explosive fanfare 'intervening from outside', in the first movement of Mahler's First Symphony, reminiscent of what is lost and desired 'of what was heard for a second between sleeping and waking'.[118] This may smack of Benjaminian dream montage, but for Adorno it is, of course, a moment which in large-scale hearing is understood as subsumed in a symphonic totality which is questioned, raising a dialectic of particular and whole, but which nonetheless retains its fundamentally dynamic character.

Constellation, the key to Benjamin's theory of knowledge, is a regrouping of concrete materials so that the 'Idea' might emerge, and the phenomena or

---

[114] Benjamin, 'The Work of Art in the Age of Mechanical Reproduction', in *Illuminations*, 214–15.

[115] Benjamin, 'Some motifs in Baudelaire', in *Illuminations*, 156–66.

[116] For discussion see 'Introduction: Esthetic Theory and Cultural Criticism', in Andrew Arato and Eike Gebhardt (eds.), *The Essential Frankfurt School Reader* (Oxford: Blackwell, 1978), 212–18.

[117] See Peter Osborne, 'Small-Scale Victories, Large-Scale Defeats: Walter Benjamin's Politics of Time', in Andrew Benjamin and Peter Osborne (eds.), *Walter Benjamin's Philosophy: Destruction and Experience* (London: Routledge, 1994), 59–109.

[118] Adorno, *Mahler*, 5.

objects themselves are redeemed. There is a focus on the particular, the micrological, and no imposition of a universal system. Its aim is a 'momentary epiphany' which 'bear(s) affinities with the surrealist search for transcendence'. In surrealist collage, the rearrangement of broken shards produces a 'profane illumination'. As such it 'would release the utopian wish images from their reified imprisonment in the fetishistic world of bourgeois cultural consumption'.[119] Adorno noted that Benjamin remained indebted to Friedrich Schlegel and Novalis for the conception of the fragment, the 'fractured' or the 'incomplete', as a philosophical form. He saw Benjamin as a 'seismograph of the moment', and seemed obsessed with the functions of Benjamin's 'gaze', which he described as variously 'melancholic', 'micrological', 'saturnine', 'medusan' and 'fixating'.[120] All of these are comparable with Adorno's image of Mahler as a prophet speaking in a fractured language, as seismographic of the modern, and melancholically preoccupied in the 'long gaze'. The 'allegorist', according to Bürger, pulls elements out of the 'totality of the life context'; the fragment, deprived of original function, is petrified, leading to an expression of melancholy and montage which is avant-gardiste and anti-classicist. This, however, does not demand a rejection of hermeneutics, as the avant-gardiste work is still to be understood as a 'total meaning'; instead, a new hermeneutics must deal with contradiction and heterogeneity.[121] Weill's musical idiom, in which broken gestures of romantic bourgeois expression are anachronistically reproduced in new structural contexts undermining or even eschewing organic unity, represents just such a challenge.

In the opening of Weill's Violin Concerto, a melodic rise and fall is accompanied by a complex chord. This is followed by silence (Example 3.5). The chord, militarized or dehumanized by the drum roll, is repeated, immediately and exactly. It always occurs in pairs (as did the similarly mechanical sounding chords at the opening of *Der neue Orpheus*). This, recall, is a night piece, a *Liebesnacht*. It might, then, be heard as a

---

[119] The contrast with Adorno's verdict on reification in surrealist montage is marked, but Richard Wolin explores Adorno's sympathies with constellation, which is coupled with an emphasis on dialectical mediation, on the 'unifying moment', as discussed in *Negative Dialectics*: 'Benjamin, Adorno, Surrealism', in Tom Huhn and Lambert Zuidervaart (eds.), *The Semblance of Subjectivity: Essays on Adorno's Aesthetic Theory* (Cambridge, Mass.: MIT, 1997), 97–8, 104.

[120] Theodor W. Adorno, 'Introduction to Benjamin's *Schriften*' (1955), trans. R. Hullot-Kentor, in Gary Smith (ed.), *On Walter Benjamin: Critical Essays and Recollections* (Cambridge Mass.: MIT, 1988), 2–17.

[121] Peter Bürger, *Theory of the Avant-Garde*, trans. Michael Shaw (Minneapolis: University of Minnesota Press, 1984), 69–70, 84.

Example 3.5 Weill, Concerto for Violin and Wind Orchestra, bb. 1–10 (piano reduction).

mechanization of the gesture of erotic yearning at the opening of *Tristan und Isolde*. It simultaneously invokes and thwarts the 'individualization of harmony' in Wagner's chromatic idiom where as Dahlhaus explains, the 'accent falls on harmonic details', on the 'momentary effect', which may be 'relieved of the responsibility for the large-scale formal structures', so that the harmony 'serves instead to establish the unique identity of one instant in the music'.[122] Weill's chord is denied the uniqueness of identity in an invariant doubling which is insistent, a reproduction which, like Adorno's recorded music, preserves the ephemeral object but in doing so leads to deprivation of its original quality.

Comparison with Schoenberg is again telling. The 'syntactic foundation' of Schoenberg's setting of Georg's 'Ich darf nicht dankend', Op. 14 no. 1 (1907), which may have been composed as a reflection upon the debt Schoenberg felt to Mahler,[123] lies in the 'sound and the characteristic succession' of its opening chords.[124] A dissonant fourth chord functions as a motive and 'symbolic entity'. On the edge of 'renunciation' or 'emancipation', it 'articulates the tonal and atonal implications that express its moment in history, an unreduplicatable instant in the evolution of

---

[122] Carl Dahlhaus, *Between Romanticism and Modernism*, trans. Mary Whittall (Berkeley: University of California Press, 1980), 73–4.

[123] See Bryan Simms, *The Atonal Music of Schoenberg* (Oxford University Press, 2000).

[124] Edward T. Cone, 'Sound and Syntax: An Introduction to Schoenberg's Harmony', *Perspectives of New Music* 13 (1974), 21–40 (at 32).

compositional technique and the history of ideas'.[125] This illustrates both the kind of combination of advanced aesthetic totality and social timeliness which Adorno sought in the authentic modern artwork, and also a dynamic whole which deprives the fetishized objects of their self-evidence. This 'solution' to the relation of particular and whole can be heard expressed negatively, 'as if', in Weill's concerto. Kim Kowalke notes that Weill's 'punctuating five-note chords ... continually recur at structural seams of the first movement', and 'near the end of the movement ... the gesture is repeated, but the sonority is a D-minor triad, related to the earlier chords by linear progressions of a minor second in almost all voices'.[126] By the end of the movement, the repeated chordal signature of Weill's concerto seems deathly and soulless. It is Eros turned to death (in Schoenberg's favourite key). The recurrences are increasingly marked, apart from the very end, as a return to sameness, not part of organic development. Out of place and time, they suggest the loss of aura. They bring a brutal end to phrases, and yet also a remembrance, through denial, of lost beautiful moments in romantic expression, which in this piece arouses no expressionistic scream, just cool counterpoint.[127]

Music's images, as those in dreams, pass – they die. Ephemeral and ghostly, their reproduction is an attempt to arrest time. The significance of residual echoes of romantic melancholy and yearning are especially apparent in the closing bars of *Der neue Orpheus*, the moments approaching suicide. Here repeated chords, whose structure and character are strikingly similar to the deathly chords of the Violin Concerto, appear to mark the death of the genius and his ability to create a masterpiece of artistic teleology in whose beginning is the seed of apotheosis, transfiguration and resolution. The Goll–Weill Orpheus, despite his diverse musical skills as Mahlerian interpreter and technological messenger, is in this reading doomed to fail. The soloist introduces him as having left behind the Hellenic pastoral arcadia with vocal lines over two simultaneous pentatonic arpeggios, a superimposition which generates sequences of disturbing major–minor clashes (1 after fig. 3). When he starts to sing his song to Eurydice, the *tranquillo* theme previously associated with her is accompanied by a

---

[125] Dahlhaus, *Nineteenth-Century Music*, 378–9.

[126] Kowalke, *Kurt Weill in Europe*, 261. For another analysis of the work see Siglund Bruhn, 'Kurt Weill: Violinkonzert', *Melos* 48 (1986), 84–105.

[127] Kowalke considers 'the straightforward tonal conclusion of the Concerto is an artificial solution to the composer's dilemma concerning how to "end" a piece rather than to "stop" it ... the final dominant-tonic cadence in F is not perceived as a large-scale resolution, but instead as a punctuation telling the listener ... that the composition had ended'. Kowalke, *Kurt Weill in Europe*, 262.

succession of lyre-like pentatonic chords. The new urban pastoral is confirmed towards the end of the work when the stylized 'lyre' chords return: this
time their close relationship to both the pentatonic and the added sixth and
seventh chords of popular song style is clear (fig. 34). The lyrical Eurydice
theme, now expressed in this context of looming loss, is cut short by mechanical rhythms of the dark industrialized underworld of the city (figs. 10–11). Its
final return leads only to punctuating chords which contain the grind of the
major–minor clash of the perverted pastoral pentatonic and suggest a muffled
echo of the mechanistic repetitions of the opening section of the work. The
tam tam announces Orpheus's suicide and the violin offers one last return of
the Eurydice theme, but now unresolved (Example 3.6). The final sounds are
lyre chords but they are deathly rehearings of the F–A♭ dyad which opposed
the organic developmental process of the opening section. By contrast with
the finale of Mahler's Fourth, this end offers no heavenly pastoral of uncount-
able violins and seraphic pentatonic song, only a lonely violin and morbid
elegy. Neither does the serenade lead to a celebratory blaze of sunrise as in
Mahler's Seventh, only to a grubby death in the shadows of a railway station
waiting room.

The final chord is a D♭ major seventh. A frozen version of the will to
resolve in the leading-note, it leads nowhere. It also resonates with the cliché
of popular harmonic styles, suggesting a mediation, or ambivalent relationship, between high and low worlds. In this way it may be compared with the
well-known added-sixth chords of the 'Moritat von Mackie Messer' from
Die Dreigroschenoper. For Lawrence Kramer 'the "mechanization" of this
particular chord via the hand-organ style signals the palpable collapse of a
subjectivity-laden romantic sound world into a disenchanted modernity'.[128]
In response to Orpheus's long gaze and his Song of the Underground, by
contrast with *Das Lied von der Erde* where, as Adorno writes, 'the girl
throws her secret lover "long yearning looks"', there is no reciprocal gesture.
For Benjamin, 'looking at someone carries the implicit expectation that our
look will be returned by the object of our gaze. Where this expectation is
met . . . there is an experience of the aura to the fullest extent.' 'Experience of
the aura', he continues, 'thus rests on the transposition of a response

---

[128] Kramer, *Musical Meaning*, 223. Kowalke makes a comparison between the C–E–G–A chord of
the Moritat, 'one of the hallmarks of Weill's early style', with the concluding chord of 'Das Lied
von der Erde', *Kurt Weill in Europe*, 140. For a characteristically provocative reading of the
Moritat's 'apotheosis' of the submediant and corresponding 'inhibition of the tonic' as a
'prolonged' 'caress', in a 'parody of . . . our conception of decadence', see Hans Keller, 'Film
Music: The Harry Lime Theme' (1951), in *Essays on Music*, ed. Christopher Wintle (Cambridge
University Press, 1994), 84–5.

Example 3.6 Weill, *Der neue Orpheus*, bb. 355–close.

Example 3.7 Weill, *Der neue Orpheus*, bb. 1–2 (reduction).

common in human relationships to the relationship between the inanimate or natural object and man ... To perceive the aura of an object we look at means to invest it with the ability to look at us in return.'[129] With the demise of the New Orpheus and the failure of his rescue mission, the irrecoverable Eurydice is an allegorical figure of lost aura. She did not return his gaze. The leading function of the pitch C is denied and the D♭ seventh chord becomes a seismograph of disenchantment and unfulfilment.

But that is just one side of this ambiguous Orpheus story. Wackers characterizes the work's opening figure as 'dissonierend-expressiven', as symbolic of the failed Orpheus and hence prophetic of the end of the work.[130] This sense in which there is a long-term relationship between the beginning and end of the work might suggest an attenuated or lamented redemptive process. The opening bars (see the reduction in Example 3.7) contain strong hints of D♭ through a combination of the leading-note to tonic C–D♭, the semitonal E–F, the viola descending chromatic line E–D–D♭ and the F–A♭ harmonic dyad. But the opening motive closes with the D♭ triad grating against the inner voice A♮ and held bass D♮, suggesting a coexistent D minor. On its *fortissimo* return (bars 15–16), the D♭ elements of the motive are absent and D minor thus emerges in more forceful clarity, and the instrumental introduction ends with transposed versions of the motive over an inner pedal D. Thus the motive becomes the driver of a fundamental tonal conflict between D♭ and D. The 'Tranquillo' entrance of the 'Eurydice' theme is prepared (at fig. 7) by the semitonal G♯–A dotted rhythm tail of the opening motive over a pedal D (see Example 3.8). This encourages a hearing of the Eurydice theme itself as containing pitch and rhythmic reminiscences of the opening motive – the minor third

---

[129] Benjamin, 'On Some Motifs in Baudelaire', in *Illuminations*, 184–5.
[130] Wackers, 'Eurydike folgt nicht mehr', 118.

Example 3.8 Weill, *Der neue Orpheus*, fig. 7 to 7 after fig. 7 (piano reduction).

fall from C♯–A♯ and the E–F semitone, the dotted quaver/semiquaver and
dotted quaver/two demisemiquaver rhythmic figures. Furthermore, the
Eurydice theme expands the C♯–D relationship and thus (enharmonically)
rekindles the D♭–D relationship of the opening. In this way organic connection between two contrasting themes can be discerned, suggesting a
process which counters Painter's modern polyphony, where 'simultaneity
was the determining attribute – that is, two musical thoughts (or themes)
are presented as clashing entities, each in its own world' (62). The theme is
also a clear intertextual reference to a central motive in Part 2 of Mahler's
Eighth (see Example 3.9), establishing the connection with that symphony's
redemptive figure. The D♭/C♯–D conflict also informs, in more complex
fashion, the final statement of the opening motive (from 1 bar after fig. 33)
and also the *fortissimo* chords which follow. This musical gesture of return
precedes the final section in which, over pastoral harp arpeggios, we hear of
Orpheus's final glance back to Eurydice in a pentatonically coloured D♭. The
last recollection of the Eurydice theme (Example 3.6) evokes a melancholic
tone. Yearning persists for the possibility of redemption encapsulated in the
unresolved leading-note C over D♭, the first two notes of the work's opening
motive. The final vocal climax had screamed of 'the unredeemed humanity'

Example 3.9 Mahler, Symphony no. 8, Part 2, 5 bars after fig. 32 to fig. 33.

(die unerlöste Menschheit!). But it remains possible to hear in Weill's music echoes not only of a rather traditional organicist process but also, through long-term tonal conflict and relationship, a sense of sustained yearning for redemptive reconciliation. Two hearings of the ending seem equally viable – one which evokes a negative vision through surrealist, mechanical montage of dead materials, another which contradicts this by evoking yearning for redemption through romantic, organic processes of relationship.

V

Wackers has constructed a persuasive narrative to reveal the relationship of the 'stylistic pluralism', 'intertextuality' and surrealism of *Der neue Orpheus* and the follow-up collaboration with Goll, the one-act opera *Royal Palace* (1926), to Weill's more famous collaborations with Brecht.[131] Hinton, too,

---

[131] Wackers, *Dialog der Künste*, 202, 280–91.

has pointed out that Weill's song style in *Mahagonny Songspiel* (1927) and *Die Dreigroschenoper* (1928) owes much to technical aspects of musical surrealism which had their genesis in the Goll works.[132] Temporal subversions, ambiguities and contradictions are once more central. In 'epic opera' Brecht insisted on the denial of dramatic growth and linear causality through the employment of techniques designed to produce jumps, shocks and montage effects.[133] Writing on *Die Dreigroschenoper* in 1929, Adorno deploys poetic critical language which resonates with the content of the Goll–Weill Orpheus. Adorno describes 'strange, unrelated juxtapositions', the 'photographic', even 'pornographic', 'rhythmic glibness' and musical expression that flirts with 'inanity'. This signalled for Adorno that 'Weill's approach penetrates all the further into the ghostly region', more advanced than that of the 'radical' Stravinsky of *L'Histoire du soldat*. Weill's music, therefore 'reflects the entire questionable order of the bourgeois overworld; rags and ruins, that's all that's left for the enlightened consciousness of that thoroughly demystified overworld; perhaps it is only rags and ruins that it can redeem in an image'.[134] And for Adorno the broken, shard-like character of Weill's music extends to 'the nature of the harmony itself, which hardly has anything to do with the principle of development, of leading-note tension or cadential functions any longer, instead omitting those smallest of communications between chords that characterize late chromaticism, so that the results of chromaticism are now simply left standing,

---

[132] Hinton, 'Weill: *Neue Sachlichkeit*, Surrealism, and *Gebrauchsmusik*', 71, 75–6. Weill, however, did not speak of surrealism (though Goll called the text of the opera *Royal Palace* 'surrealistic'), and with the more homogeneous musical style in the Brecht collaborations, including greater integration of popular idioms, the surrealistic effect may seem to diminish.

[133] Aspects of Brecht's epic theatre are comparable with the momentary 'distractions' of cinema. As Benjamin wrote, 'like the pictures in a film, epic theatre moves in spurts. Its basic form is that of the shock.' The aim is to 'impair the illusion of the audience', to generate 'astonishment' rather than 'empathy', and through interruptions lead to the 'quotable gesture', elements which are lifted out of original context. Benjamin, 'What is Epic Theatre?' (1939) in *Illuminations*, 44–151. Benjamin illustrates his essay with examples from *Happy End* and *Lindberghflug*. On the assimilation of cinematic techniques – film projection, pantomime, epic montage – in *Royal Palace*, *Der Protagonist* and *Mahagonny Songspiel*, see Bryan Gilliam, 'Stage and Screen: Kurt Weill and Operatic Reform in the 1920s', in Gilliam (ed.), *Music and Performance during the Weimar Republic*, 1–12. As Gilliam notes, Orpheus reappears in the 'Tomorrow's Lover' section of the *Royal Palace*. In a letter to Universal Edition of October 1925, Weill writes of a projected ballet *Maschinen* for Max Terpis, which David Drew suggests may have a legacy in certain motoric passages of *Royal Palace*; see Drew, *Kurt Weill: A Handbook* (London: Faber, 1987), 380.

[134] Theodor W. Adorno, 'The Threepenny Opera' [1929] trans. in Stephen Hinton (ed.), *Kurt Weill: The Threepenny Opera* (Cambridge University Press, 1990), 130–2.

devoid of any functions'.[135] If we buy Adorno's hearing, it seems clear that the ambivalent ambiguity of the music of the Goll works, in which at important moments long-range cadential or teleological implications remain symbolically in play and leading-note tensions are intensified in a manner clearly echoing romantic style, has been cast aside for a more simple, short-windedly direct idiom.

Brecht's notes to *Mahagonny* famously pointed to the 'culinary character' of opera and its roots as a hedonistic means of gaining pleasurable experience. 'Those composers who stem from Wagner', Brecht argued, 'still insist on posing as philosophers.' But this is a philosophy 'which is of no use to man or beast, and can only be disposed of as a means of sensual satisfaction'. All operatic content is 'absorbed' into this sensuous pleasure, and this is confirmed by composers' 'desperate', futile attempts to give opera 'posthumous' sense through new musical 'titillations'. The key idea for Brecht is that although *Aufstieg und Fall der Stadt Mahagonny* is 'culinary through and through' – it *is* opera – it brings this principle under critical scrutiny.[136] Adorno similarly saw the 'culinary' or sensuous element of art becoming self-serving, as an element producing illusory effects without functional or structural purpose. The question that arose for Adorno, as for Brecht, was how pleasures of the sensuous might remain part of a socially 'truthful' artwork. The self-conscious montage of ludic allusions to the illusions of operatic seduction, desire and satisfaction in *Mahagonny* suggests one answer. In this way, *Mahagonny* can be understood to produce a sort of meta-pleasure, one refusing the resolution or solution of a happy ending. Intoxications are revealed as addictions; Wagnerian music is parodied as narcotic effect. *Mahagonny*, Lydia Goehr argues, also presents a refutation of Wagner's *Gesamtkunstwerk* and the decadent illusory appearance of wholeness.[137] As is well known, Adorno considered *Mahagonny* to be the 'first surrealist opera'. Mahler figures as precursor of this character:

One hears a peculiar strain of Mahler throughout the opera, in its marches, its ostinato, its dulled major and minor chords. Like Mahler, it uses the explosive force of 'low' elements to break through the middle and partake of the highest. It smashes

[135] Theodor W. Adorno, '*Mahagonny*' (1930), in *Night Music: Essays on Music 1928–1962*, ed. Rolf Tiedemann, trans. Wieland Hoban (London: Seagull, 2009), 198.

[136] Bertolt Brecht, 'The Modern Theatre is the Epic Theatre' (Notes to the opera *Aufstieg und Fall der Stadt Mahagonny*) (1930), trans. in *Brecht on Theatre: The Development of an Aesthetic*, ed. and trans. John Willett (New York: Hill and Wang, 1964), 33–41.

[137] Lydia Goehr, 'Hardboiled Disillusionment: *Mahagonny* as the Last Culinary Opera', *Cultural Critique* 68 (2008), 3–37.

all the images present within it – not to be left with nothing, but, rather, to salvage those it has looted as flags of its own endeavour.[138]

Goehr also demonstrates how surrealism focuses on unfulfilled desire, and how surrealist art rejects or refuses art's traditional promise of satisfaction. Tantalizing and teasing, *Mahagonny* surrealistically ruminates on the ruination of bourgeois cultural edifices. The result is a liberating, fantastic polemic on intoxicating excess (Benjamin's 'profane illumination'), desire and fulfilment, romantic longing and union.[139] The Act three finale offers a parody of denouement, closure and redemption. *Mahagonny*'s false happy ending is one designed to stimulate discussion of what kind of utopia we should hope for.[140]

Hinton warns, however, that Brecht's 'Notes' to *Mahagonny*, which have accrued a degree of notoriety, diverge from Weill's views and practice. Weill believed in the primary structural and symbolic role of music and that its expressive effect was greater than that of words. (He thought that Brecht probably would admit this too, but that this was not discussed.) Weill and Brecht did nonetheless seem to agree on the 'unromantic' aims of their collaboration. Weill wrote in his 1929 'Über den gestischen Charakter der Musik': 'Romanticism as art switches off our capacity to think; it operates with narcotic means.'[141] There remains, however, an important if ambiguous and ambivalent role for a romantic type of lyricism in Weill's music, something which Adorno in his 1929 description of Weill's harmony cited above perhaps strategically ignores. Crucially, however, this romantic lyricism is exposed in plural aesthetic and stylistic contexts, in a manner Weill was already beginning to develop in works from the mid 1920s. Hinton notes that Weill's music for the Kaiser opera *Der Protagonist* (1926) foreshadows an 'aesthetic dualism' embodied by a 'combination of lyrical expressivity and ostinato-like accompaniments' which 'will form the basis of the much-vaunted song style' of the Brecht collaborations. But though these lyrical elements may suggest Schubert, they are 'not exactly romantic; they are post-romantic. *Espressivo* in quotation marks, as it were.' Kaiser, as

---

[138] Adorno, '*Mahagonny*', 199.

[139] Lydia Goehr, '*Juliette fährt nach Mahagonny* or a Critical Reading of Surrealist Opera', *The Opera Quarterly* 21 (2006), 647–74.

[140] See Foster Hirsch, *Kurt Weill on Stage: From Berlin to Broadway* (New York: Knopf, 2002), 52. On the 'happy' ending of *Dreigroschenoper*, see Peter W. Ferran 'The *Threepenny* Songs: Cabaret and the Lyrical Gestus', *Theater* 30 no. 3 ('100 Years of Kurt Weill') (2000), 5–21.

[141] Hinton, 'The Concept of Epic Opera: Theoretical Anomalies in the Brecht–Weill Partnership', in Hermann Danuser (ed.), *Das musikalische Kunstwerk. Geschichte – Ästhetik – Theorie* (Laaber-Verlag, 1988), 285–94.

a 'recovering expressionist', displayed an ambivalent attraction to the dangers of 'artistic absorption', one probably also then shared by Weill, who 'spoke two musical languages: the emotionally charged "subjective" one of late-Romanticism and its mechanically "objective", neoclassical antithesis'.[142] Even when Weill's music seems to inhabit the sentimental, kitsch end of romanticism, his mastery of the idiom is so complete and its seductive quality so powerful that the most sophisticated of listeners is left in troubled uncertainty. Donald Mitchell wrote that the piano paraphrase of the 'sentimental ballad' known as 'The Maiden's Prayer', over which Jack comments 'Das ist die ewige Kunst',

stands for the oozing sentiment and escapist romanticism of the kind of 'art' that is pleased to seek the protection of inverted commas . . . But while one smiles at the swooning, maudlin, cascading phrases of Weill's extraordinarily cunning arrangement, which wonderfully recreates the lost Lisztian skill of artful decoration, one is also oddly and perhaps rather disturbingly touched by it. It is, we come to realise, almost with a sense of guilt, rather beautiful in its own right. 'Eternal art'? Well, perhaps not that exactly, but certainly, yes, it *has* a validity. One can't, in fact, simply laugh it off, because Weill's paraphrase very subtly and even painfully reminds us that a whole tradition of romantic music, a glorious tradition, indeed, however debased it may have become, is bound up with what might easily be mistaken for a straightforward parody.[143]

Brecht would doubtless have scoffed, proclaiming that Mitchell has been duped. The inflected melodic turns in E♭ in Weill's music seem to swoon in the face of Adorno's declaration of the demise of chromatically intensified cadence and the death of the leading-note in the music of *Die Dreigroschenoper* (see Example 3.10). If Adorno had recognized that these bars overtly recall the key and melodic shaping of several prayerful passages towards the end of the second part of Mahler's Eighth, then he would undoubtedly had declared his suspicions concerning Mahler's Goethe setting to be independently verified. But though they are tawdry, Weill's cadences are disturbingly, residually alluring. This is heightened by their imperilled existence within a juxtaposition of other more directly 'anti-romantic' or realist styles. It is through the placement of romantic idioms in such pluralistic combinations, Hinton concludes, that Weill's music tells a 'story more universal in its lyrical way than the didactic parable that Brecht wanted the piece to be. Not as something readily resolvable into

---

[142] Hinton, *Weill's Musical Theatre*, 76–7.

[143] Donald Mitchell, 'Weill's *Mahagonny* and "Eternal Art"', in *Cradles of the New: Writings on Music 1951–1991* (London: Faber, 1995), 82.

Example 3.10 Weill, *Aufstieg und Fall der Stadt Mahagonny*, 2 before fig. 16 to 4 after fig. 16.

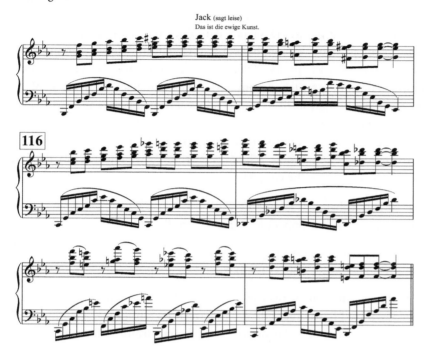

the specificity of allegory so much as an essentially nonverbal symbolic language.'[144] The sentimental cadential patterns of the Maiden's Prayer might seem to mock the redemptive aspirations of 'Art' with a capital A. They might be heard as devastating allegorical mimicry of the expressive character of the romantic symbol, to invoke the dualism to which Hinton clearly alludes, and to which Mahler's Eighth so protractedly strives. Yet even in a hostile stylistic ecosystem, this symbolic quality seems to resist total devastation: the demise of 'die ewige Kunst' might be too quickly announced.

Like Goll, Kaiser was a crucial figure in Weill's early career. They became increasingly close during 1924, and when Busoni died in July, Kaiser assumed special importance for Weill (work on *Der Protagonist* began later that year).[145] The Weill–Brecht collaboration *Happy End* (1929) was an unsuccessful attempt to continue in the mode of *Die Dreigroschenoper*'s artificial happy end. By contrast, Kaiser's *Der Silbersee*, which Weill set in

---

[144] Hinton, *Weill's Musical Theatre*, 154.   [145] See Eichhorn, 'Introduction', 13.

1932–3, offers, as Hinton summarizes, a final 'promise of escape and redemption' and conveys a message of 'hope and transcendence' that is not coloured by satirical or ironic tones. Furthermore, as Hinton points out, Fennimore's song about the Silver Lake, which returns at the end, suggests her potential status as symbolic of a Goethean 'eternal feminine'.[146] Similarly, for Ian Kemp, *Der Silbersee* 'ends with a transformation scene, in which the tone is switched from stark reality to magic – a revelation of the power of the human spirit to transcend its earthly miseries and strive after paradise. Furthermore, the agent of this catharsis is Goethe's *Ewigweibliche* (in *Der Silbersee*, the voice of the young girl Fennimore).'[147]

In Fennimore's first song, 'Ich bin eine arme Verwandte' (Act 2), the first two stanzas end with the couplet:

Das ist kein Leben, das ist nur Verduß
Den man, was soll denn werden, ertragen muß

It's no way of living, my life is a chore,
But then, you've not much option when you are poor

Weill sets these lines over an extended dominant pedal during which modally mixed harmonies add a bittersweet, regretful tone. The third and final stanza, in which she imagines a life free from tedious, restrictive, troublesome relations, ends with the couplet:

Ach das wär' ein Leben, das wär' ein Genuß,
Wenn man vergessen könnte, daß man verwandt sein muß

Now that would be living, that would be a pleasure,
If only I could manage without my kith and kin.

In the music to these lines the dominant pedal is expressively transfigured. Minor inflections largely disappear and emphasis is left on the added major sixth, C, which lends a pentatonic colour. A rising instrumental descant moves from diatonic to whole tone (bb. 103–9; see Example 3.11).

[146] Hinton, *Weill's Musical Theatre*, 126, 129, 131. Kaiser's earlier work is a theatrical exploration of vitalistic regeneration versus idealism, of the dichotomy of *Geist* versus *Leben* or a dialectics of optimism and pessimism. Instinct reveals that all ideals are illusory, raising the possibility of a nihilist conclusion but also the redemptive possibilities of love. But the 1920s sees a new, if insecure, idealism, a rejection of the ugly side of life, partially because of renewed interest in Plato, a spiritualized love, a move from vital life, from carnal desire. There is a renewed struggle between real and ideal: see Herbert W. Reichert, 'Nietzsche and Georg Kaiser', *Studies in Philology* 61 (1964), 85–108.
[147] Ian Kemp, 'Music as Metaphor: Aspects of *Der Silbersee*', in Kowalke (ed.), *A New Orpheus*, 131–46 (at 132).

Example 3.11 Weill, *Der Silbersee*, Act 2: Fennimore, 'Ich bin eine arme Verwandte', bb. 103–close.

The musical technique – transfigurative in effect; the level of discernible irony debatable – is the familiar 'salvation' dominant six-four. This becomes even more apparent when, towards the end of Act 2, Fennimore tells Severin of the path to redemption: 'Wer weiter muß, den trägt der Silbersee' (Who must go on is borne by Silver Sea), after which Weill supplies a long instrumental coda where the tonal move is from D (with major seventh C♯) to D♭ (with major seventh C) and whose final cadence is another dominant six-four overtly in the 'salvation' manner with a closing statement of a pentatonically inflected theme. The tonal shift from D to D♭

Example 3.12a Weill, *Der Silbersee* instrumental coda to Act 2, bb. 484–89.

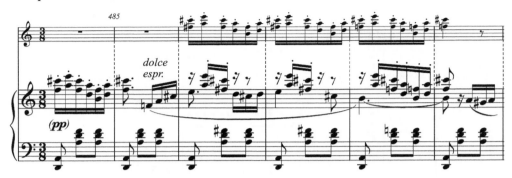

Example 3.12b Weill, *Der Silbersee* instrumental coda to Act 2, bb. 509–17.

enables the theme to be transformed from modally mixed chromaticism (bb. 484–9) to major mode pentatonicism (bb. 509–17; see Examples 12a and 12b). This music, and the D–D♭ tonal relationship, returns in the closing scene of the work where the disembodied voice of Fennimore repeats this line and Olim and Severin 'disappear over the shining surface of the lake'. Pondering the work's final chord (G–B–D–F♯), Hinton asks of the unresolved leading-note: 'leading to where?'[148] The tonic seventh chord

[148] Hinton, *Weill's Musical Theatre*, 137.

overtly recalls the ambiguous ending of *Der neue Orpheus*. But the more emphatically redemptive tone of the final cadences of *Der Silbersee* sustains the early twentieth-century investment in a romantic notion of closure through transfiguration to which Mahler's music provides a rich series of variants and negotiations. Kemp concludes that 'as far as Weill was concerned, his artistic standpoint had now shifted toward the romantic aesthetic that art embodies the universal and that messages about the universal can be transmitted subliminally and symbolically'.[149] Reading Weill's music alongside passages from Mahler has revealed that this manoeuvre was always a possibility, even though often challenged, subverted, parodied or resisted. The temporal ambiguities, which the music of Mahler and Weill share, between goal-direction and static montage are achieved by musical techniques which, through their different manipulations of expectations, denial and surprise, can offer glimpses of some future state, whether dystopian or utopian.

[149] Kemp, 'Music as Metaphor', 139.

4 | Tyranny and freedom: Henze and Mahler

I

In post-Second World War Germany, as elsewhere in Europe, a heated debate developed between those who advocated radical notions of innovative cultural advancement and those who supported conservative reconstruction. The polemical polarization of progress and restoration that structured Adorno's *Philosophie der neuen Musik* (1949), in which approval of Schoenberg's atonal expressionism as 'authentic' and advanced art was contrasted with condemnation of the music of Hindemith and especially Stravinsky as hollow, reactionary restoration, is a familiar example. A comparable division formed the basis of the contrast between the focus of the early Darmstadt meetings on the music of Stravinsky, Bartók and Hindemith, and René Leibowitz's espousal from 1948 that out of the devastation of the immediate past the new should be sought in a radical kind of neo-serialism, with its promise of abstraction and athematicism. This latter programme of renewal held strong appeal for composers who in the late 1940s and early 1950s sought a 'new German musical identity as distant as possible from both postromantic subjectivity and the political manipulation of music under the Nazis'.[1] A move to structural rigour, often allied to supposed political neutrality and the rejection of romantic expression, emerged from analysis of the music of Webern disseminated in the pages of *die Riehe* (1955–62) under the editorship of Herbert Eimert and Karl-Heinz Stockhausen.[2]

But by the mid 1950s, accusations of musical totalitarianism in the predetermined, masterful control systems of the new serialism were already being voiced. In his essay 'The Ageing of New Music' (1955), Adorno attacked the pursuit of apparently neutral musical material and the static 'abstract negation' sought by the new serialists for excluding the dynamic of subjective doubts and anxieties that he heard powerfully manifest in the

---

[1] Gesa Kordes, 'Darmstadt, Post-War Experimentation, and the West German Search for a New Musical Identity', in Celia Applegate and Pamela Potter (eds.), *Music and German National Identity* (Chicago University Press, 2002), 215.

[2] For details of this period, see M.J. Grant, *Serial Music, Serial Aesthetics: Compositional Theory in Post-War Europe* (Cambridge University Press, 2001), 11–71.

atonal expressionism of the Second Viennese School and that lay at the heart of the shock of 'authentic' new music.[3] It is arguable that by judging central European music in the aftermath of the Second World War with models from pre-First World War Viennese culture, Adorno is 'comparing totally different musical aesthetics',[4] but in 1960 he asserted that 'Viennese new music was never directly at one with its own milieu', that 'from the outset it pressed beyond the boundaries of its place of origin'. Adorno allied this music's subjective freedom and expressive complexity with its productive, dialectical relationship with the past. He raised Berg's Violin Concerto as a model of modern Viennese music, as a demonstration that 'things that are modern do not just sally forth in advance of their time. They also recall things forgotten: they control the anachronistic reserves which have been left behind and which have not yet been exhausted by the rationality of eternal sameness', by the 'ageing of modernism ... in the face of an indiscriminately expanding rationality'.[5] At this point Adorno might have repeated his pre-war convictions about the continuing relevance of Mahler (although Mahler's musical materials might not have been deemed to have contained enough that was 'advanced'). In 1930 he had observed that 'the currently dominant consciousness is at odds with Mahler', but that in the rational era of *Neue Sachlichkeit* and the cool, chic view of the past in neoclassicism 'Mahler has not been overcome, he has been repressed.'[6] The version of new objectivity he heard manifest in the complex, machine-like systems developed by post-war serialists might similarly be seen as a repression of the kind of problematized subjectivity and diversity of materials he identified in the music of Mahler. As Alastair Williams has noted, reading Adorno's 1960 Mahler monograph in the context of his writings on new music 'leads one to conclude that there are two Adornos: one is an advocate of progressive material, while the other is prepared to track multiple layers of signification. He seldom acknowledges this ambivalence, which is more indicative of simultaneous possibilities than outright contradiction.' Adorno's understanding of Mahler's music suggests a 'path for musical modernism' based upon semantic and structural interaction between esoteric 'internal configuration' and 'objects' with exoteric yet 'sedimented', intertextual meanings.[7]

---

[3] Theodor W. Adorno, 'The Aging of New Music' (1955), in *Essays*, 181–202.
[4] Grant, *Serial Music*, 68.
[5] Theodor W. Adorno, 'Vienna' (1960), in *Quasi una Fantasia*, 216.
[6] Theodor W. Adorno, 'Mahler Today' (1930) in *Essays*, 603–4.
[7] Alastair Williams, 'Adorno and the Semantics of Modernism', *Perspectives of New Music* 37 (1999), 31, 36; see also Paddison, *Adorno's Aesthetics of Music*, 269–70.

Henze's well-known rejection in the 1950s of the Darmstadt line was in part motivated by an aversion to the apparently 'mechanical' and 'inexpressive' qualities of Boulez's brand of 'Webernism'.[8] Henze shunned this objectified, monological image of Webern. 'My antipathy was not directed against Webern's music', he wrote, 'but against the misuse and misinterpretation of his aesthetic and indeed, of his technique and its motivation and significance. Thanks to the initiative of Boulez and Stockhausen this had become institutionalized as official musical thinking.' This led to music which Henze considered barren and lifeless:

Everything had to be stylized and made abstract: music regarded as a glass-bead-game, a fossil of life. Discipline was the order of the day. Through discipline it was going to be possible to get music back on its feet again, though nobody asked what for. Discipline enabled form to come about: there were rules and parameters for everything. Expressionism and (left-wing) Surrealism were mystically remote; we were told that these movements were already obsolete before 1930 and had been surpassed. The new avant-garde would reaffirm this.[9]

Henze preferred a more polyvalent and polymorphous reading of Webern. He sought both a more worldly music and a music in which the tensions between affirmation and wholeness and negation and fragment take central place. Behind the abstractions of Webern, so attractive to Darmstadt neo-serialists, lie transformations of musical topics of nature and loss in a Utopian search for universal affirmation in new organic order which coexists with the tendency to fragment and symbiosis. In this, Webern's music compares closely with Mahler, with whom Webern shared an aesthetic preoccupation with memory, and the coexistence of idealizing content, referential gesture, subjective expression and abstract form.[10] While Webern's 'classicist' obsession with unity and connection apparently smooths out Mahler's characteristic heterogeneity (in *The Path to New Music*, he particularly admired Mahler's 'polyphony' created by secondary voices that were no longer merely accompanying figures but were part of the motivic web of material), this should not mask the elements of polarity and fragmentation, and the symbiotic balance of discontinuities which complement coherence and stability in

---

[8] Hans Werner Henze, 'German Music in the 1940s and 1950s', in *Music and Politics*, 27–56.

[9] *Ibid.*, 38, 43. Henze is here alluding to Hermann Hesse's novel *Das Glasperlenspiel* (1943); the game was practised in an environment in which, detached from the world, its players pursued aesthetic purity, a visionary serenity, an abstract perfection.

[10] See Julian Johnson, *Webern and the Transformation of Nature* (Cambridge University Press, 1999).

Webern's atonal and serial works.[11] This sustains the dialectic between the freedom of singular particulars and the demands of formal wholeness which is often especially intensified in Mahler's music. Such precarious coexistence of order and disorder would become a prominent, indeed stylistically defining, feature of much of Henze's music.

Leibowitz's 1948 lectures on Schoenberg's Op. 31 had previously convinced Henze that serialism 'enabled us to create new concepts of freedom and beauty'.[12] But he soon became uncomfortable with Leibowitz's espousal of a serialist aesthetic of the 'individual note', which by contrast with the coherence of the thematic phrase seemed only to generate 'disjointed meaninglessness'.[13] Henze also baulked at the feeling that 'the existing audience ... was to be ignored. Their demand for "plain language" music was to be dismissed as improper ... Any encounter with the listeners that was not catastrophic and scandalous would defile the artist.' He considered Adorno to be an ally of this trend: 'as Adorno decreed, the job of the composer was to write music that would repel, shock, and be the vehicle for "unmitigated cruelty" ... Thus spake Adorno; this was supposed to be the point of departure for the new international generation of composers.'[14] By contrast, Henze sought a comprehensible language of expression which rejected the molecular structures and subjective vacuum of post-Leibowitzian pointillism. In Hans Keller's words, in the face of the chronic crisis of communication in the 'atonal trauma', Henze wished to recover compositionally implied or suppressed backgrounds of 'well-defined expectations'. Thus speaking dissidently against the apparent Stockhausen–Boulez hegemony, Henze seemed to represent an 'untimely, downright lonely musicality'.[15]

This artistic alienation, combined with his personal predicament as a homosexual in post-war Germany, precipitated his move to Italy in 1953. Here he sensed a recovery of subjective 'freedom' and also an alternative view of artistic rigour and purity, 'a concept of beauty that had something to do with the notion of truth – inner truth, one's own private truth'.[16] Paradoxical ramifications emerged from this new search for 'authentic'

[11] Arnold Whittall, 'Webern and Atonality: the Path from the Old Aesthetic', *The Musical Times* 124 (1983), 733–7.

[12] Hans Werner Henze, *Bohemian Fifths: An Autobiography*, trans. Stewart Spencer (London: Faber, 1998), 74.

[13] Henze, *Music and Politics*, 84; Grant notes that this aesthetic split is evident in Rudolf Stephan's essay on Henze in *die Riehe* IV, 32–7; *Serial Music*, 199.

[14] Henze, 'German Music in the 1940s and 1950s', 40–1.

[15] Hans Keller, *Music, Closed Societies and Football* (reprint of *1975 (1984 minus 9)*) (London: Toccata Press, 1986), 136, 145, 170, 210, 245.

[16] Henze, *Bohemian Fifths*, 121.

expressive identity. First, 'instead of turning into an Italian' as Henze declared was his initial desire, he confessed that he 'became more and more of a German' whilst in Italy, 'a German who read Hegel, Marx, Benjamin and Adorno in the original'. Looking back in 1971, Henze sought to distinguish his experience as a German in Mediterranean climes with the tradition of the Central European artist's 'Italian Experience'; what mattered to him was isolation, freedom and search for self-identity – not 'Italy' itself.[17] Second, after what Henze called the 'unruly' music of *König Hirsch* (1953), the *Five Neapolitan Songs* (1956) and *Nachtstücke und Arien* (1957), there was a reaction, in a group of works from the late 1950s written in Naples (for example, *Antifone*, 1960), as, 'alarmed and exhausted after dealing with the unknown and with the temptations and dangers of free-style composition', he 'kept returning to serialism' and its 'constraints', in a reconfrontation with order and system which had a 'traumatic quality'.[18]

At this time it was the music of Mahler, dismissed by the Darmstadt faithful as 'Art nouveau kitsch, suited at best only to provoke laughter'[19] and resisted by influential sectors of Vienna's intellectual elite until well after the Second World War (Keller admitted that he only came to an understanding of Mahler when in Britain, through the music of Britten),[20] which offered Henze the prospect of a consistently productive response to what he called the 'restrictive . . . one dimensional approach to music which many adopted in the period following the Second World War, in the post-fascist world' and to his own desire to develop a musical style of more overt and varied subjective expression:[21]

[17] Hans Werner Henze, 'Art and Revolution', (1971), in *Music and Politics*, 178.

[18] Douglas Jarman (ed.), 'Looking Back' (1990), in *Henze at the Royal Northern College of Music: A Symposium* (Todmorden: Arc, 1998), 9, 13. As is often recounted, at the 1958 performance of *Nachtstücke und Arien*, Boulez, Stockhausen and Nono all very publicly left after just a few bars, apparently to register their disdain for the work. See Henze's description in 'German Music in the 1940s and 1950s', 46.

[19] Henze, 'German Music in the 1940s and 1950s', 44.

[20] Hans Keller, 'National Frontiers in Music' (1954), in *Essays on Music*, 24.

[21] Within the Darmstadt domain, the only reference to Mahler in *die Reihe* is from Diether Schnebel, who cites him as a composer of 'layers' in musical space comparable with Debussy's vertical sound textures, and appropriates him, in stark contrast to Henze, for a quasi-Leibowitzian project: 'the consequences of Mahler are . . . [that] traditional modes of thought like melody, accompaniment, theme, etc., lose their meaning; and the traditional form-schemes are equally unsuited to this kind of music'. Mahler, like Webern, 'had little immediate effect on musical history', and was 'denied disciples'; but 'the tendencies of their music', like those of Debussy's, 'are being fulfilled today'. '*Brouillards*. Tendenzen bei Debussy', *die Reihe* VI (1958), 30–5.

My encounter with Mahler's art came then, at just the right moment to give me a different perspective, and enabled me to find a wholly personal approach to the music of the present and of the past, the trivial and the ritual music of all periods, on the basis of personal experiences and decisions. I was then able to pursue this personal path outside the 'acceptable' aesthetic course of the mainstream of self-styled modern music.[22]

The exploration of Mahler's music, which as Henze has recalled, was '*years after the Second World War*' (his emphasis perhaps indicates frustration that this did not occur sooner), was often pursued via a car radio. With records of Mahler scarce at that time, Henze the new Mahlerian enthusiast had to seek out distant concert performances and broadcasts.[23] Mahler became crucial for the sustenance of Henze's compositional projects and to the development of his aesthetic and technique, in particular because he heard in it a direct expression of both desperate loss and redemptive amorous aspiration. As Henze later wrote, Mahler's music 'contains much grief for things that have been lost, but messages for the future of mankind should also be discerned: one of them is hope; another, directed at the very essence of music itself, love . . . Its provocation lies in its love of truth and its consequent lack of extenuation.'[24]

II

In musical terms, the problematic post-war issue of German identity was – Wagner apart – most closely associated with the genre of the symphony. The nineteenth- and early twentieth-century symphonic legacy of Beethoven, Schumann, Brahms and Bruckner (though the 'Germanness' of the last of course is highly debatable) remained a potent symbol of a 'heroically' German, nationalist – indeed imperialist – artistic achievement. In romantic discourse, the 'symphonic' had become the characteristic of German music which, it was claimed, raised it above other musical types into an 'absolute' or metaphysical plane, to a Universal status which the music of other (peripheral, marginal) nations was unable to reach. In such spirit was the supposedly 'symphonic' quality of Wagner's music dramas, *Tristan* especially, often identified. Wagner himself, of course, saw his stage

---

[22] Henze, *Language, Music and Artistic Invention*, 7.
[23] Jarman (ed.), 'Conversations with Henze 1', in *Henze at the RNCM*, 42.
[24] Henze, 'Gustav Mahler' (1975), *Music and Politics*, 157–8.

works as the next essential step beyond Beethoven's Ninth.[25] It is unsurprising therefore, that many German composers of the post-Second World War period shunned both the symphony as a genre and the 'symphonic' as a broader idea, or at least sought to place it at a controlled distance through techniques of parody or ironic critique. Henze, by deliberate, dissenting contrast, continued to interrogate the symphony and the symphonic, in a sympathetic if ambivalent manner. In 1947 the Darmstadt summer school was attended by Karl Amadeus Hartmann, whose moral, political and communicative commitments enthralled Henze. Later, during 1952–3, he enthused over Hartmann's *musica viva* concerts in Munich. Hartmann's technical expansion of orchestral timbre and commitment to large-scale symphonic forms were important examples for Henze's own symphonic ambitions.[26] In pursuing those ambitions he was engaging with a tradition which for many of his contemporary compatriots had become irrevocably tarnished through distasteful ideological or historical associations. As Karen Painter has commented, 'after the collapse of the Third Reich it would be difficult to pick up a tradition that had been so laden with political expectation and eventually with debased political programs ... For postwar German composers the rehabilitation of a musical tradition led them back to the Second Viennese School and the modernist Weimar Left, with its recourses to montage and brevity.'[27] Henze is the notable exception. But, as Painter notes, he engaged with this legacy from a position of increasing and self-imposed exile. Henze's geographical and creative distance from the current 'orthodoxies' of the German *Heimat* raises a centrally important issue. Henze's feeling of being an outsider was confirmed by his increasing desire to rebel against the rule of German avant-garde ideologues.

From his youth, Henze had developed a refined appreciation for the taboo literature of the so-called 'degenerates':

the voices of decay and decline that entered German poetry through Georg Trakl's lyric verse struck a chord with us: our evenings passed in a haze of blue; crystalline tears would fall from our eyelids; shed for a bitter world. Shivering bluely, the night wind swept down the hillside like a mother's dark lament, only to die away again, and for a moment we glimpsed the blackness at the centre of our hearts, whole

---

[25] See Carolyn Abbate, 'Opera as Symphony, a Wagnerian Myth', in Carolyn Abbate and Roger Parker (eds.), *Analyzing Opera: Verdi and Wagner* (Princeton University Press, 1989), 92–124.

[26] See Hanns-Werner Heister, 'Zur Bedeutung Karl Amadeus Hartmanns für Hans Werner Henze', *Hamburger Jahrbuch für Musikwissenschaft* 20 (2003), 205–14.

[27] Painter, *Symphonic Aspirations*, 243.

minutes of shimmering silence. We lived completely bound up in this world of forbidden pleasures.[28]

He also developed an enthusiasm for the 'young German bourgeoisie of the early nineteenth century, with its discoveries concerning not only the language of music and music of language, but also the significance of our folk tales and myths and the soulscapes that they conceal, since it seems to me that such ideas may help us to escape from our benighted state of spiritual underdevelopment and into the light and lucidity of classical culture'.[29] Henze is clearly speaking of the romantic culture of Rückert, the Schlegels, von Platen, Novalis and Tieck. If it all seemed so untimely and desperately out of fashion, then so did Mahler's enthusiasm for the same early romantics in *fin-de-siècle* Vienna.[30]

Moving to Italy allowed Henze to revalue the potential furtherance of German legacies. In a famous study of exile, Edward Said argued that alienation and agonizing distance from dominant cultural processes are essential if a critically informed consciousness is to emerge. Paradoxically, however, the 'critic' (and, by extension for argument, the artist) nonetheless remains an inseparable part of this culture. There is no escape. Said's prime example is Erich Auerbach's classic text of the post-war years, *Mimesis* (1947), written when the author was in Istanbul and thus exiled from Western European culture, the very topic of the work. The condition of exile generates the risk of not writing, because as an outcast from home, nation and milieu, the author experiences a 'loss of texts, traditions and continuities that make up the very web of culture'. The question for Said is how Auerbach was able to transform this predicament into the creative production of a critically voiced text. He finds an answer in a later essay of Auerbach, 'Philologie der *Weltliteratur*': 'The most priceless and indispensable part of a philologist's heritage is still his own nation's culture and heritage. Only when he is first separated from this heritage, however, and then transcends it does it become truly effective.' Auerbach analyses culture's aggressive fortification, the affirmation of identity through silencing or excluding alterity, as an 'affirmation of the known at the expense of the knowable'.[31] All this is strikingly resonant with Henze's position, with his exclusion from the homeland's dominant musical culture and his flaunting

---

[28] Henze, *Bohemian Fifths*, 26.   [29] *Ibid.*, 55.
[30] See Solvik, 'Mahler's Untimely Modernism'.
[31] Erich Auerbach, 'Philology and *Weltliteratur*', trans. M. and E.W. Said, *Centennial Review* 13 (Winter 1969), 17; cited in Said, *The World, The Text and The Critic*, 7. On exile as a central experience of modernity, see Said, 'Reflections on Exile', in *Reflections on Exile and other Literary and Cultural Essays* (London: Granta Books, 2000), 173–86.

of a deliberately provocative alterity which ultimately allows him to develop a new creative, 'transcendent' if ambivalent relationship with the culture of the *Heimat*. In summary, it led to a combined sense of freedom and critical relationship.

Henze approached the German traditions with a sense of what we might, to evoke Schoenberg, call '*Erwartung*' – anxious or nervous expectation. Nonetheless, Henze has repeatedly sought to challenge these 'German' features with apparently oppositional styles and techniques. In particular he has attempted to find a way of creatively engaging with Stravinsky without jettisoning the Germanic legacy. Through the 1950s he was drawn to Stravinsky as the 'diametrical opposites of those of the expressionistic Schoenberg. Enslaved by one, enthralled by the other, I have tried ever since, for decades, to sustain a double life, a contradiction, a dualism within myself, and to draw the aesthetic consequences.'[32] On the surface this seems to counter the famous chasm in modern music opened up in Adorno's *Philosophie der neuen Musik*. But it is rather too pat to assume that Henze achieved, or even sought, an organic synthesis of Adorno's opposition. Indeed the sense is often one of an approach towards a kind of negative dialectic. In this tensed, anti-organic position, the music of Mahler powerfully suggested to Henze modes of engagement with the German tradition which can move between dissenting, conflicting or more indulgently accommodating coexistence with alternative traditions.

Several key works from the late 1950s reveal how Henze's engagement with traditions rejected by the contemporary avant-garde was sustained, enriched, counterpointed and inflected. Such works include *Kammermusik 1958* and *Der Prinz von Homburg* (also composed during 1958). In *Kammermusik 1958*, Henze set the romantic poetry of Friedrich Hölderlin and, inspired by the poetic allusions to myths of Greek antiquity and the landscapes he saw on a trip to Greece, explored what he called an 'art of metaphor' and 'tragedy'. Henze dedicated the work to Britten, 'whose music', Henze recalled, 'I admired so much at that time that the results of that admiration may be heard at various points in my own music and nowhere more so than in the present piece.'[33] Unsurprisingly, Britten's music was another topic on which Henze fell out with Adorno, who dismissed Britten as a 'helpless' epigone engaged in a failed quest for the

---

[32] Henze, *Language, Music and Artistic Invention*, 7.

[33] Henze, *Bohemian Fifths*, 155–6. The ensemble for the work's Hamburg premiere included Peter Pears and Julian Bream. Henze's admiration for Britten goes back to him seeing the first German production of *Peter Grimes*.

past, one whose music demonstrates a 'pretentious meagreness'.[34] The multi-movement *Kammermusik 1958* includes a setting of Hölderlin's late hymn 'In lieblicher Bläue' and it is in parts of these and especially in the three 'Tentos' for solo guitar which form the third, fifth and eleventh movements that Henze composes in a notably simple, directly expressive idiom which exploits overtly tonal and pentatonic materials. It is possible that Henze's inclusion of the year of composition in the work's title is a declaration that such an idiom could remain relevant in the late 1950s. The avant-garde composer Helmut Lachenmann could not abide such a style. In a public debate with Henze broadcast by Stuttgart radio in the early 1980s, he condemned the guitar solos in *Kammermusik 1958* for creating a 'simple utopia' through the deployment of a 'lyrical' style which is 'intact', 'unreflective' and 'naïve' rather than transformed, mediated or 'experienced'. Lachenmann is 'suspicious' of their effect, in which the 'idyll' is exploited in an 'unaltered' state. Henze replied, after playing to the gallery through humorous allusion to Adorno, that it is 'permitted to portray utopias, to sketch out and prepare models of utopias'.[35] Hölderlin was frequently either set by or an inspiration for composers associated with the avant-garde (Nono, Kurtág, Rihm, for example). But though Hölderlin's poetry was curiously eschewed by nineteenth-century romantic composers, Henze's settings clearly evoke romantic traditions. (The title of the first 'Tento', 'Du schönes Bächlein', inevitably recalls Schubert's *Die schöne Müllerin*.) It is striking that Lachenmann's diatribe alludes explicitly to Schiller's naïve and sentimental and therefore to a seminal dualism for romantic art. And in focusing on the guitar solos, in which diatonic and pentatonic materials are often employed in provocative simplicity, he probably identifies those passages that most overtly reveal Henze's admiration for Britten's music. As we saw in Chapter 2, Britten's diatonic simplicity plays a vital role in his extensions and interrogations of the naïve and sentimental as well as redemptive or utopian notions which draw upon aspects of the romantic tradition. In Schiller's view of modern art, idyll and elegy are necessary counterparts of course, and it is significant that in 1963, when his enthusiasm for Mahler was of particularly strong creative importance, Henze added

---

[34] Adorno, *Philosophy of Modern Music*, 10. Henze recalled a conversation of 1961 in which Adorno would not be budged from his condemnation of Britten: 'Teddy was a queer bird, I did not like him, there was something about him that I found disagreeable.' *Bohemian Fifths*, 168. Henze dedicated his Fifth String Quartet (1976) to Britten's memory.

[35] The dialogue is transcribed and translated in an appendix to Helmut Lachenmann, 'Open Letter to Hans Werner Henze', trans. Jeffrey Stadelman, *Perspectives of New Music* 35 (1997), 189–200.

as an Epilogue to *Kammermusik* an instrumental Adagio whose sustained chromatic counterpoint and expansive rhetoric are of elegiac articulation. The dualism invoked by the final line of Hölderlin's hymn, which precedes this Adagio, 'Leben ist Tod, und Tod ist auch ein Leben', is one which clearly parallels the refrain of 'Das Trinklied vom Jammer der Erde', the first song of Mahler's *Das Lied von der Erde* ('Dunkel ist das Leben, ist der Tod!'). The romantic, Schubertian resonances in Henze's Hölderlin work are refracted through elegiac evocations of Mahler and idyllic echoes of Britten's diatonic simplicity. The Adagio, an elegiac afterthought written for a work composed five years earlier and whose title explicitly located the composition in a moment in history, might be called doubly late: its lateness is overtly both chronological and stylistic. Lachenmann would doubtless dismiss it as an epigone's epilogue.

In *Der Prinz von Homburg*, Heinrich von Kleist's exemplification of a move out of Prussianism into Greece provided a Mediterranean impetus for Henze's interest in early nineteenth-century Italian opera and allowed him to 'free my musical technique from the burden of Expressionism'.[36] During the composition of this opera in the 'seductive Naples' of the late 1950s, Henze recalled that he 'had to nail my windows shut in order not to hear the siren songs of tonality reaching up to me on the fifth floor from a thousand guitars and mandolins'.[37] Again, a sustained, unresolved contradiction or lack of resolution between opposing styles is characteristic. In the essay 'Instrumental Composition' (1963), he noted alternations between contrapuntal and *cantabilità* pieces:

a polyphonic North German temperament in the *arioso* South . . . could be interpreted as indecisiveness, but also as an artistic means of clarifying tension and resolution, rigour and effortlessness, brightness and darkness; as something theatrical, perhaps even as the intention to interweave things that are irreconcilable. There is no attempt at synthesis. The resulting frictions produce a dramatic effect which differs from work to work.

Everything here tends towards the 'theatrical', though 'the characteristics of certain symphonic traditions are not lost sight of'.[38] Henze declared that many works composed up to this point in his career – he lists *Ode an den Westwind* (1953), *Quattro poemi* (1955), *Nachtstücke und Arien*, and *Antifone* (1960) – 'incorporate different formal experiments in the greatest Central European form of instrumental music, the sonata'. But the

---

[36] Hans Werner Henze, 'Der Prinz von Homburg' (1960), *Music and Politics*, 102.
[37] Henze, *Language, Music and Artistic Invention*, 8.
[38] Hans Werner Henze, 'Instrumental Composition' (1963), *Music and Politics*, 131.

symphonies he composed between the late 1940s and early 1960s are far from consistent in their relationship to Austro-German symphonism. He considered his First Symphony to be a failure in its original version (he revised it in 1963); the Second (1949) and Third (1949–50) are really '*sinfonias*', suggesting a preclassical form or style; the Fourth (1955) is a 'five movements in one' structure incorporating overture, sonata, variations, scherzo and rondo finale with theatrical origins (its material is drawn from Act 2 of *König Hirsch*). The Fifth (1962) has a very much clearer engagement with the Classical symphony, but in a highly condensed form, obviously comparable with Stravinsky's Symphony in C and Symphony in Three Movements. Resistance remained to a more fulsome feeding upon the Austro-German symphonic tradition.

An urgent sense of a need for new musical freedoms was widely in the air in the mid to late 1950s. The desire was heightened for new informal modes of subjective expression rather than total, objective construction. Writing in 1960, Adorno considered Henze's pursuit of freedom to be mired in failure because the composer had succumbed to a retreat to the comforts of old forms of restriction. Adorno noted that:

> total constructivism, as a taboo on the subjective need for expression, stirs up opposing forces ... Some of the most talented German composers ... suffer so terribly under determinism that they attempt to break free of it; the foremost of these is Henze. In such works as the opera *König Hirsch*, however, this attempt led not to the longed-for realm of freedom, a true 'musique informelle' but, rather, backwards: to compromise. The laments about the compulsion of constructivism can become a mere pretext to withdraw into the more comfortable bondage of convention.[39]

Adorno's statements, in which he hankered for a new type of expressive and formal freedom akin to that he heard in Schoenberg's radical atonal scores of the years from 1908, played a powerful part in a discourse in which Henze's position was becoming increasingly figured as one of retrenchment in opposition to his more obviously avant-garde contemporaries.

Henze's growing enthusiasm for Mahler nonetheless encouraged a sustained creative dialogue with the Austro-German symphonic legacy (though not, for some years, in a work entitled 'Symphony'). He saw in Mahler's music examples of how the exploration of apparently 'dead' forms and styles can lead to innovation. Henze became convinced that it was possible to 'develop the line of thought of [Mahler's] music, for above and

---

[39] Adorno, 'On the State of Composition in Germany' (1960), in *Night Music*, 408–9. See 'Vers une musique informelle' (1961), in *Quasi una Fantasia*, 269–322.

beyond its incontestable necrological qualities, it contains many new starting-points, challenges and stimuli'.[40] A central attraction lay in the eclectic idiom, the productive yet critical relationship with tradition and subjective complexity exhibited by Mahler's music. In an essay written upon conducting Mahler's Second Symphony, he describes how this music can be heard interrogating itself, how the tradition is continued but also critiqued, that it is music both 'knowing' and 'tragic', thus sharing a state of consciousness similar to that also exposed by Freud, Kafka and Musil.[41] Henze summarized thus:

My music draws what strength it has from its inherent contradictions. It is like a thorny thicket full of barbs and other unpleasant things. It is as poisonous as any serpent's sting. Its embraces may be dangerous, they may turn out to be a form of betrayal and frustrate one's expectations. People may feel repelled by its often garish colours and the infernal din that it seems constrained to produce ... My music has an emotional dimension that is unfashionable, an emotional untimeliness.[42]

III

Henze's compositional engagement with Mahler's music is strongly manifested in works of the early and mid 1960s. Mahler's music offered precedents for Henze's stylistic and expressive aims and his apparently anachronistic eclecticism. In particular it confirmed for Henze that there remained much creative mileage in a reinvestigation of diatonic elements. This is reflected in Henze's frequent employment of a 'traditional principle of dissonance and resolution' to 'dramaturgical ends', in his drawing up apparently 'obsolete grammatical order' to generate a 'sense of impending cadence'.[43] Technically, this leads to his employment of 'major and minor modes and dominants and subdominants quite experimentally, as if they were something altogether new'.[44] Aesthetically and thematically, Henze's relationship to Mahler is reflected in his preoccupation with the conjunction of beauty, love, death and regeneration, in a visionary art that promises the possibility of 'redemption' but one which is 'multilayered' in its 'illusions and Utopias'.[45]

---

[40] Henze, 'Instrumental Composition', *Music and Politics*, 131–2.
[41] Hans Werner Henze, 'Gustav Mahler' (1975), *Music and Politics*, 157–8.
[42] Henze, *Bohemian Fifths*, 56.   [43] *Ibid.*, 56.
[44] Henze, *Language, Music and Artistic Invention*, 9.   [45] Henze, *Bohemian Fifths*, 57.

During the Roman summer of 1963, Henze turned to Rimbaud's 'Being Beauteous', a poem which expresses notions of creativity, eroticism, and the beauty of old and new forms. The poem is from *Illuminations* (1872–3), a cycle whose poems are suggestive of hallucinations of shifting colours and shapes, an interaction of dynamism, splintering and control, the liberation of language, and of forms which grow out of an internal necessity. 'Being Beauteous' is part of a group in the cycle concerned with the inauguration of new life by *le nouvel amour*, a regeneration of self, a new physical experience, a new body.[46] Rimbaud's poem speaks of metamorphosis through destruction and creation. Sounds (music and whistlings) cause the adored, beautiful body to expand and burst open into vibrant colours, movement and sensuality. The spectators become acolytes, initiates intoxicated by the new beauty, embraced and reclothed by it. But the whole is mingled with death and violence. In the final lines the 'Being Beauteous' becomes a grotesque dummy:

Devant une neige un Etre de Beauté de haute taille. Des sifflements de mort et des cercles de musique sourde font monter, s'élargir et trembler comme un spectre ce corps adoré. Les couleurs propres de la vie se foncent, dansent, et se dégagent autour de la vision, sur le chantier. Des blessures écarlates et noires éclatent dans les chairs superbes. Et les frissons s'élèvent et grondent, et la saveur forcenée de ces effets se chargeant avec les sifflements mortels et les rauques musiques que le monde, loin derrière nous, lance sur notre mère de beauté, – elle recule, elle se dresse. Oh! Nos os sont revêtus d'un nouveau corps amoureux. Ô la face cendrée, l'écusson de crin, les bras de cristal! Le canon sur lequel je dois m'abattre à travers la mêlée des arbres et de l'air léger!

(Against the snow a high-statured Being of Beauty. Whistlings of death and circles of faint music cause this adored body to rise, expand, and quiver like a ghost. The colours proper to life deepen, dance, and detach themselves round the vision in the making. Scarlet and black wounds burst in the fine flesh. And shudders rise and rumble, and the frenetic flavour of these effects is filled with the mortal whistlings and the raucous music which the world, far behind us, hurls at our mother of beauty – she recedes, she rears herself up. Oh! Our bones are clothed with a new and amorous body. O the ashen face, the escutcheon of horsehair, the crystal arms! The cannon at which I must charge across the skirmish of the trees and the light air!)[47]

Henze's setting is for high soprano, harp and four cellos.[48] Its opening Adagio (Example 4.1), in which the harp initiates a gradual expansion of

---

[46] The experience expressed in these poems can be identified with that of homosexual love, which for Rimbaud had personal resonances in his relationship with Paul Verlaine.

[47] Translation by Oliver Bernard, from the CD Henze, *Versuch Über Schweine*, etc., Dietrich Fischer-Dieskau, *et al.* DG 449 869–2, (1996).

[48] For a useful, though brief analysis of the work's formal functions and symmetries, motivic content and instrumentation, see Hans Vogt, *Neue Musik seit 1945* (Stuttgart: Philipp Reclam, 1972), 311–17.

Example 4.1 Hans Werne Henze, *Being Beauteous* (Rimbaud), bb. 1–9.

harmonic and textural space from top to bottom as an introduction to an expressive, yearning string melody, immediately suggests the Adagietto of Mahler's Fifth Symphony (which, by 1963, Henze had conducted on several occasions). Given Henze's enthusiasm for Mahler at this time, this opening gesture and the instrumentation are together sufficient to invoke a loose but highly suggestive parallel. Positioning Mahler's movement as the adored, beautiful musical body as a parallel to Henze's setting allows a close analytical and hermeneutic exploration of the structural and expression in Henze's piece.

The tonal ambiguity of the opening C–A figurations of Mahler's Adagietto has often attracted comment, but the significance of these pitches is sustained by the fact that the expressive highpoints of the succeeding violin melody are generated by their two upper neighbour notes, B♭ and D (see Example 4.2). These two pitches are made especially pungent through chromatic alteration to B♮ and D♭/C♯ in bar 6. The first of these pairs (B♭/B♮) occurs in close melodic juxtaposition, the second (D/D♭) in strikingly dissonant superimposition (producing a kind of false relation). These chromatic disturbances return at the first climax of the movement (bb. 29–33; see Example 4.3). After the return to F major (in b. 24) the harmony becomes more turbulent as a powerfully directional chromatic bass line moves up to B♭ (bb. 27–9). The sense of diatonic major-mode stability is undermined. The D♭ turns the subdominant B♭ harmony to minor, and at bars 29–30 the descending melody, completed by the G♭ in the violas and cellos, suggests both whole-tone and pentatonic configurations (A–G–F–E♭–D♭ and E♭–D♭–B♭–G♭ respectively). The ecstasy and expanded duration of the climactic dominant six-four chord seems cathartic, promising a purging of all dissonant disturbance, only for the D♭ of bar 32 to ripple further the pool of pure consonance. Clearly, this is far from the end of things. Indeed, the most pungent melodic motion – E♭–D♭–B♭–G♭ pentatonic – is reinterpreted in the interrupted cadence of bars 46–7, where the harmony moves to G♭ major, here functioning as the flat submediant of B♭. In the return of the climactic cadence in the movement's final bars, the melodic descent is cut short at F and after the six-four chord there are no D♭s, only full-toned D♮s (suggesting the pentatonic) and a final, fading resolution of B♭ to A. To summarize, the lyrical expressivity of Mahler's movement is based largely upon the manner in which highlighted dissonant pitches colour tonal commonplaces (climactic dominant six-fours and interrupted cadences), in an amorous suggestion, perhaps, of Mahler's interpretation of old chords as 'cryptograms of modernism', to use a famous quote from Adorno's address at the Mahler centenary in 1960. Adorno felt that the Adagietto 'borders on genre prettiness through its ingratiating sound'[49] – that is, it flirts with the dangers of kitsch – but even within this music of apparently serene beauty, traditional tonal formulae, through subtle destabilizations, become powerfully expressive of subjective pain

[49] Adorno, *Mahler*, 136.

Example 4.2 Mahler, Symphony no. 5, fourth movement, bb. 1–11.

Example 4.3 Mahler, Symphony no. 5, fourth movement, bb. 23–38.

and anxiety.[50] In a prolonged glance backwards to a nineteenth-century sentimental style, the inflection, dissolution and reinterpreted return of cadential six-fours, all of which are hallmarks of Mahler's slow movement style (recall the examples in Chapter 1), become authentic expressive signature and defining structural feature.

Henze's Adagio establishes referential pitches (particularly E♭ in upper registers and D in the bass) that foreshadow simulations of Bachian, neo-baroque counterpoint in the following *più mosso* (b. 23). It is a clear example of Henze's desire to reinterpret old tonal processes through processes of allusion, dissolution and reformation. The diatonicism of Henze's pseudo-baroque G minor is imbued with expressive conventions which have attached to the flattened sixth (here E♭) and the ninth (here A). The opening vocal phrase, which introduces the 'Being' ('un Être'), stretches the E♭ in a traditionally expressive manner (Example 4.4). The following vocal line ('de beauté') expands the association of E♭ and A in a rising line structured on the resolution of an A–C–E♭–F♯ diminished seventh, via A♭, to G. The shape of this line is then employed as a model for the more expansive enunciation of the text 'Des sifflements de mort et des cercles de musique sourde font monter, s'élargir . . . ce corps adoré', (Example 4.5). This melodic phrase is supported by clear allusion to a tonal cadence. A diatonic model for this modally mixed passage is proposed in Example 4.6. Henze employs diminished sevenths in sequences and superimposition as a (Bachian?) means of intensification towards arrival of the dominant six-four of G. This altered or disfigured six-four, dissonantly intensified by the 'suspension' of the D♯ (enharmonic E♭) and an 'appoggiatura' A♭ (b. 58), initiates a descending bass whose implied goal is B♭. But the progression is halted and expanded by the 'trembling' of the chord built on C (bb. 61ff.). A second attempt at the progression is again suspended (bb. 63ff.) as the voice intones the spectre of the adored body. These expressive delays are coloured by the yearning dissonance of, first, E♭–D (b. 61) and, second, A–G (bb. 58, 62–3, 67–8).

As in Mahler's Adagietto, cadential commonplaces are expanded and enriched by neighbour-note relationships (invoking modal mixture) which have been set up and highlighted in opening melodic material, defining a tension between the demands of expressive truth and those of formal closure. Motivic process can be demonstrated to operate on several levels (especially the E♭–D motive) suggesting post-tonal middleground structures as part of a complex 'organic' unity in a manner that may recall Allen

---

[50] See Franklin, "'. . . his fractures are the script of truth'", 271–94, and Alastair Williams, *New Music and the Claims of Modernity* (Aldershot: Ashgate, 1998), 28–31.

Example 4.4 Henze, *Being Beauteous*, bb. 27–41.

Forte's famous analysis of Mahler's Adagietto.[51] The passage also reflects
Henze's concern to communicate a background of well-defined but

---

[51] Allen Forte, 'Middleground Motives in the *Adagietto* of Mahler's Fifth Symphony',
    19th-Century Music 8 (1984), 153–63.

Example 4.4 (cont.)

suppressed expectations (to recall Keller's definition). However, this is not sustained across the whole piece. Organic connection and 'deep' structural processes are fragile and break down, at times as part of a potentially explosive expressive mode. Like the beautiful statue in Rimbaud's poem, Mahler's music can be positioned as an adored and amorous body, because it offers precedents for an expressive style based on rejuvenating aged, crumbling tonal forms. One might say that Henze's piece, in which Rimbaud's text is at one point itself broken and dissolved into crazy, worldless melisma, is a sacrilegious *Ave verum corpus*, in which agape is replaced by Eros in worship of beautiful forms that are broken, reborn but always threatened with rejection or destruction. Despite the setting's small scale, it is a typically ambitious and provocative project from Henze. The parade of styles, gestures and emotions deliberately flaunts with excess and chaos. Henze wrote, in words and images which echo the vision of Rimbaud's poem:

The sight of . . . beauty moves us, we feel a sacred awe, it plucks a string within us which vibrates and reverberates. It causes something to happen inside us, perhaps it's a kind of conversion. Wounds and sores disturb this harmony, as we know. We cannot prevent our thoughts from turning from the sight of a handsome human face

Example 4.5 Henze, *Being Beauteous*, bb. 53–70.

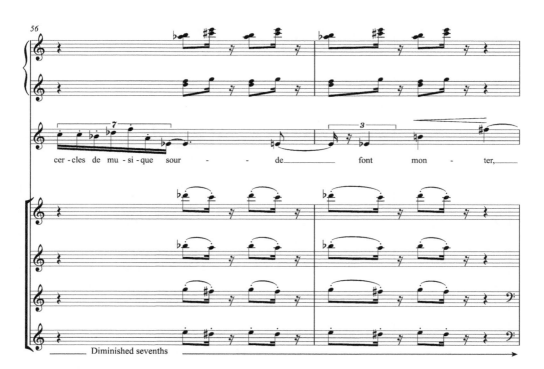

Example 4.5 (cont.)

Example 4.5 (cont.)

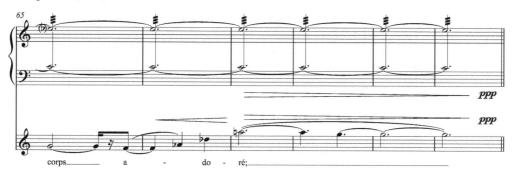

Example 4.6 Henze, *Being Beauteous*, bb. 58–70, diatonic model.

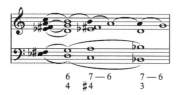

to pictures of its destruction. And we cannot prevent mourning and regret sounding like an incessant dissonance, distracting us from the contemplation of beauty, a steadily dripping poison which clouds our sight and makes our eyes smart. 'Whoever looks on beauty is already in death's hands.'[52]

Henze's final line is a quotation from the 'Tristan' *Venetian Sonnet* of August von Platen (1824). It is characteristic of Henze to recall and quote a beloved predecessor at moments of heightened expression. This cultural legacy and technique is also manifest in an embedded allusion to the opening of Wagner's *Tristan* towards the final section of *Being Beauteous* (bb. 189–92, Example 4.7). The allusion occurs as the beautiful form in Rimbaud's text is most imperiled and yet also most alluring. It emerges from the texture after the line 'Oh! Nos os sont revêtus d'un nouveau corps amoureux' (Oh! Our bones are clothed with a new and amorous body). The melody, when compared to Wagner's original, is transposed, rhythmically altered and textually camouflaged, but it is in Wagner's register, retains a suggestion of the expressive rhetoric of resolution to the dominant of A minor, and the cello of course is the instrument that carries the erotically charged melos of Wagner's opening gesture. This again links the piece with

[52] Henze, *Language, Music and Artistic Invention*, 22.

Example 4.7 Henze, *Being Beauteous*, bb. 187–92.

Mahler's Adagietto through the latter's apparent allusions – clear enough
for Alma, so thought Gustav – to Wagner's 'glance' motive.[53] Henze's
Tristan allusion here suggests that the Wagnerian erotic tone might be
borrowed to clothe the skeletal, deathly body as a source of new beauty
and new life. *Being Beauteous* is in effect a miniature, small-scale and

[53] The whole movement is often heard as love music to the beloved Alma. One of the more
infamous backward glances now associated with Mahler's movement is in the final frames of
Luchino Visconti's *Death in Venice* (1971). Mann's Aschenbach, who had earlier, like Henze,
recalled von Platen's poetry, now – in make-up whose colours and lines break up in the throes of
fatal disease – looks on as, in an inversion of the birth of Venus, the beautiful young body of
Tadzio slowly enters the Venetian waters. Visconti's concerns map closely with Henze's
(although Henze fell out with Visconti over the interpretation of Nazism in *The Damned* (1969),
they had a long and close relationship): beauty coexistent with decay, with transformation,
aspiration, inspiration, chaos and plenitude vying with a decadence in which traditional forms
are exhausted. In such contexts, Mahler's Adagietto seems to express a 'yearning for unity of
serenity and sensuousness', as the function of its recurrences in the film soundtrack is to set up
flashbacks, gazes and nightmares; see Henry Bacon, *Visconti: Explorations of Beauty and Decay*
(Cambridge University Press, 1998), 165. Of course, Visconti's movie has attracted much vitriol
for its identification of Aschenbach with Mahler and for misreading Mann. But is it a total
misreading of Mahler's Adagietto, which itself alludes to a Tristanesque Eros and the
vulnerability of beauty? Philip Reed certainly thinks so: in his view, the use of Mahler's music
creates confusion between Apollonian coolness and emotional liberation. He concludes that
Visconti's vision – which he describes as 'naïve' and 'chaotic' – is a 'corruption' of the meaning of
the music. See Philip Reed, 'Aschenbach Becomes Mahler: Thomas Mann as Film', in Mitchell
(ed.), *Benjamin Britten: 'Death in Venice'*, 181. Mann's text is itself replete with ironic and
parodic gestures, a flux of genre and style in which evocations of beautiful neoclassical forms
coexist with destruction and decay, tensions between old and new literary codes, with allusions
overlaid in the build-up to the 'orgiastic climax'; see Gerald Gillespie, 'Mann and the Modernist
Tradition', in Jeffrey B. Berlin (ed.), *Approaches to Teaching Mann's 'Death in Venice' and Other
Short Stories* (New York: Modern Language Association of America, 1992), 98–103.

intimate exploration of eroticism and death partially viewed through a lens more or less overtly stolen, via Mahler's example, from Wagner. Both of Henze's *Tristan* allusions (the literary one in his essay and the musical one in the Rimbaud setting) are examples of non-satirical intertextuality. (They are comparable, say, with Berg's *Tristan* reference in the *Lyric Suite* rather than Debussy's *Tristan* allusion in the *Golliwog's Cakewalk*). Neither irony nor alienation is the prime interest here for Henze.

Mahler is evoked to more biting, ironic and dark effect in the opera *Der junge Lord*, composition of which began in 1964. In two essays on this opera, Henze highlights the 'knowing' quality of Mahler's music and explains that he employs quotes from Mahler's Fourth Symphony to express the potentially unsettling character of childhood memories and the 'deathly' which lies within superficial bourgeois *Gemütlichkeit* (cosiness). The mood these Mahler passages create, as Henze describes it, is one of 'malaise – uncanny, bitter'.[54] The opera is set in 1830 in small-town Germany. Civic officials and other worthies of the town are waiting to greet the arrival of the visiting Sir Edgar, a rich and cultured Englishman. Edgar, however, spurns the invitations of genteel society and instead fraternizes with the performers of a travelling circus. A meeting of two young lovers, Luise and Wilhelm, is interrupted by terrible noises coming from Edgar's house. It is, the towns-folk are told, the noises of the young Lord Barrat, Edgar's nephew, straining to learn German and being punished for his ineptitude. But when his 'education' is complete, Barrat is presented at a reception at which he dazzles the assembled pillars of small-town society with his eccentric man-ners and elegance. Luise is lined up by the Baroness to marry the young Lord. But at the succeeding ball Barrat's dance with Luise becomes more and more uncontrolled and disturbing. In the mounting frenzy, Barrat hurls her against a wall. Sir Edgar reveals, to gasps of shock and distress, that the young Lord is the dancing ape from the travelling circus. At the climax the duped townsfolk exclaim 'It's an ape!' – a quote, Henze confirms, from Mahler's 'Das Trinklied vom Jammer der Erde', the first song of *Das Lied von der Erde*.[55]

The textual quote (the libretto is by Bachmann) inevitably encourages comparison with Mahler's musical treatment of the disturbing simian

---

[54] Hans Werner Henze, '*Der junge Lord* (2): The Spectre of Mendacity' (1965, 1972) and '*Der junge Lord* (3): Hints on Staging' (1973), in *Music and Politics*, 138–42.

[55] Henze, *Bohemian Fifths*, 192. Another possible allusion is to Nietzsche: 'What is the ape to men? A laughing stock or a painful embarrassment . . . Once you were apes, and even now man is more of an ape than any ape.' *Thus Spoke Zarathustra*, trans. R.J Hollingdale (Harmondsworth: Penguin, 1969), 41–2.

Example 4.8 Mahler, 'Das Trinklied vom Jammer der Erde', *Das Lied von der Erde* (Bethge–Mahler), 4 after fig. 32 to fig. 33.

figure. The third verse of 'Das Trinklied' contains the lines 'Das Firmament blaut ewig und die Erde wird lange fest steh'n und auf blüh'n im Lenz' (The heavens are forever blue, and the Earth shall long stand firm and blossom in spring), an overt foreshadowing of the poetic end of the whole cycle. Adorno listed this verse as an example of 'fulfilment'.[56] At the extolling of the eternal beauty of nature in spring (it is interesting to note that the poetic clause at this moment of 'anticipated transformation', as Hefling calls it, is one of Mahler's own interpolations into Bethge's Chinese paraphrase[57]) there is a full statement of the symbolic six-four /five-three with pentatonic descending melodic line in A♭ which Chapter 1 revealed to be a Mahler musical paradigm of the symbolic transcendent state (4 after fig. 32; see Example 4.8). But the song has been repeatedly informed by grotesque, upper register chromatic trills. The final verse reveals the identity of these figures as the shrieks of a ghastly ape who sits in the moonlit graveyard. The climactic statement of these shrieks leads to a plunge, a cataclysmic collapse onto a *fortissimo* A♭ triad in low register (4 after fig. 44), a dark negation of the A♭ fulfilment field of the third stanza and functioning as the precursor to a whole-tone and chromatically inflected progression back to the tonic A. The refrain 'Dunkel ist das Leben, ist der Tod', first heard in an unambiguous G minor at the end of stanza 1 (fig. 11), then in A♭ minor with Tierce de Picardie at the end of stanza 2 (fig. 24), is absent in the third stanza. The transcendent A♭ cadence might be heard temporarily to take its place to offer an affirmative alternative. After this passing moment of hope, the refrain's final statement, which follows the revelation of the terrible ape and the musical debasement of the previously beautiful A♭ harmony,

---

[56] Adorno, *Mahler*, 44.
[57] Stephen E. Hefling, *Mahler: Das Lied von der Erde* (Cambridge University Press, 2000), 90–1.

Example 4.9 Mahler, 'Das Trinklied vom Jammer der Erde', figs. 47–8.

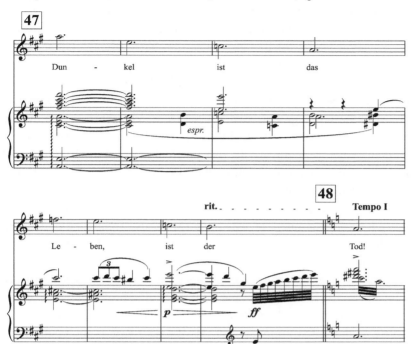

sounds as a mordant echo of the fulfilment cadence (see Example 4.9). The vocal line outlines a chromatic-minor mode variant of the previously pentatonic-major mode descent over the dominant six-four/five-three cadence. The music of the shrieking ape has mocked and corrupted the vision of transcendent, eternal beauty glimpsed, fleetingly, in the third stanza.

So, what of Henze's ape? Henze was especially pleased with the music of the duet between the young lovers Luise and Wilhelm in scene 4. He described this music as 'recalling the world of early German Romanticism, an ideal world, innocent and carefree, into which a tempest sweeps, bringing with it snow and pain and illusion, grim forebodings and blindness and truth'. This disturbance of the lover's apparent idyll is caused by offstage noises of 'the crack of a whip and the screams of the ape being flayed, an ape whose existence is still unsuspected'.[58] Henze also described the duet's music as 'unbroken tonality ... but not entirely'.[59] On the lovers' entry,

---

[58] Henze, *Bohemian Fifths*, 191.
[59] Henze, '*Der junge Lord*: (2) The Spectre of Mendacity', in *Music and Politics*, 140.

the music is a lyrical Andante for strings in Henze's most overtly romantic manner (bb. 121ff.). But this music is repeatedly interrupted by the wailing chromatic motives and dissonant instrumental din of the ape's screams, so that when the 'idyllic' tonal music returns it is heard (though not at first by the lovers who are, as the score indicates, initially 'lost to the world' – recalling the inner state of Mahler's setting of 'Ich bin der Welt abhanden gekommen') as a 'second' diatonicism, as 'sentimental' in Dahlhaus's Schillerian terminology discussed in Chapter 2. When their duet moves to its conclusion with motives lifted virtually intact from the first movement of Mahler's Fourth (compare the instrumental material in bb. 196–208 of Henze's scene with motives informing the development section of Mahler's movement), the 'unbroken tonality' is revealed as sharing the reconstructed quality of the diatonic idiom of Mahler's symphony (as explored in Chapter 3; see Example 3.1). The ape's shriek also recalls the destructive intrusions of the 'grell' motives of 'Um Mitternacht' and the *Schattenhaft* scherzo of the Seventh Symphony, which, as we saw in Examples 1.10 and 3.4 respectively, negate the forces of redemption and teleological process. In the opera, the lovers' glimpse of fulfilment, of unbroken, blissful union, is shattered by the ape's grotesque vocalizations. Their hopes prove as illusory as the initial impression of the ape disguised as the young Lord Barrat.

As Henze was composing *Being Beauteous* in August 1963, W.H. Auden and Chester Kallman completed the libretto to *The Bassarids*, the opera which would quickly follow *Der junge Lord*. (The libretto is based on Euripides's *The Bacchae*, replacing the original name for female followers of Dionysus with the inclusive version embracing female and male Dionysians.) Henze recalled that while he was writing the score of *The Bassarids*, Mahler 'was my daily life, my bread, my creed'.[60] Other 'Germanic' precursors were more ambivalently encountered. During the early stages of Henze's collaboration with Auden and Kallman on the opera, his librettists urged Henze to reconsider his disdain and distaste for Wagner's music. They insisted Henze listen to *Götterdämmerung* and that

---

[60] Paul Griffiths, 'Hans Werner Henze Talks to Paul Griffiths', *The Musical Times* 115 (1974), 831. The opera's inspiration – 'the highly unreliable muse of *The Bassarids*' – was Henze's own 'Tadzio', Hans Schmidt-Isserstedt, who entered his life in November 1964 with 'a spring in his step and a condescending glance'; 'my monastic life as a composer was once again undermined by a hedonistic component'; 'seduction, deception and promiscuity, someone in league with the Devil or with the God of wine, smiling the smile of the Bassarids'. When Schmidt-Isserstedt did not return Henze's phone calls, imagined nocturnal repetitions of the transformation of Frère Jacques from Mahler's First Symphony kept Henze awake at night. See Henze, *Bohemian Fifths*, 204–5.

he should learn to overcome political and aesthetic aversions to Wagner's music. But on attending a production conducted by Herbert von Karajan in Vienna, Henze heard

silly and self-regarding emotionalism, behind which it is impossible not to detect a neo-German mentality and ideology. There is something of an imperialistic threat, of something militantly nationalistic, something disagreeably heterosexual and Aryan in all these rampant horn calls, this pseudo-Germanic *Stabreim*, these incessant chords of a seventh, and all the insecure heroes and villains that people Wagner's librettos.

However, *Tristan* was a special case. This work was exempt from Henze's sceptical if not downright toxic view of Wagner's work. Writing on the genesis of *The Bassarids* in 1966, he notes that, despite attempting to avoid Wagner's work out of a certain antipathy, 'I am well aware what Wagner signifies, wherein his greatness lies; *Tristan*, which I have never seen, although I have studied the score in detail, has subsequently become a kind of bible for me.' The libretto for *The Bassarids* arrived as Henze 'was beginning to discover the great forms of nineteenth-century symphonic music'. He wrote:

I believe that the road from Wagner's *Tristan* to Mahler and Schoenberg is far from finished, and with *The Bassarids* I have tried to go further along it. I am not prepared to relinquish what the centuries have passed on to us. On the contrary; 'One must also know how to inherit; inheriting, that, ultimately, is culture.' That was Thomas Mann's view and I willingly subscribe to it.[61]

There is, however, hardly anything of Wagner in *The Bassarids*. There *is* much that relates the opera to Mahler and also to Berg.[62] In a manner comparable with Berg's employment of instrumental formal procedures in *Lulu*, Henze structured the opera as four symphonic movements – sonata, scherzo, slow movement (including a fugue) and a passacaglia finale. Henze wished to contrast his musical processes and structures with Wagnerian leitmotivic techniques and 'endless melody'. Instead, he declared, there is 'symphonic form', but 'done in a very analytic, psychoanalytic way, with closed forms interpolated into it all the time'.[63] This symphonic combination of formal and psychological complexity chimes with Henze's characterization of Mahler's achievement. Indeed, Henze might legitimately be placed within the psychoanalytically informed reception history of Mahler

---

[61] Hans Werner Henze, '*The Bassarids*: (1) Tradition and Cultural Heritage' (1966), in *Music and Politics*, 144–5.

[62] But these *Tristan* 'seeds', though they would lie dormant for several years, were now firmly planted, and would flourish (and explode, if seeds might do this) in Henze's own *Tristan* of 1973 for piano, orchestra and electronic tape.

[63] Griffiths, 'Henze Talks to Paul Griffiths', 831.

and his music.[64] As noted in Chapter 2, Keller saw Mahler as 'the first to develop a consistent, "ruthlessly" self-observing as well as expressive' music. The Freudian Keller called this 'superego music'.[65] In its explorations of a man and his psychological and sexual discontents, *The Bassarids* is in many ways something of a period piece. John Bokina characterizes it as 'an expression of a specific conflict in a specific age', the political and sexual revolution at the heart of the aims of the countercultural movement of the 1960s. But Henze's opera 'retains a dialectical edge' for Bokina, and reveals the dangerous consequences of total submission to sensual immediacy, of the 'tyranny of the instincts'.[66] In this light, the dialectical principle of sonata form which underpins the 'first movement' of the opera parallels the conflict between the super-rational Pentheus and the liberation embodied by Dionysus. (The tradition of a gendered description of sonata form suggests that Dionysus is, as so often, feminized, as the 'other' second subject.) Ritualistic order is set against sensual abandon, but the traditional expectation of resolution achieved through bringing the unruly second subject into the tonal realm of the first is not fulfilled. The unresolved confrontation between Pentheus and Dionysus is sustained through the bacchanalian dances which occur in the 'second movement'.

In the Adagio first part of the 'third movement', Pentheus becomes charmed by the dangerously seductive beauty of Dionysus (still posing at this point as the Stranger) and demands to 'know' what has so enchanted and enraptured his people (including his mother, Agave). Henze's setting of Auden and Kallman's dialogic text, through its shaping, pacing and material disposition, carries strong suggestions of bar form:

Stollen I

PENTHEUS: You were right. Yes. We can see. Yes. You must know.

DIONYSUS (STRANGER): I know what he knows. He has made you see I know.

PENTHEUS: See. Yes. I would see. Yes. You know. Yes.

---

[64] This tradition often takes Mahler's brief consultation (or stroll) with Freud in 1910 as a starting point or justification, but it also begins with Max Graf, a close colleague of Freud, in his *Die innere Werkstatt des Musikers* (1910). It moves through Theodore Reik's *The Haunting Melody* (1953), Jack Diether, 'Mahler and Psychoanalysis', *The Psychoanalytic Review* 45 (1959–60), 3–14, David Holbrook, *Gustav Mahler and the Courage to Be* (London: Vision, 1975), George H. Pollock, 'Mourning through Music: Gustav Mahler', in Stuart Feder, Richard L. Karmel and George H. Pollock (eds.), *Psychoanalytical Explorations in Music* (Madison, Conn.: International Universities Press, 1990), 321–39, and Feder's own *Gustav Mahler: A Life in Crisis* (New Haven: Yale University Press, 2004).

[65] Keller, 'The Unpopularity of Mahler's Popularity', in *Essays on Music*, 69–70.

[66] John Bokina, *Opera and Politics: from Monteverdi to Henze* (New Haven: Yale University Press, 1997), 167–97.

Stollen II

PENTHEUS: Tell me: when are these rites most . . . you know, yes, *you* know . . .
  most themselves?

DIONYSUS: At night. The dark blood best in darkness glows to woo the darkness to
  itself. We dance. Come, night! Mine! Me!

PENTHEUS: You dance. I know that step. Who cares with whom they dance? You
  are beautiful. No doubt you dance with much success.

Abgesang

DIONYSUS: What should my beauty matter were the rites what you believe they are?
  The chaste are chaste, the unchaste unchaste there as elsewhere.

PENTHEUS: The chaste are chaste you say, the unchaste . . . which are you?

DIONYSUS: I? I am I.

PENTHEUS: My mother?

DIONYSUS: You know her. *She* told *you*, you know.

PENTHEUS: I know.

DIONYSUS: Then see.

PENTHEUS: See. I would see. Yes. Yes. I had forgotten. See.

DIONYSUS: He will help you as he helped before. To see. To know.

THE BASSARIDS: To know.

By the end of this dialogue Pentheus is gripped by the prospect of fulfilling
his desire for knowledge. As we saw in Chapter 1, Adorno related the
Mahlerian category of musical fulfilment closely to the *Abgesang* of bar
form, where fulfilment and 'emotional discharge' are characteristically
achieved through the introduction of intensifying and closing material.
Crucially, as James Buhler has explained, an *Abgesang* in Mahler's hands
is also characteristically the site of new material which, while it responds to a
preceding theme is also an area of freedom and surplus as much as closure.[67]
Henze's *Abgesang* exhibits just such a combination of intensification, closure and enfolding of new yet familiar material as a correlate of Pentheus's
desire for fulfilment. From its beginning, the *Abgesang* is saturated with
quotations from the second movement of Mahler's Fifth Symphony (particularly overt are repeated statements of accompanimental woodwind
figures from Mahler's movement, bb. 1475–7). These are combined with a
heightened expressive melody which, through sequences and turns of
overtly Mahlerian cut, builds towards an ardent climactic cadence
(Example 4.10). For Henze, quotations such as those found here function
as 'landmarks' and 'associations', a technique which 'can be found to a

---

[67] James Buhler, 'Theme and Form in the Andante of the Sixth Symphony', in Barham (ed.),
Perspectives on Gustav Mahler, 291–3.

Example 4.10 Henze, *The Bassarids*, third movement, bb. 1473–93.

high degree in Mahler's works', where, for Henze, it is especially notable for its 'conscious and psychologizing extent'.[68] Pentheus's compulsion

[68] Hans Werner Henze, '*The Bassarids*: (2) Psychology in Music' (1966), in *Music and Politics*, 151. Keller was wary of the use of quotations as a 'crutch' to 'replace, strengthen or clarify backgrounds', as a 'creative hope' which succeeds only rarely; Keller, *Music, Closed Societies and Football*, 226–7.

Example 4.10 (cont.)

'to know' is paralleled by the use of material from Mahler's 'knowing music'. Furthermore, the quotation plays with the response of a 'knowing' audience. The recourse to quotation, self-consciously derived from Mahler, is employed as a communicative strategy through the evocation of 'continuity' with tradition.[69] This continuity on the surface of musical quotation

---

[69] Hans Werner Henze, '*The Bassarids*: (3) Symphony in One Act' (1975), in *Music and Politics*, 153.

Example 4.10 (cont.)

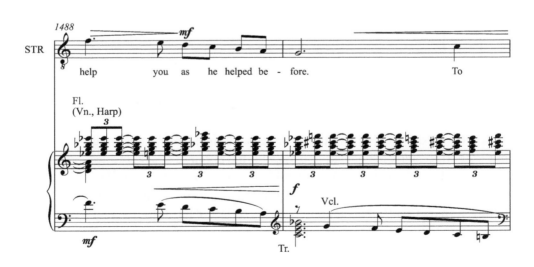

Example 4.10 (cont.)

is paralleled by the subsurface evocation of a traditional formal configuration (bar form) as vehicle for the promise of fulfilment.

But this heightened moment of expectation is followed by the image of negation which sounds in direct conflict with Pentheus's desire for fulfilment. Pentheus is revealed to be self-observing as he looks for enlightenment in the reflections in his mother's mirror. A long-prepared tonal resolution and its associated thematic statement are interrupted by mocking laughter which is decidedly Nietzschean as it decrees, to use Alan White's phrase, that all meanings 'are putative, all orders merely ostensible'.[70] The D and A tonalities which until now prevailed (and supported the allusions to the second movement of Mahler's Fifth) shift abruptly upwards to E♭/B♭ (b. 1507), a rise of tonal centre in response to the dramatic change of emotional temper. The moment suggests a hysterical version of 'breakthrough' as a previously established developmental process with large-scale formal and tonal implications is ruptured. This breakthrough offers no vision of redemption or revitalization: it is empty to grasp too soon the transcendent secret or scent the victory of a higher coherence, for the Pentheus–Dionysus dialogue scene is followed (in the 'Intermezzo', which was cut in the 1986 version of the score) by a burlesque parody of eighteenth-century rococo style, 'an artificial, farce-like representation of the sexual fantasies and hallucinations'.[71] Pentheus sees only his own inner fantasies, in which, as Auden and Kallman explain, 'Dionysian life is not, as in reality, passionate and dangerous but decadent and difficult to take seriously.'[72]

The Bassarids, meanwhile, wait expectantly in the night for their own Dionysian 'fulfilment', but the moment, the enchanting spell, is broken by the intrusion of the cross-dressed Pentheus. A long, fevered search for Pentheus (who is now the stranger, the outsider) is set over a long B♭ pedal. The broken D–A tonal axis and its characteristic expressive counterpoint returns long after Pentheus's vision has dissolved and, hounded down, he faces his dreadful fate at the hands of the Bassarids (led by his mother). In the final section of the third movement (letter N; b. 831), the discovered Pentheus, who has been covering his eyes with his hands, sings 'I looked into eyes that were my own' to Adagio D minor music of overtly post-Bachian counterpoint. The tonality rises to E♭ as, to no avail, he implores his mother to remember him. The moment of his slaying by the Bassarids, including Agave, is a brutal, bitonal combination of E♭ and D with descending arpeggiations directly recalling the cadence of Example 4.10 but sounding as its negative fulfilment. In the final movement, the Stranger finally identifies himself as Dionysus and he and *his* mother, Semele, are granted a final apotheosis. Thus the opera is, in the composer's words, a 'tragedy, a funeral symphony, a requiem (ending with a Gloria). Its goal is truth, and truth is

[70] Alan White, *Within Nietzsche's Labyrinth* (London: Routledge, 1990), 123.

[71] *Hans Werner Henze: ein Werkverzeichnis, 1946–96* (Mainz: Schott, 1996), 54; cited in Virginia Palmer-Fochsel, 'Henze on the Stage of Berlin', in Jarman (ed.), *Henze at the RNCM*, 34n.

[72] W.H Auden and Chester Kallman, 'Euripides for Today', *The Musical Times* 115 (1974), 833–4.

serious, difficult and cruel – not culinary.' The final term in this description is probably an allusion to Brecht; but lest there be any misunderstanding Henze immediately states that 'neither "irony" nor "alienation" are the objects of my musical interest'.[73] Henze's central concern is to underscore the contrast between the 'passionate and dangerous' quality of the faithful Dionysian, and the 'decadent' falsity of Pentheus's illusion. The essential conflict lies between musical voices which we are urged to hear as revealing psychological truth and those which are revealed as mendacious fantasy. The play of allusions and quotations is a primary technical method of producing these voices, carefully positioned within structural processes of development, fulfilment, breakthrough, collapse, disintegration and apotheosis. Fragmentations and discontinuities on the surface of Henze's music combine with polyglot signals suggesting intertextuality in the Kristevan sense – providing a dynamic dimension to structuralism (through intersections, transformations and juxtapositions which are textually and politically subversive) and, furthermore, generating an intensified, celebratory heteroglossia, a transposition of various signifying systems stimulating reading or listening beyond overt, intentional allusions.[74]

Der junge Lord and *The Bassarids* are comparable through their exposing of the hypocrisy of bourgeois society. To know is necessarily also to forget: Henze wrote that

> with Mahler too there occurs a self-forgetting; there too conformity to a sham civilization is cast aside. In my eyes this is such a significant achievement that I really don't understand why even some of his admirers feel the need to defend those eruptions into an immense new freedom, almost as if they were defending the acts of a musical rapist.[75]

Such freedom is, however, but one side of the coin. In 1901 Mahler expressed to Bauer-Lechner his desire to write '*Bachisch*' music, a possible pun encapsulating both the legacy of Bach and the Dionysian (Bacchic).[76] Frisch has suggested that the 'Bachian' polyphony in the finale of the Fifth Symphony is an effect different from related procedures in the music of other German modernists (for example, in Reger's version of 'historicist

---

[73] Henze, '*The Bassarids*: (2)', 149.

[74] See 'Introduction' to Michael Worton and Judith Still (eds.), *Intertextuality: Theories and Practices* (Manchester University Press, 1990), 16–17, and Julia Kristeva, *Desire in Language: A Semiotic Approach to Literature and Art*, ed. Leon S. Roudiez, trans. Thomas Gora, Alice Jardine and Leon S. Roudiez (Oxford: Blackwell, 1982).

[75] Henze, '*The Bassarids*: (1) Tradition and Cultural Heritage', in *Music and Politics*, 145.

[76] La Grange, *Gustav Mahler vol. 2.*, 360.

modernism') because of its comic (Nietzschean?) manner, a 'new, more detached attitude toward the music of the past'.[77] For many artists working at the turn of the century, Bach was a symbol of regeneration, healing and the medicinal. His music was heard as a 'cultural balm'. Recourse to the 'Bachian' idiom established a distance from late romantic unhealthiness by evoking, in an earnest not parodic manner, a more distant past. In the finale of Mahler's Fifth, the energetic contrapuntal passages contribute to the evocation of a Nietzschean comic sublime as antidote to decadent dissolution. As I have shown elsewhere, the dangers and seductions of de-energizing, sensuous beauty in the transformed return of material from the Adagietto in the finale are resisted. Mahler's 'Bachic' in the Fifth evokes both control through contrapuntal mastery and the intoxicating abandon of the Bacchic/Dionysian, a 'doubleness' reflected in the symphony's kaleidoscopic, frenzied final bars.[78] In the third and fourth movements of *The Bassarids*, Henze's recourse to Bachian counterpoint of melancholic resonance similarly suggests not only the Freudian process of mourning, of recuperation through grieving, but also the hope of redemptive restoration of wholeness following the horrific and hysterical scene of dismemberment.

The writings of Erich Neumann were very important to the conception of *The Bassarids*.[79] Neumann's *Depth Psychology and a New Ethic* (1949) was conceived and written during the Second World War and published as the nuclear nightmares of the Cold War took hold, to which the horrors of Nazism seemed to be only a dark prelude. In Jungian terms, Neumann argued that in the face of evil, mankind must acknowledge and listen to the inner voice of the dark 'shadow' in each and every individual. Neumann moves from Jungian psychology to develop an ethics capable of transforming these inner forces and their destructive potential. He proposed a new ethic of the total unit – a state of wholeness that is not perfection but is beyond opposites, where rather than project evil onto the 'Other' a

process of transformation . . . bound up with the shadow throughout its course . . . the creative grace of renewal, healing and transformation, which emerges unexpectedly from the darkness of the unconscious, retains to the last its connection with the paradox of the *deus absconditus*, that unaccountable and inscrutably numinous

---

[77] Walter Frisch, *German Modernism: Music and the Arts* (Berkeley: University of California, 2005), 182–5.

[78] See Downes, *The Muse as Eros*, 119–34.

[79] Henze quotes from Neumann's *The Origins and History of Consciousness* near the beginning of his essay 'The Bassarids (2) Psychology in Music' originally published as 'Tiefenpsychologie in der Musik' (1966).

power which may encounter the human ego under the guise of the Devil, the shadow of God, in the very citadel of the psyche.[80]

Neumann acknowledged that, given the dark spectre of the most horrific 'dance of death', such a new ethic may seem anachronistic or obsolete in the second half of the twentieth century. Henze, in whose music the employment of intertextual allusions to generate tension between heteroglossia and unity becomes a central expressive strategy, has frequently been judged in these very terms. The important essay 'Music as a Means of Resistance' (1963) provided a riposte. Henze writes that in a world 'which leans towards self-destruction' its music is too often one of 'denial', negation and 'rejection', it is 'given little opportunity for glorification and flooding people with illumination'. He finds creative tension between engagement with a world in which there is little 'cause for affirmation' but 'there is no harm in this', though again this leads to his isolation from the 'aesthetic puritanism' of the 'progressives' who, in their 'foolish response to the nineteenth-century' stand by the hopes of technical innovation, mechanization and depersonalization and esotericism. Compositional 'recourse to older worlds of sound' is more invigorating and promising than the 'colloquial', 'learnable language of modernism espoused in the academy and the electronic studio'.[81] Henze's music of the early to mid 1960s also epitomizes his striving to 'recapture' classical 'ideals of beauty', his yearning 'to restore' in the face of 'utterly unfathomable grief' and 'experiences both terrible and wonderful'.[82] As in Mahler, the move beyond the necrological is an ambitious quest in which the dangers of heroic failure, ostracism, or ridicule are not shirked. In this sense Henze may be pictured as the passionate poet of Plato's *Ion*, who, like a Bacchic disciple, is inspired to sing or speak with a transgressive plurality of languages with a licence against authority: creative, affirmative, yet dangerous and potentially destructive – struggling to find beautiful forms for expression of delirium and death, love and horror, a nomad banished by the ruling powers of the repressive Republic.

In Henze's plural systems of structure and signification, old materials sometimes appear to defy integration. Part/whole relationships become contingent and scrutinized. Organicism can no longer be uncritically affirmed as the counter to dehumanizing mechanistic and materialistic trends. In *Being Beauteous*, the G minor material does not gradually emerge

---

[80] Erich Neumann, *Depth Psychology and a New Ethic*, trans. Eugene Rolfe (London: Harper & Row, 1973), 146.

[81] Hans Werner Henze, 'Music as a Means of Resistance' (1963), in *Music and Politics*, 123–7.

[82] Henze, *Bohemian Fifths*, 55, 65.

like that in the opening paragraph of Berg's Violin Concerto, nor is it a long-range, and long-denied, confirmation of the background structural focus as achieved with the Bach evocations in *The Bassarids*. The shock of the old is more akin to Berg's juxtaposition of the tonality of the 'Es ist genug' chorale, or, even more closely, to the discontinuities characteristic of Stravinsky. But in Henze's setting this is succeeded by a move beyond bald anachronism, to suggest, through establishing the possibility of exchange between past and present, 'genuine renewal' and a 'revivalist impulse'.[83] In their subsequent treatment, these old materials become part of, indeed generative of, Henze's symbolically expanded, fragmented and expressive progressions. The fragmentations in Henze's music, whether through their search for new beauty in old forms they are redolent of Berg or Stravinsky, shift between exotericism and processes driven by immanent expressive impulses towards wholeness.[84] This dialectic of whole and particular, crucial for Adorno's understanding of modernism, emerges particularly strongly in his essays on Berg and Mahler. In the essay 'Berg's Discoveries in Compositional Technique' (1961), he recalls how in the early 1950s it seemed that every German composer, in apparently following Webern's 'footsteps', felt the need to construct from scratch, from 'primal' rather than preformed materials. But now (in 1961), Adorno argued, 'the question simply of the evolution of musical material is less urgent'; now we can hear the resemblances between Berg's Three Pieces for Orchestra and Stravinsky's *Rite of Spring*, and Mahler's montages built from the 'molecules' of marches.[85]

IV

In his works of the 1960s and 1970s, Henze made particularly wide use of quotations and allusions.[86] In *Natascha Ungeheuer* (1971), Henze quotes

[83] On this aspect of anachronism, see Martha M. Hyde, 'Neoclassic and Anachronistic Impulses in Twentieth-Century Music', *Music Theory Spectrum* 18 (1996), 205.

[84] On Adorno's contrast between Berg and Stravinsky, see *Alban Berg: Master of the Smallest Link*, trans. with introduction and annotation by Juliane Brand and Christopher Hailey (Cambridge University Press, 1991), 74–5.

[85] Theodor W. Adorno, 'Berg's Discoveries in Compositional Technique' (1961) in *Quasi una Fantasia*, 179–200. As Jonathan Cross has said, when the 'kinds of musical modernism' identified with Stravinky 'intersect' with the seemingly 'oppositional modernisms' of Mahler and Berg, and when 'similarities do emerge', the effect is 'all the more arresting'. *The Stravinsky Legacy*, 15–16.

[86] For an interesting survey of the function of quotations in twentieth-century music, though one that mentions Henze only briefly and in passing, see David Metzer, *Quotation and Cultural Meaning in Twentieth-Century Music* (Cambridge University Press, 2003).

again, for example, from Mahler's Fifth Symphony (the first movement funeral march is heard on the gramophone) as part of a pervasive montage technique (the score specifies '*bruitage*'). Chopin's funeral march is quoted in the vaudeville *La Cubana oder ein Leben für die Kunst* (1973) 'in a depraved version for military band' amongst a collage of funeral marches.[87] The level of 'assimilation' of quoted material differs across and within works, depending on the manner in which the source materials are manipulated. Certain contexts may actually heighten the sense that these are 'external' materials being worked upon (or in some cases obviously being attacked). In *Tristan* (1973), materials from works by Wagner, Chopin and Brahms are subjected to degrees of assimilation, dissolution and destruction through which they play a central role in the work's 'drama'.[88] The ambiguous status of Henze's *Tristan* as part symphony and part musical 'theatre' is especially interesting and has wide resonances in Henze's work of the 1970s and 1980s.[89] (*The Bassarids* offers a reverse precedent through its placing of symphonic structures in the opera house.) As Peter Petersen explains, the musical form of Henze's *Tristan* was 'underlaid and directed by a dramaturgical plan, based both on the dreams and fantasies of the compositional subject, and on "imaginary" scenarios'. Furthermore, the 'formal plan and the dramaturgical concept influence each other, the former based on alternation, the latter intended to create sudden reversals and surprises'. Quotation from Brahms's First Symphony, for example, generates a 'peripeteia', after which there is a plunge into dark psychological regions ('Tristan's Madness'). The use of quotations and external materials move Petersen to approach *Tristan* as Brechtian epic theatre applied to concert music, with two coexisting communication systems, one internal the other external. 'Immanent communication' exists between the motivic or instrumental characters in the work, but the work breaks out of this internal sphere into quotation, as in the sixth movement of Berg's *Lyric Suite*, in a kind of musical aside to the audience, in a

---

[87] See Peter Petersen, *Hans Werner Henze. Ein politischer Musiker* (Hamburg: Argument Verlag, 1988), 194.

[88] On Henze's *Tristan*, see Lawrence Kramer, *Opera and Modern Culture: Wagner and Strauss* (Berkeley: University of California Press, 2004), 120–4, and my *Hans Werner Henze: 'Tristan'* (Aldershot: Ashgate, 2011), from which the following paragraphs are derived.

[89] Two later works have actually carried the title 'imaginary theatre', *El rey de Harlem* (Imaginäres Theater I) of 1979 and *Le miracle de la rose* (Imaginäres Theater II) of 1981. This is a kind of hybridity also exemplified by Weill's *Der neue Orpheus*: Wackers discusses Weill's use of the title 'Kantata' for this work as reflecting the fact that the composer considered the cantata genre to lie in an ambiguous position between concert and dramatic music: *Dialog der Künste*, 175; see also Eichhorn, 'Introduction', 14. Of course, the 'theatricality' of passages in Mahler's symphonies are often noted by commentators.

reflection of Henze's fascination for 'music's capacity to step outside itself, to be figurative and meaningful'.[90] Henze's work demonstrates that this mode of communication is not only viable in stage works or vocal music but also in instrumental concert music. It is precisely in this aspect that Petersen invests his notion of the work as an example of imaginary epic theatre. In his notes to *Mahagonny* (discussed in Chapter 3), Brecht explains how he sought to exclude traditional theatrical concepts of catharsis and empathy – the Aristotelian purging of emotions by the spectator identifying with the protagonist on stage – and in the notes on *Dreigroschenoper* he famously emphasized the role of interruptions, montage and externalization, of 'Verfremdung', which is often translated as alienation but is perhaps better rendered as distanced detachment.[91] The quotations in Henze's *Tristan* are, for Petersen, like the staged entries of three nineteenth-century dramatic figures: Wagner (the representative of musical drama), Chopin (the representative of artificial salon music) and Brahms (the representative figure of symphonic music), who together form a triangle analogous to that of Tristan, Isolde and King Marke in Wagner's music drama.[92]

Petersen's aim is to illuminate Henze's 'epic' strategies for opening up the internal aesthetic world of symphonic music to 'real life'. This theatricality extends to the 'subjective' identities heard in the music. For Petersen, Henze is an artist who 'opens up his whole being', but in a manner which has 'nothing to do with romantic or Biedermeieresque escapes into inwardness. His subjectivity does not burst out of him uncontrolled: it is, in some sense, staged ... his staging of the subject is always a way of communicating objective social reality.'[93] Henze is in this manner comparable with Mahler through their shared 'equivocation over the unitary subject', as Monelle has put it, manifest in the curious absence in Mahler's music of the subjective voice and the rupture of romantic expression behind which is the construction of 'himself'. Monelle emphasizes Mahler's 'realization of the frailty of Romantic subjectivity', his 'loss of faith in the essentially sentimental identification of the composer with the subjectivity of the work'.[94]

---

[90]   Peter Petersen, '"... eine Form und ein Name: Tristan". Strukturelle und semantische Untersuchungen an Hans Werner Henzes Préludes für Klavier, Tonbänder und Orchester', in Otto Kolleritsch (ed.), *Verbalisierung und Sinngehalt: Über Semantische Tendenzen im Denken in und Über Musik Heute* (Vienna: Universal Edition, 1989), 148–76 (149).

[91]   The classic explication in English is John Willett, *The Theatre of Bertolt Brecht* (London: Methuen, 1977), especially 165–81.

[92]   Petersen, '"... eine Form und ein Name: Tristan", 162.   [93] *Ibid.*, 152.

[94]   Monelle, *The Sense of Music*, 229–31.

In Henze a similar equivocation or pluralism extends to undermining the 'epic' quality of the work. But this, too, is achieved through allusion and affirmation of tradition. Robert Hatten, writing on *We Come to the River*, the opera which Henze composed in 1975, soon after *Tristan*, comments that Henze's art of surface and gesture is a confirmation of the legitimacy of pluralism since at least Mozart. For Hatten 'the real issue is whether the network of opposing styles supports significant oppositions in meaning'. In *We Come to the River*, generic conflicts between Aristotelian tragedy and Brechtian epic theatre undermine the distancing effect achieved by parody, pastiche and the simultaneous use of, or disjunctive shifts between, different styles. Henze's pluralism in *We Come to the River* is an attempt to solve the problem of the compatibility of opera and modern theatre, a task aligning Henze with three of his great heroes, Monteverdi, Mozart and Mahler.[95] Henze's pluralism in *Tristan* is an attempt to solve the problem of the competing legacies of Wagnerian music drama, Brechtian 'epic theatre' and the tradition of concert music in a modern era of horror. The dangers, as Whittall has noted, are that the resulting 'extravagance of expression creates an aura, if not of insincerity, then of contrivance', of 'artificial, calculated, wilful exaggeration' of 'feigned and pretentious' melancholia. In this music of masks, in the distancing from romantic expression, distancing from the 'objects of his desire', and the pursuit of a vanishing classical perfection of beautiful forms, where, Whittall asks after Paul Griffiths, might one hear the 'real' Henze?[96] An answer may ultimately lie in Henze's allegiance to Pablo Neruda's *poesía impura*:

A poetry impure as the clothing we wear, or our bodies, soup-stained, soiled with our shameful behaviour, our wrinkles and vigils and dreams, observations and prophecies, declarations of loathing and love, idylls and beasts, the shocks of encounter, political loyalties, denials and doubts, affirmations and taxes.

'Let no one forget them'. Neruda urges. 'Melancholy, old mawkishness impure and flawed, fruits of a fabulous species lost to the memory, cast away in a frenzy's abandonment – moonlight, the swan in the gathering darkness, all hackneyed endearments: surely that is the poet's concern, essential and absolute. Those who shun the "bad taste" of things will fall flat on the ice.'[97]

---

[95] Robert Hatten, 'Pluralism of Theatrical Genre and Musical Style in Henze's *We Come to the River*', *Perspectives of New Music* 28 (1990), 292–311.

[96] Whittall, 'Henze's Haunted Sensibility', *The Musical Times* 147, no. 1895 (Summer 2006), 5–15 (at 5); Paul Griffiths, 'Henze', in *The Substance of Things Heard: Writings about Music* (University of Rochester Press, 2005), 155.

[97] Pablo Neruda, 'Toward an Impure Poetry', in *Five Decades: A Selection (Poems: 1925–1970)*, ed. and trans. Ben Belitt (New York: Grove Press, 1974), xxi–xxii. On Henze's allegiance

The images of death and destruction in Henze's *Tristan* function as portals to hope through the rekindling of processes of mourning and memorialization (processes also importantly rekindled in the final parts of *The Bassarids*). In this respect, Henze sustains a typical 'German' metaphysics of music. Applegate, for example, has noted that 'German composers and performers have been leaders in the use of music as a means to memorialize the suffering their own country brought about in the twentieth century.'[98] This is also one way in which Henze flirts with the 'discredited' nineteenth century, with the 'gloomy and afflicted grandeur' which Mann saw as the 'essence and hallmark' of the nineteenth-century artwork, a melancholy 'monumentalism' which 'curiously enough, goes hand in hand with a love of the very small and painstaking, the psychologically detailed'.[99] *Tristan*, *The Bassarids* and other works express a striving for memorial eloquence in the face of despair and disgust at the dark horrors of modern times. The structural ambition and ambiguity of Henze's *Tristan* (part symphonic poem after the German late romantic tradition, part concerto, part epic theatre transposed to the concert hall) and *The Bassarids* (opera as four-movement symphony) amount to hybrid conflations of formal traditions offered as an alternative to avant-garde examples of iconoclastic nominalism. Both these expressive and structural aspects can be summarized as processes of attempted recovery, but also as a confrontation with deep-seated creative anxieties. Whittall characterizes Henze's music as 'a music haunted by the need to be something else, to find itself in the impossible role of total identity with what has been lost'. The music often evokes 'lost' tonal artefacts, whether these are chords, melodies or forms. However, Whittall argues that by contrast with a tonal composer such as Britten, for the 'post-tonal' Henze 'what can be recovered from the past – save by direct quotation – is even more elusive'. Ultimately, for Whittall, Henze's music 'tends to express "shades" of its models and meanings rather than their essence'. This suggests that this is music seeking the fading shadows of past forms. Indeed, Whittall continues, 'the main quality of his music might even be characterized as the aspiration to confront dissolution by representing it as a viable and sustainable reality, thereby indefinitely deferring its inevitable triumph'. However, quotation is not the

to Neruda, see Henze, *Language, Music and Artistic Invention*, 17; see also 'Art and Revolution' (1971), in *Music and Politics*, 182.

[98] Celia Applegate, 'Saving Music: Enduring Experiences of Culture', *History and Memory* 17 (2005), 217–37 (231).

[99] Thomas Mann, 'The Sorrows and Grandeur of Richard Wagner', in *Pro and Contra Wagner*, trans. Allan Blunden, with an introduction by Erich Heller (London: Faber, 1985), 92.

only means available to Henze to evoke these lost, beloved models and 'post-tonal' is a label which to some extent obscures the ambiguous harmonic character of some of Henze's most powerful passages, where the tonal background remains important, even if it is in some fragile or perilous state. The overcoming of the horror of the 'cry' in *Tristan*, where in the face of the electronic and symphonic cataclysm there is still a tonal drive and tension elusively evoking the expressive and functional qualities of the leading-note and hence the desire to resolve (in short, a residual yet powerful sense of tonal cadence), confirms that Whittall is elsewhere on the mark when he notes that symphonic works such as the *Requiem* (1990–2) and the Ninth Symphony (1995–7), appear to be 'getting close to exorcising the nightmare, relieving the (hyper)-tension, making it possible for later works to advance to a means of expression governed less by bitterness and grief and more by acceptance and forgiveness'.[100]

The Seventh Symphony (1983–4) is crucial in this regard. It is often, justifiably, identified as the symphony in which Henze turns to overt and sustained engagement with the Austro-German late romantic symphonic tradition, by contrast with the more or less defiant eschewal of this tradition in his earlier symphonies. As Hans-Klaus Jungheinrich notes, this dialogue had previously informed two works for large orchestra, *Heliogabalus Imperator* (1972) and *Barcarola* (1979), both in essence symphonic poems explicitly composed after the nineteenth-century tradition. Jungheinrich describes Henze's symphonic music as pervasively concerned with Mahlerian 'formal openness' and a 'multidimensional tonal language', in which 'uninhibited autobiographical diction' coexists with 'confusion, brokenness, affliction', but also 'yearning and self-assertion'.[101] Writing in the mid 1990s, Jungheinrich considers Henze's opposition to the view that 'today it is impossible still to write symphonies'. But in the face of the avant-garde's vigorous, optimistic and uncompromising allegiance to the abolition of 'symphonic' composition as a necessary part of a rupture from the past and breakthrough into radical newness, any such attempt produces, without exception, 'last' symphonies. In this regard they sustain an aspect of

---

[100] Whittall, 'Henze's Haunted Sensibilty', 7–9. The tone of the anti-fascist Ninth (it is based upon Anna Seghers's *Das siebte Kreuz*) approaches the melodramatic – with a climactic use of the organ which does not quite escape evoking a sense of *Grand Guignol* – as Henze once again engages with violence, conflict and the utopian; on the Ninth, see Benedikt Vennefrohne, *Die Sinfonien Hans Werner Henzes* (Hildesheim: Georg Olms Verlag, 2005), 215–70 – especially 257–66 on its anti-fascism.

[101] Hans-Klaus Jungheinrich, '"A World of Freely Invented Orders of Magnitude": Hans Werner Henze and the Problem of the Symphony', *Contemporary Music Review* 12 (1995), 125–43 (at 136).

the symphonic tradition itself, which throughout the nineteenth century struggled with – and yet was inspired by – the suspicion that the 'last' symphony had already been composed. For Jungheinrich, indeed, Beethoven wrote several 'last' symphonies. Beethoven's Ninth is an obvious candidate, but his Fourth and Eighth are, Jungheinrich argues, already 'symphonies after the symphony'. Jungheinrich explains:

the paradox that since Beethoven 'last' symphonies are composed, again and again and without any loss of credibility, becomes more comprehensible. The new beginnings are at the same time late and second flowerings, 'last' urges of a species laden with problems, and this burden cannot be shaken off. Whoever begins to work on symphonies is always working 'at the end', on something extreme, final.

Every symphony is therefore an 'emergency'. Jungheinrich evokes a somewhat apocalyptic tone, but one can easily see here how the example of Mahler (composer of at least nine and a half 'last' symphonies) was important as a precedent for Henze.

How is this sense of 'lastness' evident in Henze's Seventh Symphony? For Jungheinrich, its four movements lead to a 'catastrophe'. He hears the symphony as 'a labyrinth with four entrances, and no exit to it, only the "black hole" into which the music plunges'; 'terror appears to have the last word'.[102] The elegiac tones of the last two movements of the symphony have provoked comparison with the *Lamentations* of the fictional composer Adrian Leverkühn in Mann's *Doctor Faustus*.[103] As we saw in Chapter 2, the final sections of Mann's book tell of the death of Leverkühn's beloved five-year-old nephew Nepomuk (suggestively nicknamed 'Echo') whom the narrator Zeitblom describes as a 'seraphic', pure and precious 'manifestation' – in 'extraordinary completeness' – of 'the child'. The tragic loss leads Leverkühn to declare that he will 'take back' Beethoven's 'Ode to Joy' from the Ninth Symphony in a giant 'lamento', in a work 'very certainly non-dynamic, lacking in development'. 'The echo', he continues, is 'the giving back of the human voice as nature-sound, and the revelation of it as nature-sound, is essentially a lament . . . Purely orchestral is the end: a symphonic adagio . . . it is, as it were, the reverse of the "Ode to Joy", the negative, equally a work of genius, of that transition of the symphony into vocal jubilation. It is the revocation.'[104] The link between Henze's Seventh and Leverkühn's fictional work has been sanctioned by the composer, but for

[102] *Ibid.*, 143.
[103] On the Seventh Symphony see also Vennefrohne, *Die Sinfonien Hans Werner Henzes*, 153–214.
[104] Mann, *Doctor Faustus*, 447, 459, 466–7, 470.

Björn Heile there is no such negation of the Beethovenian symphonic tradition in Henze's symphony.[105] There is also a sense of subjective recovery in Henze's symphony which contradicts Leverkühn's pessimistic revocation, and this is perhaps where one can identify a profound relationship between Henze's Seventh and his *Tristan*. On the second movement of the symphony, Henze wrote: 'never before had I known music of such darkness nor been able to capture it in writing with so great a degree of intensity'. In the third movement, inspired by Hölderlin's horrific predicament in an asylum for the insane, Henze portrays the poet's 'screams, louder and louder and ever more terrifying, until they finally break off'.[106] The slow movement and finale can be heard as movements in search of apotheosis, convalescence or restoration (if not quite a post-Wagnerian *Erlösung*) after this protracted musical scream. In the finale, resonances of Mahler and Berg are especially evident, but with the tone often reaching further 'back' to a desperate expressive tone of *Sehnsucht* recalling, in pained or strained form, that of Wagner's *Tristan*. The movement is an orchestral interpretation of Hölderlin's poem 'Half of Life' (*Hälfte des Lebens*):

Mit gelben Birnen hänget
Und voll mit wilden Rosen
Das Land in den See
Ihr holden Schwäne,
Und trunken von Küssen
Tunkt ihr das Haupt
Ins heilignüchterne Wasser.

Weh mir, wo nehm´ ich, wenn
Es Winter ist, die Blumen, und wo
Den Sonnenschein,
Und Schatten der Erde?
Die Mauern stehn
Sprachlos und kalt, im Winde
Klirren die Fahnen.

With its yellow pears
And wild roses everywhere
The shore hangs into the lake,

---

[105] Björn Heile, Review of Vennefrohne, *Die Sinfonien Hans Werner Henzes, Music & Letters* 88 (2007), 545–7. By contrast, see Henze's explicitly 'Leverkühnian' Third Violin Concerto, three portraits from Thomas Mann's *Doctor Faustus*, (1996).
[106] Henze, *Bohemian Fifths*, 412.

O gracious swans,
And drunk with kisses
You dip your heads
In the sobering holy water.

Ah, where will I find
Flowers, come winter,
And where the sunshine
And shade of the earth?
Walls stand cold
And speechless, in the wind
The weathervanes creak.[107]

One could easily imagine Mahler setting this poem (Britten did so in 1958). Passages of Henze's symphonic response to this text strive for a utopian luminosity: he was, he recalled, 'inspired by Hölderlin's lovely swans as they dip their heads in the sacramentally sobering water, an ideal image of redemption and harmony'.[108] With Hölderlin's unheard poetic lines as its prompt, the music approaches a hymn-like transfiguration. But the symphony's closing sections reconfirm– as Henze's *Being Beauteous* and *Tristan* had previously confirmed – that horror is always at hand.[109]

The utopian, redemptive aspect to this artistic project resurfaced when Henze returned to overtly Mahlerian inspiration in the *Sechs Gesänge aus dem Arabischen* (1999), written for Ian Bostridge and Julius Drake. In the first five songs, Henze sets his own texts (which are frequently explosive and dramatically tragic) with often rich post-romantic piano textures and complex dissonant aggregates and counterpoint. The writing for voice moves between arioso, *Sprechgesang* and (at the end of the fifth) extended melismata overtly suggesting the arabesque. The sixth and final song is a setting of a paraphrase of Hafiz by Rückert, 'Das Paradies'[110] in which the call 'Komm, dass ich dich fasse, reich mir deine Hand' is an invitation to withdraw from the world, but also offers redemption for the beloved, through averting the eyes of the threatening fiend. The first stanza reads:

---

[107] Trans from Friedrich Hölderlin, *Hymns and Fragments*, trans. Richard Sieburth (Princeton University Press, 1984), 46.

[108] Henze, *Bohemian Fifths*, 414.

[109] For more discussion of the Hölderlin aspects of the symphony, see Peter K. Freyberg, 'Henzes Siebte – eine Hölderlin-Symphonie', *Hamburger Jahrbuch für Musikwissenschaft* 20 (2003), 91–110.

[110] Rückert's reputation had reached its nadir in the post-Second World War period, when it was seen as 'reactionary sentimentalism'; see La Grange, *Mahler vol. 2*, 783.

Komm, dass ich dich fasse, reich mir deine Hand,
Und dich nicht mehr lasse, reich mir deine Hand!
Sieh die Finsternis, die meine Zeit bedroht,
In der dunklen Gasse reiche mir die Hand!
Von der Schicksals Schlusse ward mir Arges kund –
In schwindelnden Höhen – reich mir die Hand!

Come, let me hold you, give me your hand,
And may I nevermore leave you, give me your hand!
Behold the darkness that threatens my days,
In the sunless alleyway give me your hand!
Of destiny's plans I have heard dread tales –
In dizzying heights – give me your hand![111]

In Henze's setting, Whittall identifies 'music close enough to tonal and triadic traditions to make its ultimate inability to resolve on to consonant triads after the Wagnerian paradigm a telling factor, but the music is also post-tonal enough to make that non-resolution inevitable and right'. In Whittall's hearing, while the chromatic tensions characteristic of late Wagner are strongly evoked, Wagnerian redemption through resolution is no longer possible: such aspirations have a 'poignant futility', in the face of which Henze 'seeks strategies of coping, co-existing, surviving', in cadences which evoke an 'aura of aesthetic consolation fraught with ambivalence'.[112] Whittall's emphasis on cadential function is apposite, but the lack of diatonic resolution in these cadences, though sustaining harmonic ambiguity, does not negate the possibility of evoking a tone suggesting the redemptive. The setting of the first four lines of the poem builds towards the most powerful of these cadence points (see Example 4.11; note that the example follows Henze's notational style in this song, where accidentals only pertain to individual notes and are not operative through a whole bar, but Henze's use of straight lines as ties in the original score is replaced by ties drawn in traditional fashion). The opening vocal line is set in counterpoint with a single piano line. Both lines are shaped to generate manifold tonal allusions and references to the melodic idiom of the late romantic *lied*. The vocalist's opening B♭ sounds as though it is decorated by its lower neighbour, A, before a scalic ascent of a fourth to the peak E♭.

[111] Trans. Stewart Spencer from the CD, Hans Werne Henze, *Sechs Gesänge aus dem Arabischen/Three Auden Songs*, Ian Bostridge (tenor), Julius Drake (piano) EMI 7243 57112 29 (2001).
[112] Whittall, 'Henze's haunted sensibility', 10–15.

Example **4.11** Henze, 'Das Paradies' (Rückert, after Hafiz), *Sechs Gesänge aus dem Arabischen*, bb. 1–24.

The returning descent to B♭ incorporates a melodic turn (B–A♯–B–C♯), almost a cliché of romantic melody. The parallels with the opening melodic phrase of Mahler's setting of Rückert's 'Nun seh' ich wohl, warum so dunkle Flammen' from the *Kindertotenlieder* are very strong (compare

Example 4.11 (cont.)

Example 4.12). The parallels extend to the harmonic character. G minor is strongly implied by Henze's opening bar, but the piano line's continuation to E♭, followed by an ascending perfect fourth challenge this by allusion to a cadential move in A♭, a harmonic moment strengthened by the voice's coincident rise to E♭. In Mahler's song the opening G minor is similarly

Example 4.12 Mahler, 'Nun seh' ich wohl, warum so dunkle Flammen',
Kindertotenlieder (Rückert), bb. 1–8.

challenged by the dissonant A♭ triad under the peak melodic E♭. The setting
of the next three lines in Henze's song broadly represents a gradual filling
out of the texture through two-, three- and four-part counterpoint to a
richly textured romantic piano idiom. This textural development coexists
with a continuous motivic developmental process. For example, the piano
phrase of bars 5–7 is clearly a developed variant of bars 1–4. This process
again raises parallels with the second of Mahler's *Kindertotenlieder* which,
as Agawu has demonstrated, exhibits an overtly developmental melodic
process.[113] Henze's song also displays careful deployment of contrasting
triadic and fourth/fifth-based chords. The latter inform all the climactic
points, right from the first phrase. (In Mahler's song, too, the appoggiatural
style produces fourth chords at several expressive climaxes.) Henze's climactic fourth line ('in der dunklen') alludes to the motivic content of the
opening line (rise from B♭, climactic falling semitone, B♭–A). Its climactic
C♯ becomes the goal of the chromatically descending bass octaves (bb. 22–
3), another motivic recollection of the opening of the song. Above this bass
line the piano peaks on an A♭ triad. This triad is then composed out by the
falling upper melodic line of bar 23 (with passing B♭). Triadic and quartal

---

[113] Agawu, 'The Musical Language of *Kindertotenlieder* No. 2', 81–93.

chords now sound in climactic juxtaposition. The cadence suggests intensification through combination of diatonic, chromatic and potentially pentatonic (fourth chords) materials. To recall Henze's words cited earlier, this
moment is a fine example of music which, 'multilayered' in its 'illusions and
Utopias', promises the possibility of 'redemption'.[114] It is even possible,
through the connection of the voice's climactic C♯ to the piano's falling A♭
arpeggiation, to create a further motivic parallel – the resulting C♯–C–A♭–
E♭ descent being a clear relative of the motive characterizing the closing bars
of both 'Liebst du um Schönheit' and 'Ich bin der Welt abhanden gekommen'. Through this intertextual resonance Henze's cadence offers an intimation of the transcendent moment characteristic of Mahler's romantic
symbol.

Five of Henze's own verses precede his setting of Rückert's Hafiz paraphrase, establishing Henze as a composer-poet much as Mahler did through
his substantial additions within the Bethge paraphrases from the Chinese
which form *Das Lied von der Erde*.[115] The passage generated by Mahler's
poetic interpolations at the end of Bethge's 'In Erwartug des Freundes', a
paraphrase of Mong-Kao-Yen which is the first of the two poems which
Mahler revised and synthesized to form the text of 'Der Abschied' ('O
Schönheit; O ewigen Liebens, Lebens trunk'ne Welt!' (O beauty; O eternal
Love and life, drunken world!)), exhibits musical techniques, expressive
qualities and poetic content particularly resonant with Henze's song. The
vocal line with which Mahler set these lines (to which the melodic turns and
ascents of Henze's 'Das Paradies' again sound like attenuated echoes) and
the upper orchestral line combine to form an impassioned expansion of the
pentatonic ascent and C–B♭ descent previously exposed, in a clear allusion
to the opening of the setting of Rückert's 'Ich bin der Welt abhanden
gekommen', from fig. 23. Between figs. 30 and 32 there is gradual 'evolution'
from simple pentatonic melodic elements to a more extended diatonic
scalar rise from F to D followed by a leap to G. This shape then forms the
basis of the climactic cadence. At fig. 34 (Example 4.13) the D is embellished
by an E♭–D–C♯–D turn. The upper G, taken by the orchestra, then rises
further to A. The cadence strongly implied by the long, chromatically
enriched dominant ninth of C (which will of course be the final tonic of
the movement) is then interrupted (both the flat and the natural submediant – A♭ and A – appear), so that although the melody incorporates the

---

[114] Henze, *Bohemian Fifths*, 57.
[115] See Arthur B. Wenk, 'The Composer as Poet in *Das Lied von der Erde*', *19th-Century Music* 1 (1977), 33–47.

Example 4.13 Mahler, 'Der Abschied' (Bethge–Mahler), *Das Lied von der Erde*, 5 after fig. 33 to fig. 36.

potentially closing D–C (2–1 in C) there is no harmonic closure. (In the final bars of the piece this is reversed: the harmony reaches C, but the resolution of D to C is famously unheard.) This D–C upper voice 'resolution' in two registers is linked by an embellished descent through a complete whole-tone scale. In the earlier version of this cadence (figs. 11–13), intensification of

Example 4.13 (cont.)

the diatonic cadential model is achieved through chromatic embellishment which Agawu has compared with Bach's chromatic practice and modal mixture.[116] In this later version, the cadence is intensified not only through chromatic enrichment of the diatonic model but also through the embedded presence of non-diatonic pentatonic and whole-tone materials. In Henze's cadence (Example 4.11, bars 20–3), the motivically significant chromatic descending bass generates strong progressive motion, halting on the pitch C♯. Over this bass line the elaboration of the A♭ triad in the upper voice has already been noted (as well as the melodic shape's Mahlerian echoes, generated by its deployment in the cadential gesture). At the climax the upper parts of the piano deploy triads and fourth chords in counterpoint: after the peak an A♭ triadic descent in the melody is achieved in the upper texture through three parallel fourth chords (which together complete an A♭–B♭–C–E♭–F pentatonic collection). In a lower register triadic chords persist and E♭ and B♭ triads combine with the bass C♯ (enharmonic D♭) to suggest an unresolved dominant ninth in fourth inversion under the upper voice's melodically exposed A♭ triad. The bass C♯ picks up the elongated last pitch of the vocal line, which the piano's top C♮ on the downbeat of bar 23 had 'resolved' in the A♭ diatonic realm, but the bass descent (ending on enharmonic D♭, the seventh over the dominant according to this diatonic context) seems incomplete. In this way Henze's cadence is incomplete in a manner comparable with Mahler's cadence in 'Der Abschied' in Example 4.13, where the upper melody closes but is 'opened' up by the whole-tone infusion and the progression is harmonically unfinished.

---

[116] Agawu, 'Prolonged Counterpoint in Mahler', *Mahler Studies*, 217–47.

In the last chapter of his Mahler monograph, Adorno cites the vocal line in the final bars of 'Liebst du um Schönheit' as a precursor of the cadential incompleteness characteristic of Mahler's late works. In such cadences traditional tonal materials are deployed to generate new expressive significance, in particular the regret, the 'sobbing' (Adorno's word), of profound yet incomplete utterance.[117] As discussion of Example 1.6 showed, the vocal line ends on the submediant pitch, invoking the pentatonically inflected dominant six-four which possesses such strong symbolic status and sense of impending ending. Yet it then remains silent, leaving the instrumental lines to work through to tonal closure. There is a tension between, in new expressive terms, a necessary incompleteness, sounded vocally and, in older (traditional, historical) terms, a necessary finality, sounded instrumentally. The fleeting moment of ambiguity between ending and endlessness may be an insinuation of the allegorically inexpressible or an intimation of immortality. As Franklin says, after invoking Adorno's reading of 'Liebst du um Schönheit', in Mahler's vision the 'baggage' of romantic art, the expectation that music resonantly enacts transcendence through affirmative resolution remains disquietingly definitive.[118] Adorno wrote that in Mahler's music 'the absolute is conceived, felt and longed for, and yet it does not exist'.[119] Ultimately, must we be so pessimistic? The darkest moments of negation in Mahler's music seem to demand that we ask, after Wordsworth, 'Whither is fled the visionary gleam?'[120] In contemplating Mahler's death mask, Adorno wrote:

in Mahler's face, which seems both imperious and full of a tender suffering, there is a hint of cunning triumph, as if he wished to say: I have fooled you after all. Fooled us how? If we were to speculate we might conclude that the unfathomable sorrow of his last works had undercut all hope in order to avoid succumbing to an illusion, rather as if hope were not unlike the superstitious idea of tempting fate, so that by hoping for something you prevent it from coming true.[121]

Mahler's last expression is captured as suggesting the 'cunning' victory of 'hope' in the face of intense suffering. The profound ambiguity in the cadences of the last two works Mahler lived to complete, the Ninth Symphony and *Das Lied von der Erde*, 'translated the uncertain outcome between destruction and its alternative into music'.[122] Where there is doubt,

---

[117] Adorno, *Mahler*, 146–7.   [118] Franklin, "'... his fractures are the script of truth'", 278–9.

[119] Theodor W. Adorno, 'Afterthoughts' (1961), in *Quasi una Fantasia*, 109.

[120] William Wordsworth, 'Intimations of Immortality from Recollections of Early Childhood' (1807).

[121] Adorno, 'Afterthoughts', 110.   [122] Ibid., 109–10.

faith; where there is despair, hope? Those cadences in Mahler's Ninth (Example 1.15) and *Das Lied* (Example 4.13), the 'heavenly sounds of unimagined beauty' that Weill heard in the former and the 'beauty of loneliness and of pain' yet also of 'strength and freedom' that Britten heard in the latter, suggest that perhaps, after all, the answer to such questions is an endless artistic task. Henze wrote:

Once he has managed to reformulate and refashion all his ideas about beauty and horror, hell and paradise and to express them in faultless, unique and matchless metaphors – only then may he perhaps retire, relieved, from the field of battle.[123]

But such fulfilment always lies tantalizingly beyond the horizon. Henze died on 27 October 2012, just as this book was being completed. Famously, he remained prolific until his last years of ill health. 'Der Abschied' is never final in music after Mahler. It is a story surely to be continued.

---

[123] Henze, *Bohemian Fifths*, 208.

Bibliography

Abbate, Carolyn, *In Search of Opera*, Princeton University Press, 2001.

    'Opera as Symphony, a Wagnerian Myth', in Carolyn Abbate and Roger Parker (eds.), *Analyzing Opera: Verdi and Wagner*, Berkeley: University of California Press, 1989, 92–124.

Adorno, Theodor W., *Aesthetic Theory*, trans. Robert Hullot-Kentor, Minneapolis: University of Minnesota Press, 1997.

    Alban Berg: Master of the Smallest Link, trans. with introduction and annotation by Juliane Brand and Christopher Hailey, Cambridge University Press, 1991.

    Beethoven. The Philosophy of Music, ed. Rolf Tiedemann, trans. Edmund Jephcott, Stanford University Press, 1998.

    Essays on Music, Selected with Introduction, Commentary and Notes by Richard Leppert, Berkeley: University of California Press, 2002.

    In Search of Wagner, trans. Rodney Livingstone, London: Verso, 1984.

    'Introduction to Benjamin's *Schriften*' (1955), trans. R. Hullot-Kentor, in Gary Smith (ed.), *On Walter Benjamin: Critical Essays and Recollections*, Cambridge, Mass.: MIT, 1988, 2–17.

    Mahler: A Musical Physiognomy, trans. Edmund Jephcott, Chicago University Press, 1991.

    Night Music. Essays on Music 1928–1962, ed. Rolf Tiedemann, trans. Wieland Hoban, London: Seagull, 2009.

    'On Some Relationships between Music and Painting' (1965), trans. Susan Gillespie, *The Musical Quarterly* 79 (1995), 66–79.

    Philosophy of Modern Music, trans. Anne G. Mitchell and Wesley V. Blomster, London: Sheed & Ward, 1973.

    Prisms, trans. Samuel and Shierry Weber, London: Spearman, 1967.

    Quasi una fantasia: Essays on Modern Music, trans. Rodney Livingstone, London: Verso, 1992.

    'Schubert' (1928), trans. Jonathan Dunsby and Beate Perrey, *19th-Century Music* 29 (2005), 7–14.

    'The Threepenny Opera' (1929) trans. in Stephen Hinton (ed.), *Kurt Weill: The Threepenny Opera*, Cambridge University Press, 1990, 130–2.

Adorno, Theodor W. and Walter Benjamin, *The Complete Correspondence 1928–1940*, ed. Henri Lonitz, trans. Nicholas Walker, Cambridge: Polity Press, 1999.

Agawu, Kofi, 'The Musical Language of *Kindertotenlieder* no. 2', *The Journal of Musicology* 2 (1983), 81–93.

'The Narrative Impulse in the Second *Nachtmusik* from Mahler's Seventh Symphony', in Craig Ayrey and Mark Everist (eds.), *Analytical Strategies and Musical Interpretation*, Cambridge University Press, 1996, 226–41.

'Prolonged Counterpoint in Mahler', in Stephen Hefling (ed.), *Mahler Studies*, Cambridge University Press, 1997, 217–47.

Allen, Stephen Arthur, '*Benjamin Britten and Christianity*', unpublished PhD, University of Oxford, 2002.

Applegate, Celia, 'Saving Music: Enduring Experiences of Culture', *History and Memory* 17 (2005), 217–37.

Arato, Andrew and Gebhardt, Eike (eds.), *The Essential Frankfurt School Reader*, Oxford: Blackwell, 1978.

Ashby, Arved, 'Britten as Symphonist', in Mervyn Cooke (ed.), *The Cambridge Companion to Benjamin Britten*, Cambridge University Press, 1999, 217–32.

Attali, Jacques, *Noise*, trans. Brian Massumi, Minneapolis: University of Minnesota Press, 1985.

Auden, W.H. and Kallman, Chester, 'Euripides for Today', *The Musical Times* 115 (1974), 833–4.

Bacon, Henry, *Visconti: Explorations of Beauty and Decay*, Cambridge University Press, 1998.

Bailey, Robert, 'Musical Language and Formal Design in Weill's Symphonies', in Kim H. Kowalke and Horst Edler (eds.), '*A Stranger Here Myself*': *Kurt Weill-Studien*, Hildesheim: Georg Olms Verlag, 1993, 206–15.

Banfield, Stephen, *Sensibility and English Song*, vol. 2, Cambridge University Press, 1985.

Barringer, Tim, '"I am a native, rooted here": Benjamin Britten, Samuel Palmer and the Neo Romantic Pastoral', *Art History* 34 (2011), 126–65.

Barry, Barbara R., 'Schiller's (and Berlin's) "Naïve" and "Sentimental": Propensity and Pitfalls in the Philosophical Categorization of Artists', in Christoph Asmuth, Gunter Scholtz and Franz-Bernhard Stammkötter (eds.), *Philosophischer Gedanke und musikalischer Klang: Zum Wechselverhältnis von Musik und Philosophie*, Frankfurt/Main: Campus, 1999, 155–61.

Bauer, Karen, *Adorno's Nietzschean Narratives: Critiques of Ideology, Readings of Wagner*, State University of New York Press, 1999.

Bauer-Lechner, Natalie, *Recollections of Gustav Mahler*, trans. Dika Newlin, edited and annotated by Peter Franklin, London: Faber, 1980.

Bauman, Zygmunt, *Modernity and Ambivalence*, Cambridge: Polity Press, 1991.

Baxandall, Michael, *Patterns of Intention: On the Historical Explanation of Pictures*, New Haven: Yale University Press, 1985.

Beechey, James and Stephens, Chris (eds.), *Picasso and Modern British Art*, London: Tate, 2012.

Benjamin, Walter, *The Arcades Project*, trans. Howard Eiland and Kevin McLaughlin, Cambridge: Mass.: Harvard University Press, 1999.

Illuminations, ed. Hannah Arendt, trans. Harry Zohn, London: Fontana, 1973.

One-Way Street and Other Writings, trans. Edmund Jephcott and Kingsley Shorter, London: New Left Books, 1979.

The Origin of German Tragic Drama, trans. John Osborne, London: Verso, 1998.

Berefelt, Gunnar, 'On Symbol and Allegory', *The Journal of Aesthetics and Art Criticism* 28 (1969), 201–12.

Berman, Jill, 'History can Restore Naivety to the Sentimental: Schiller's Letters on Wallenstein', *The Modern Language Review* 81 (1986), 369–87.

Bernstock, Judith E., *Under the Spell of Orpheus: The Persistence of a Myth in Twentieth Century Art*, Carbondale: Southern Illinois University Press, 1991.

Black, Joel D., 'Allegory Unveiled', *Poetics Today* 4 (1983), 109–26.

Blanchot, Maurice, 'Reflections on Surrealism', in *The Work of Fire*, trans. Charlotte Mandell, Stanford University Press, 1995, 85–97.

Bloch, Ernst, *Essays on the Philosophy of Music*, trans. Peter Palmer, with an introduction by David Drew, Cambridge University Press, 1985.

Bohrer, Karl Heinz, *Suddenness: On the Moment of Aesthetic Appearance*, trans. Ruth Crowley, New York: Columbia University Press, 1994.

Bokina, John, *Opera and Politics: From Monteverdi to Henze*, New Haven: Yale University Press, 1997.

Bonds, Mark Evan, *After Beethoven: Imperatives of Originality in the Symphony*, Cambridge: Mass.: Harvard University Press, 1996.

'Idealism and the Aesthetics of Instrumental Music at the Turn of the Nineteenth Century', *Journal of the American Musicological Society* 50 (1997), 387–420.

Bork, Camilla, 'Musical Lyricism as Self-Exploration: Reflections on Mahler's "Ich bin der Welt abhanden gekommen"', trans. Irene Zedlacher, in Karen Painter (ed.), *Mahler and His World*, Princeton University Press, 2002, 159–72.

Botstein, Leon, 'Whose Mahler? Reception, Interpretation and History', in Karen Painter (ed.), *Mahler and His World*, Princeton University Press, 2002, 1–53.

Bray, Trevor, 'Bridge's *Novelletten* and *Idylls*', *The Musical Times* 117, no. 1605 (1976), 905–6.

Frank Bridge: A Life in Brief, http://trevor-bray-music-research.co. uk/Bridge.

Brecht, Bertolt, 'The Modern Theatre is the Epic Theatre' (Notes to the opera *Aufstieg und Fall der Stadt Mahagonny*) (1930), in *Brecht on Theatre: The Development of an Aesthetic*, ed. and trans. John Willett, New York: Hill and Wang, 1964, 33–41.

Breton, André, *Manifestoes of Surrealism*, trans. Richard Seaver and Helen R. Lane, Ann Arbor: University of Michigan Press, 1972.

Brett, Philip, *Music and Sexuality in Britten: Selected Essays*, ed. George E. Haggerty, Berkeley: University of California Press, 2006.

Brinkmann, Reinhold, *Late Idyll: The Second Symphony of Johannes Brahms*, trans. Peter Palmer, Cambridge, Mass.: Harvard University Press, 1995.

Britten, Benjamin, 'Conversation with Benjamin Britten', *Tempo* 6 (1944), 4–5.

'The Folk-Art Problem', *Modern Music* 18 (1941), 71–5.

Bruhn, Siglund, 'Kurt Weill: Violinkonzert', *Melos* 48 (1986), 84–105.

Buck-Morss, Susan, *The Origin of Negative Dialectics*, Hassocks: Harvester Press, 1977.

Buhler, James, '"Breakthrough" as a Critique of Form: The Finale of Mahler's First Symphony', *19th-Century Music* 20 (1996), 125–43.

'Theme, Thematic Variant Form Process in the Andante of Mahler's Sixth Symphony', in Jeremy Barham (ed.), *Perspectives on Gustav Mahler*, Aldershot: Ashgate, 2005, 261–94.

Bürger, Peter, 'The Decline of the Modern Age', trans. David J. Parent, *Telos* 62 (1984–5), 117–30.

Theory of the Avant-Garde, trans. Michael Shaw, Minneapolis: University of Minnesota Press, 1984.

Burkholder, J. Peter, 'The Historicist Mainstream in Music of the Last Hundred Years', *The Journal of Musicology* 2 (1983), 115–34.

'Musical Time and Continuity as a Reflection of the Historical Situation of Modern Composers', *The Journal of Musicology* 9 (1991), 412–29.

Burnham, Scott, 'Landscape as Music, Landscape as Truth: Schubert and the Burden of Repetition', *19th-Century Music* 29 (2005), 31–41.

Butler, Christopher, *Early Modernism: Literature, Music and Painting in Europe 1900–1916*, Oxford: Clarendon Press, 1994.

Carpenter, Humphrey, *Benjamin Britten: A Biography*, London: Faber, 1992.

Cone, Edward T., 'Sound and Syntax: An Introduction to Schoenberg's Harmony', *Perspectives of New Music* 13 (1974), 21–40.

Cook, Susan C., *Opera for a New Republic: The 'Zeitopern' of Křenek, Weill, and Hindemith*, Ann Arbor: UMI, 1988.

Cooke, Deryck, *Gustav Mahler: An Introduction to his Music*, London: Faber, 1980.

Cross, Jonathan, *The Stravinsky Legacy*, Cambridge University Press, 1998.

Cunningham, David, 'The Futures of Surrealism: Hegelianism, Romanticism, and the Avant Garde', *SubStance* 34 (2005), 47–65.

Dahlhaus, Carl, *Between Romanticism and Modernism*, trans. Mary Whittall, Berkeley: University of California Press, 1980.

Foundations of Music History, trans. J.B. Robinson, Cambridge University Press, 1983.

Nineteenth-Century Music, trans. J.B. Robinson, Berkeley: University of California Press, 1989.

Richard Wagner's Music Dramas, trans. Mary Whittall, Cambridge University Press, 1979.

Danuser, Hermann, *Gustav Mahler und seine Zeit*, Laaber-Verlag, 1991.

Darcy, Warren, 'Rotational Form, Teleological Genesis, and Fantasy Projection in the Slow Movement of Mahler's Sixth Symphony', *19th-Century Music* 25 (2001), 49–74.

Daverio, John, *Crossing Paths: Schubert, Schumann and Brahms*, Oxford University Press, 2002.

Nineteenth-Century Music and the German Romantic Ideology, New York: Schirmer, 1993.

Decsay, Ernst, 'Stunden mit Mahler', *Die Musik* 40 (1911), 143–4.

Diether, Jack, 'Mahler and Psychoanalysis', *The Psychoanalytic Review* 45 (1959–60), 3–14.

Drew, David, *Kurt Weill: A Handbook*, London: Faber, 1987.

'Weill and Schoenberg', *Kurt Weill Newsletter* 12, no. 1 (Spring 1994), 11.

Downes, Stephen, *Hans Werner Henze: 'Tristan'*, Aldershot: Ashgate, 2011.

The Muse as Eros: Music, Erotic Fantasy and Male Creativity in the Romantic and Modern Imagination, Aldershot: Ashgate, 2006.

Music and Decadence in European Modernism: The Case of Central and Eastern Europe, Cambridge University Press, 2010.

'Musical Languages of Love and Death: Mahler's Compositional Legacy', in Jeremy Barham (ed.), *The Cambridge Companion to Mahler*, Cambridge University Press, 2007, 226–42.

'Modern Maritime Pastoral: Wave Deformations in the Music of Frank Bridge', in Matthew Riley (ed.), *British Music and Modernism 1895–1960*, Aldershot: Ashgate, 2010, 93–107.

Dube, Wolf-Dieter, *The Expressionists*, trans. Mary Whittall, London: Thames and Hudson, 1972, 206.

Eichhorn, Andreas, 'Introduction' to Kurt Weill, *Music with Solo Violin (The Kurt Weill Edition Series II, volume 2)*, New York: Kurt Weill Foundation for Music, 2010, 13–31.

Eisenberg, Evan, *The Recording Angel: Music, Recordings and Culture from Aristotle to Zappa*, London: Pan, 1988.

Eliot, T.S., 'Tradition and the Individual Talent' (1920), in *The Sacred Wood: Essays on Poetry and Criticism*, London: Methuen, 1950, 47–59.

Elliott, Graham, *Benjamin Britten: The Spiritual Dimension*, Oxford University Press, 2005.

Engh, Barbara, 'Adorno and the Sirens: Tele-phono-graphic Bodies', in Leslie C. Dunn and Nancy A. Jones (eds.), *Embodied Voices: Representing Female Vocality in Western Culture*, Cambridge University Press, 1995, 120–35.

Evans, John (ed.), *Journeying Boy: The Diaries of the Young Benjamin Britten 1928–1938*, London: Faber, 2009.

Evans, Peter, *The Music of Benjamin Britten*, London: Dent, 1979.

Farneth, David, Juchem, Elmar and Stein, Dave (eds.), *Kurt Weill: A Life in Pictures and Documents*, Woodstock, NY: The Overlook Press, 2000.

Feder, Stuart, *Gustav Mahler: A Life in Crisis*, New Haven: Yale University Press, 2004.

Ferran, Peter W., 'The *Threepenny* Songs: Cabaret and the Lyrical Gestus', *Theater* 30, no. 3 ('100 Years of Kurt Weill') (2000), 5–21.

Fischer, Jens Malte, *Gustav Mahler*, trans. Stewart Spencer, New Haven: Yale University Press, 2011.

Floros, Constantin, *Gustav Mahler: The Symphonies*, trans. Vernon Wicker, Aldershot: Scolar Press, 1995.

Forte, Allen, 'Middleground Motives in the *Adagietto* of Mahler's Fifth Symphony', *19th Century Music* 8 (1984), 153–63.

Franklin, Peter, '". . . His fractures are the script of truth" Adorno's Mahler', in Stephen Hefling (ed.), *Mahler Studies*, Cambridge University Press, 1997, 271–94.

The Idea of Music: Schoenberg and Others, London: Macmillan, 1985.

'A Soldier's Sweetheart's Mother's Tale? Mahler's Gendered Musical Discourse', in Karen Painter (ed.), *Mahler and his World*, Princeton University Press, 2002, 111–25.

Freud, Sigmund, *Beyond the Pleasure Principle* (1920), trans. James Strachey, *The Penguin Freud Library*, vol. 11 '*On Metapsychology*', Harmondsworth, Penguin, 1991, 269–338.

'Delusions and Dreams in Jensen's *Gradiva*' (1907), trans. James Strachey, *The Penguin Freud Library vol. 14 'Art and Literature'*, Harmondsworth, Penguin, 1985, 27–118.

Freyberg, Peter K., 'Henzes Siebte – eine Hölderlin-Symphonie', *Hamburger Jahrbuch für Musikwissenschaft* 20 (2003), 91–110.

Frisch, Walter, 'Bach, Brahms, and the Emergence of Musical Modernism', in Michael Marissen (ed.), *Bach Perspectives III: Creative Responses to Bach from Mozart to Hindemith*, Lincoln: University of Nebraska Press, 1998, 109–31.

German Modernism: Music and the Arts, Berkeley: University of California Press, 2005.

'Reger's Bach and Historicist Modernism', *19th-Century Music* 25 (2002), 296–312.

Gay, Peter, 'The Outsider as Insider', in D. Fleming and B. Bailyn (eds.), *The Intellectual Migration: Europe and America 1930-1960*, Cambridge, Mass.: MIT Press, 1969, 11–93.

Geck, Martin, *Von Beethoven bis Mahler*, Reinbek: Rohwolt, 2000.

Gifford, Terry, *Pastoral*, London: Routledge, 1999.

Gillespie, Gerald, 'Mann and the Modernist Tradition', in Jeffrey B. Berlin (ed.), *Approaches to Teaching Mann's 'Death in Venice' and Other Short Stories*, New York: Modern Language Association of America, 1998, 98–103.

Gilliam, Bryan, 'Stage and Screen: Kurt Weill and Operatic Reform in the 1920s', in Gilliam (ed.), *Music and Performance during the Weimar Republic*, Cambridge University Press, 1994, 1–12.

Goehr, Lydia, 'Hardboiled Disillusionment: *Mahagonny* as the Last Culinary Opera', *Cultural Critique* 68 (2008), 3–37.

'*Juliette fährt nach Mahagonny* or a Critical Reading of Surrealist Opera', *The Opera Quarterly* 21 (2006), 647–74.

The Quest for Voice: Music, Politics, and the Limits of Philosophy, Oxford University Press, 1998.

Goethe, Johann Wolfgang von, *Maxims and Reflections* [1827], trans. Bailey Saunders, New York: Macmillan, 1906.

Goll, Ivan, Preface to 'Methusalem, or the Eternal Bourgeois' (1922), in *Seven Expressionist Plays*, trans. J.M. Ritchie and H.F. Garten, London: Calder, 1968, 79–80.

Grant, M.J., *Serial Music, Serial Aesthetics: Compositional Theory in Post-War Europe*, Cambridge University Press, 2001.

Griffiths, Paul, 'Hans Werner Henze Talks to Paul Griffiths', *The Musical Times* 115 (1974), 831–2.

The Substance of Things Heard: Writings about Music, University of Rochester Press, 2005.

Hailey, Christopher, 'Rethinking Sound: Music and Radio in Weimar Germany', in Bryan Gilliam (ed.), *Music and Performance during the Weimar Republic*, Cambridge University Press, 1994, 13–36.

Halmi, Nicholas, *The Genealogy of the Romantic Symbol*, Oxford University Press, 2007.

Harper-Scott, Paul, 'Made you Look! Children in *Salome* and *Death in Venice*', in Lucy Walker (ed.), *Benjamin Britten: New Perspectives on his Life and Work*, Woodbridge: Boydell, 2009, 116–37.

Harris, Alexandra, *Romantic Moderns: English Writers, Artists and the Imagination from Virginia Woolf to John Piper*, London: Thames & Hudson, 2010.

Hatten, Robert, *Interpreting Musical Gestures, Topics and Tropes: Mozart, Beethoven, Schubert*, Bloomington: Indiana University Press, 2004.

Musical Meaning in Beethoven, Bloomington: Indiana University Press, 1994.

'Pluralism of Theatrical Genre and Musical Style in Henze's *We Come to the River*', *Perspectives of New Music* 28 (1990), 292–311.

Hefling, Stephen E., *Mahler: Das Lied von der Erde*, Cambridge University Press, 2000.

'The Rückert Lieder', in Donald Mitchell and Andrew Nicholson (eds.), *The Mahler Companion*, Oxford University Press, 2002, 338–65.

'Siegfried Lipiner's *On the Elements of a Renewal of Religious Ideas in the Present*', in Erich Wolfgang and Morten Solvik (eds.), *Mahler im Context, Contextualizing Mahler*, Vienna: Bohlau Verlag, 2011, 91–114.

Heile, Björn, Review of Vennefrohne, *Die Sinfonien Hans Werner Henzes*, *Music & Letters* 88 (2007), 545–7.

Heister, Hanns-Werner, 'Zur Bedeutung Karl Amadeus Hartmanns für Hans Werner Henze', *Hamburger Jahrbuch für Musikwissenschaft* 20 (2003), 205–14.

Henri, Adrian, McGough, Roger and Patten, Brian, *The Mersey Sound: Penguin Modern Poets 10*, Harmondsworth: Penguin, 1967.

Henze, Hans Werner, *Bohemian Fifths: An Autobiography*, trans. Stewart Spencer, London: Faber, 1998.

Language, Music and Artistic Invention (The Prince of Hesse Memorial Lecture), trans. Mary Whittall, Aldeburgh: Britten-Pears Library, 1996.

Music and Politics: Collected Writings 1953–81, trans. Peter Labanyi, London: Faber, 1982.

Hillman, James, *The Dream and the Underworld*, New York: Harper & Row, 1979.

Hindley, Clifford, 'Contemplation and Reality: A Study in Britten's *Death in Venice*', *Music & Letters* 71 (1990), 511–23.

'Platonic Elements in Britten's *Death in Venice*', *Music & Letters* 73 (1992), 407–29.

Hinton, Stephen, 'The Concept of Epic Opera: Theoretical Anomalies in the Brecht-Weill Partnership', in Hermann Danuser (ed.), *Das musikalische Kunstwerk. Geschichte – Ästhetik – Theorie*, Laaber-Verlag, 1988, 285–94.

'Weill: *Neue Sachlichkeit*, Surrealism, and *Gebrauchsmusik*', in Kim Kowalke (ed.), *A New Orpheus, Essays on Kurt Weill*, New Haven: Yale University Press, 1986, 61–82.

Weill's Musical Theatre: Stages of Reform, Berkeley: University of California Press, 2012.

Hirsch, Foster, *Kurt Weill on Stage: From Berlin to Broadway*, New York: Knopf, 2002.

Hirsch, Marjorie W., *Romantic Lieder and the Search for Lost Paradise*, Cambridge University Press, 2007.

Hoeckner, Berthold, '*Music as a Metaphor of Metaphysics: Tropes of Transcendence in 19th-century Music from Schumann to Mahler*', unpublished PhD, Cornell University, 1994.

Programming the Absolute: Nineteenth-Century German Music and the Hermeneutics of the Moment, Princeton University Press, 2002.

'Schumann and Romantic Distance', *Journal of the American Musicological Society* 50 (1997), 55–132.

Holbrook, David, *Gustav Mahler and the Courage to Be*, London: Vision, 1975.

Hölderlin, Friedrich, *Hymns and Fragments*, trans. Richard Sieburth, Princeton University Press, 1984.

Poems and Fragments, trans. Michael Hamburger, London: Anvil Press, 2004.

Hyde, Martha M., 'Neoclassic and Anachronistic Impulses in Twentieth-Century Music', *Music Theory Spectrum* 18 (1996), 200–35.

Jarman, Douglas, *Kurt Weill: An Illustrated Biography*, London: Orbis, 1982.

(ed.), *Henze at the Royal Northern College of Music: A Symposium*, Todmorden: Arc, 1998.

Johnson, Julian, 'The Breaking of the Voice', *Nineteenth-Century Music Review* 8 (2011), 179–95.

'Mahler and the Idea of Nature', in Jeremy Barham (ed.), *Perspectives on Gustav Mahler*, Aldershot: Ashgate, 2005, 23–36.

Mahler's Voices: Expression and Irony in the Songs and Symphonies, Oxford University Press, 2009.

Webern and the Transformation of Nature, Cambridge University Press, 1999.

Josipovici, Gabriel, *On Trust: Art and the Temptations of Suspicion*, New Haven: Yale University Press, 1999.

Jungheinrich, Hans-Klaus, '"A World of Freely Invented Orders of Magnitude": Hans Werner Henze and the Problem of the Symphony', *Contemporary Music Review* 12 (1995), 125–43.

Kangas, Ryan R., 'Classical Style, Childhood and Nostalgia in Mahler's Fourth Symphony', *Nineteenth Century Music Review* 8 (2011), 219–36.

Keller, Hans, *Essays on Music*, ed. Christopher Wintle, Cambridge University Press, 1994.

   Music and Psychology, ed. Christopher Wintle, London: Plumbago, 2003.

   Music, Closed Societies and Football (reprint of *1975 (1984 minus 9)*), London: Toccata Press, 1986.

   'The Musical Character', in Donald Mitchell and Hans Keller (eds.), *Benjamin Britten: A Commentary on his Works from a Group of Specialists*, London: Rockliff, 1952, 319–51.

   'Operatic Music and Britten', in David Herbert (ed.), *The Operas of Benjamin Britten*, London: Hamish Hamilton, 1979, xii–xxxi.

   '*Peter Grimes* II: The Story; the Music not excluded', in Donald Mitchell and Hans Keller (eds.), *Benjamin Britten: A Commentary on his Works from a Group of Specialists*, London: Rockliff, 1952, 111–24.

Kelley, Theresa M., *Reinventing Allegory*, Cambridge University Press, 1997.

Kemp, Ian, 'Music as Metaphor: Aspects of *Der Silbersee*', in Kim Kowalke (ed.), *A New Orpheus: Essays on Kurt Weill*, New Haven: Yale University Press, 1986, 131–46.

Kildea, Paul (ed.), *Britten on Music*, Oxford University Press, 2003.

Kittler, Friedrich, *Gramophone, Film, Typewriter*, trans., with an introduction, by Geoffrey Winthrop Young and Michael Wutz, Stanford University Press, 1999.

   'World-Breath: On Wagner's Media Technology', in David J. Levin (ed.), *Opera Through Other Eyes*, Stanford University Press, 1994, 215–35.

Klein, Michael, *Intertextuality in Western Art Music*, Bloomington: Indiana University Press, 2005.

Knapp, Raymond, 'Suffering Children: Perspectives on Innocence and Vulnerability in Mahler's Fourth Symphony', *19th Century Music* 22 (1999), 233–67.

Knittel, K.M., *Seeing Mahler: Music and the Language of Anti-Semitism in Fin-de-Siècle Vienna*, Aldershot: Ashgate, 2010.

Kokoschka, Oskar, *My Life*, trans. David Britt, New York: Macmillan, 1974.

Kordes, Gesa, 'Darmstadt, Post-War Experimentation, and the West German Search for a New Musical Identity', in Celia Applegate and Pamela Potter (eds.), *Music and German National Identity*, Chicago University Press, 2002, 205–17.

Korsyn, Kevin, 'Towards a New Poetics of Musical Influence', *Music Analysis* 10 (1991), 3–72.

Kovnatskaya, Ludmilla, 'Notes on a Theme from *Peter Grimes*', in Philip Reed (ed.), *On Mahler and Britten*, Woodbridge: Boydell Press, 1995, 172–85.

Kowalke, Kim, *Kurt Weill in Europe*, Ann Arbor: UMI, 1979.

'Looking Back: Toward a New Orpheus', in Kowalke (ed.) *A New Orpheus: Essays on Kurt Weill*, New Haven: Yale University Press, 1986, 1–20.

Kramer, Lawrence, *Interpreting Music*, Berkeley: University of California Press, 2011.

Music and Poetry: The Nineteenth Century and After, Berkeley: University of California Press, 1984.

Musical Meaning: Towards a Critical History, Berkeley: University of California Press, 2002.

Opera and Modern Culture: Wagner and Strauss, Berkeley: University of California Press, 2004.

Kramer, Richard, 'The Hedgehog: Of Fragments Finished and Unfinished', *19th-Century Music* 21 (1997), 134–48.

Křenek, Ernst, 'Gustav Mahler', in Bruno Walter, *Gustav Mahler*, trans. James Galton, with a biographical note by Ernst Křenek, New York: The Greystone Press, 1941, 155–220.

Kristeva, Julia, *Desire in Language: A Semiotic Approach to Literature and Art*, ed. Leon S. Roudiez, trans. Thomas Gora, Alice Jardine and Leon S. Roudiez, Oxford: Blackwell, 1982.

Kubik, Reinhold, 'Mahler's Revisions and Performance Practice', in Jeremy Barham (ed.), *Perspectives on Gustav Mahler*, Aldershot: Ashgate, 2005, 401–15.

La Grange, Henry-Louis de, 'The Eighth: Exception or Crowning Achievement?', in Jos van Leeuwen (ed.), *A 'Mass' for the Masses: Proceedings of the Mahler VIII Symposium, Amsterdam 1988*, Rijswisk: University of Rotterdam Press, 1992, 131–44.

Gustav Mahler Vol. 2 Vienna: The Years of Challenge (1897–1904), Oxford University Press, 1995.

Mahler: Volume 1, London: Gollancz, 1976.

'Music about Music in Mahler: Reminiscences, Allusions, or Quotations?' in Stephen Hefling (ed.), *Mahler Studies*, Cambridge University Press, 1997, 122–68.

La Grange, Henry-Louis de and Weiss, Günther (eds.), *Gustav Mahler: Letters to his Wife*, trans. Antony Beaumont, London: Faber, 2004.

Lachenmann, Helmut, 'Open Letter to Hans Werner Henze', trans. Jeffrey Stadelman, *Perspectives of New Music* 35 (1997), 189–200.

Lea, Henry A., *Gustav Mahler: Man on the Margin*, Bonn: Bouvier, 1985.

Leppert, Richard, 'Music "Pushed to the Edge of Existence" (Adorno, Listening, and the Question of Hope)', *Cultural Critique* 60 (2005), 92–133.

Lethem, Jonathan, *The Ecstasy of Influence*, New York: Doubleday, 2011.

Levi, Erik, 'The Rehabilitation of Kurt Weill', *Kurt Weill Newsletter* 18 (2000), 17–24.

Levin, Thomas Y., 'For the Record: Adorno on Music in the Age of Its Technological Reproducibility', *October* 55 (1990), 23–47.

Levitz, Tamara, *Teaching New Classicality: Ferruccio Busoni's Master Class in Composition*, Frankfurt: Peter Lang, 1996.

Lipiner, Siegfried, 'Über die Elemente einer Erneuerung religiöser Ideen in der Gegenwart/On the Elements of a Renewal of Religious Ideas in the Present', trans. Stephen Hefling, in Erich Wolfgang and Morten Solvik (eds.), *Mahler im Context, Contextualizing Mahler*, Vienna: Bohlau Verlag, 2011, 115–51.

Longobardi, Ruth Sara, 'Multivalence and Collaboration in *Death in Venice*', *twentieth-century music* 2 (2005), 53–78.

'Reading Between the Lines: An Approach to the Musical and Sexual Ambiguities of *Death in Venice*', *The Journal of Musicology* 22 (2005), 327–64.

Mahler, Alma, *Gustav Mahler: Memories and Letters*, trans. Basil Creighton, ed. Donald Mitchell and Knud Martner, London: Cardinal, 1990.

Mann, Thomas, *Doctor Faustus: The Life of the German Composer Adrian Leverkühn as Told by a Friend* (1947), trans. H. T. Lowe-Porter, Harmondsworth: Penguin, 1968.

'The Sorrows and Grandeur of Richard Wagner' (1933), in *Pro and Contra Wagner*, trans. Allan Blunden, with an introduction by Erich Heller, London: Faber, 1985, 91–148.

Mark, Christopher, *Early Benjamin Britten: A Study of Stylistic and Technical Evolution*, New York: Garland, 1995.

'Juvenilia (1922–32)', in Mervyn Cooke (ed.), *The Cambridge Companion to Benjamin Britten*, Cambridge University Press, 1999, 11–35.

'Simplicity in Early Britten', *Tempo* 147 (1983), 8–14.

Martin, Bernice, *A Sociology of Contemporary Cultural Change*, Oxford: Blackwell, 1981.

Martner, Knud (ed.), *Selected Letters of Gustav Mahler*, London: Faber, 1979.

McClatchie, Stephen, 'Mahler's Wagner', in Erich Wolfgang and Morten Solvik (eds.), *Mahler im Kontext/Contextualizing Mahler*, Vienna: Böhlau Verlag, 2011, 407–16.

'The Wagnerian Roots of Mahler's Eighth Symphony', in Elisabeth Kappel (ed.), *The Total Work of Art: Mahler's Eighth Symphony in Context*, Vienna: Universal Edition, 2011, 152–68.

McColl, Sandra, 'Max Kalbeck and Gustav Mahler', *19th-Century Music* 20 (1996), 167–84.

McConkey, Kenneth, *Memory and Desire: Painting in Britain and Ireland at the Turn of the Twentieth Century*, Aldershot: Ashgate, 2002.

Mellers, Wilfrid, 'Paradise, Panic and Parody in Britten's Frank Bridge Variations', *Tempo* 217 (2001), 26–36.

Metzer, David, *Quotation and Cultural Meaning in Twentieth-Century Music*, Cambridge University Press, 2003.

Micznik, Vera, 'Music and Narrative Revisited: Degrees of Narrativity in Beethoven and Mahler', *Journal of the Royal Musicological Society* 126 (2001), 193–249.

Mitchell, Donald, *Britten and Auden in the Thirties: The Year 1936*, London: Faber, 1981.

    Gustav Mahler: Songs and Symphonies of Life and Death, Berkeley: University of California Press, 1985.

    Gustav Mahler: The Wunderhorn Years, London: Faber, 1975.

    'The Modernity of Gustav Mahler', in Günther Weiss (ed.), *Neue Mahleriana*, Berne: Peter Lang, 1997, 175–90.

    'The Musical Atmosphere', in Donald Mitchell and Hans Keller (eds.), *Benjamin Britten: A Commentary on his Works from a Group of Specialists*, London: Rockliff, 1952, 9–58.

    'Swallowing the Programme: Mahler's Fourth Symphony', in Donald Mitchell and Andrew Nicholson (eds.), *The Mahler Companion*, Oxford University Press, 2002, 187–216.

    'Weill's *Mahagonny* and "Eternal Art"', in *Cradles of the New: Writings on Music 1951–1991*, London: Faber, 1995, 82–6.

    'What do we Know about Britten Now?', in Christopher Palmer (ed.), *The Britten Companion*, London: Faber, 1984.

    (ed.), *Gustav Mahler: Facsimile Edition of the Seventh Symphony*, Amsterdam, Rosbeek, 1995.

    (ed.), *Letters from a Life: The Selected Letters and Diaries of Benjamin Britten vol. 1*, London: Faber, 1991.

Monahan, Seth, 'Success and Failure in Mahler's Sonata Recapitulations', *Music Theory Spectrum* 33 (2011), 37–58.

Monelle, Raymond, *The Sense of Music: Semiotic Essays*, Princeton University Press, 2000.

Móricz, Klára, *Jewish Identities: Nationalism, Racism, and Utopianism in Twentieth-Century Music*, Berkeley: University of California Press, 2008.

Nelson, Thomas, '*The Fantasy of Absolute Music*', unpublished PhD, University of Minnesota, 1998.

Neruda, Pablo, *Five Decades: A Selection (Poems: 1925–1970)*, ed. and trans. Ben Belitt, New York: Grove Press, 1974.

Neumann, Erich, *Depth Psychology and a New Ethic*, trans. Eugene Rolfe, London: Harper & Row, 1973.

Newcomb, Anthony, 'Action and Agency in Mahler's Ninth Symphony, Second Movement', in Jenefer Robinson (ed.), *Music and Meaning*, Ithaca: Cornell University Press, 1997, 131–53.

    'Narrative Archetypes and Mahler's Ninth Symphony', in Steven Paul Scher (ed.), *Music and Text: Critical Inquiries*, Cambridge University Press, 1992, 118–36.

Niekerk, Carl, 'Mahler *contra* Wagner: The Philosophical Legacy of Romanticism in Gustav Mahler's Third and Fourth Symphonies', *The German Quarterly* 77 (2004), 188–209.

    Reading Mahler: German Musical Culture and Jewish Identity in Fin-de-Siècle Vienna, Rochester, NY: Camden House, 2010.

Nietzsche, Friedrich, *Thus Spoke Zarathustra*, trans. R.J. Hollingdale, Harmondsworth: Penguin, 1969.

Norris, Christopher, 'Utopian Deconstruction: Ernst Bloch, Paul de Man and the Politics of Music', in Norris (ed.), *Music and the Politics of Culture*, London: Lawrence & Wishart, 1989, 305–47.

Nussbaum, Martha C., *Upheavals of Thought: The Intelligence of Emotions*, Cambridge University Press, 2001.

Osborne, Peter, 'Small-Scale Victories, Large-Scale Defeats: Walter Benjamin's Politics of Time', in Andrew Benjamin and Peter Osborne (eds.), *Walter Benjamin's Philosophy: Destruction and Experience*, London: Routledge, 1994, 59–109.

Paddison, Max, *Adorno, Modernism and Mass Culture*, London: Kahn & Averill, 1996.

    Adorno's Aesthetics of Music, Cambridge University Press, 1993.

    'Adorno's *Aesthetic Theory*', *Music Analysis* 6 (1987), 355–77.

    'Stravinsky as Devil: Adorno's Three Critiques', in Jonathan Cross (ed.), *The Cambridge Companion to Stravinsky*, Cambridge University Press, 2003, 192–201.

Painter, Karen, 'The Sensuality of Timbre: Responses to Mahler and Modernity at the *Fin de siècle*', *19th-Century Music* 18 (1995), 236–56.

    Symphonic Aspirations: German Music and Politics 1900–45, Cambridge, Mass.: Harvard University Press, 2007.

Palmer, Christopher, 'Towards a Genealogy of *Death in Venice*', in Philip Reed (ed.), *On Mahler and Britten*, Woodbridge: Boydell Press, 1995, 213–27.

Parmée, Margaret A., *Ivan Goll: The Development of His Poetic Themes and their Imagery*, Bonn: Bouvier Verlag, 1981.

Peattie, Thomas, 'In Search of Lost Time: Memory and Mahler's Broken Pastoral', in Karen Painter (ed.), *Mahler and His World*, Princeton University Press, 2002, 185–98.

Petersen, Peter, '"… eine Form und ein Name: Tristan". Strukturelle und semantische Untersuchungen an Hans Werner Henzes Préludes für Klavier, Tonbänder und Orchester', in Otto Kolleritsch (ed.), *Verbalisierung und Sinngehalt: Über Semantische Tendenzen im Denken in und Über Musik Heute*, Vienna: Universal Edition, 1989, 148–76.

    Hans Werner Henze. Ein politischer Musiker, Hamburg: Argument Verlag, 1988.

Plato, *The Symposium*, trans. Walter Hamilton, Harmondsworth: Penguin, 1951.

Pollock, George H., 'Mourning through Music: Gustav Mahler', in Stuart Feder, Richard L. Karmel and George H. Pollock (eds.), *Psychoanalytical Explorations in Music*, Madison, Conn.: International Universities Press, 1990, 321–39.

Reed, Philip, 'Aschenbach Becomes Mahler: Thomas Mann as Film', in Donald Mitchell (ed.), *Benjamin Britten: 'Death in Venice'*, Cambridge University Press, 1987, 178–83.

Reichert, Herbert W., 'Nietzsche and Georg Kaiser', *Studies in Philology* 61 (1964), 85–108.

Reilly, Edward R., *Gustav Mahler and Guido Adler: Records of a Friendship*, Cambridge University Press, 1982.

Revers, Peter, 'The Seventh Symphony', in Donald Mitchell and Andrew Nicholson (eds.), *The Mahler Companion*, Oxford University Press, 2002, 376–99.

Reynolds, Christopher, *Motives for Allusion: Context and Content in Nineteenth-Century Music*, Cambridge, Mass.: Harvard University Press, 2003.

Ringer, Alexander L., '*Kleinkunst* and *Küchenlied* in the Socio-Musical World of Kurt Weill', in Kim Kowalke (ed.), *A New Orpheus: Essays on Kurt Weill*, New Haven: Yale University Press, 1986, 37–50.

'Schoenberg, Weill and Epic Theatre', *Journal of the Arnold Schoenberg Institute* 4 (1986), 77–98.

Roberts, David and Murphy, Peter, *Dialectic of Romanticism: A Critique of Modernism*, New York: Continuum, 2004.

Robertson, Ritchie, 'Introduction' to Sigmund Freud, *The Interpretation of Dreams*, trans. Joyce Crick, Oxford University Press, 1999, vii–xxxvii.

Robinson, Lisa Brooks, '*Mahler and Postmodern Intertextuality*', unpublished PhD, Yale University, 1994.

Roman, Zoltan, 'Allegory, Symbolism, and Personification in Selected "Night Songs" by Liszt, Mahler, and Strauss', *Studia Musicologica Academiae Scientiarum Hungaricae* 41 (2000), 407–39.

'Song and Symphony (I). *Lieder und Gesange* Volume 1, *Lieder eines fahrenden Gesellen* and the First Symphony: Compositional Patterns for the Future', in Jeremy Barham (ed.), *The Cambridge Companion to Mahler*, Cambridge University Press, 2007, 72–88.

Roseberry, Eric, 'The Concertos and Early Orchestral Scores: Aspects of Style and Aesthetic', in Mervyn Cooke (ed.), *The Cambridge Companion to Benjamin Britten*, Cambridge University Press, 1999, 233–44.

'A Debt Repaid? Some Observations on Shostakovich and his Late Period Reception of Britten', in David Fanning (ed.), *Shostakovich Studies*, Cambridge University Press, 1995, 229–53.

'Tonal Ambiguity in *Death in Venice*: A Symphonic View', in Donald Mitchell (ed.), *Benjamin Britten: 'Death in Venice'*, Cambridge University Press, 1987, 86–98.

Rupprecht, Philip, *Britten's Musical Language*, Cambridge University Press, 2001.

Said, Edward, *Reflections on Exile and Other Literary and Cultural Essays*, London: Granta Books, 2000.

The World, The Text, and the Critic, Cambridge, Mass.: Harvard University Press, 1983.

Sample, Colin, 'Adorno on the Musical Language of Beethoven', *The Musical Quarterly* 78 (1994), 378–93.

Samuels, Robert, *Mahler's Sixth Symphony: A Study in Musical Semiotics*, Cambridge University Press, 1995.

'Narrative Form and Mahler's Musical Thinking', *Nineteenth-Century Music Review* 8 (2011), 237–54.

Schebera, Jürgen, *Kurt Weill: An Illustrated Life*, trans. Caroline Murphy, New Haven: Yale University Press, 1995.

Schiff, David, 'Jewish and Musical Tradition in the Music of Mahler and Schoenberg', *Journal of the Arnold Schoenberg Institute* 9 (1986), 217–31.

Schiller, Friedrich von, *'Naïve and Sentimental Poetry'* and *'On the Sublime': Two Essays*, trans, with introduction and notes by Julius A. Elias, New York: Frederick Ungar, 1966.

Schnebel, Diether *'Brouillards*. Tendenzen bei Debussy', *die Reihe* VI (1958), 30–5.

Seelig, Harry E., '"Wozu (lieder) in dürftiger Zeit": Britten's *Sechs Hölderlin-Fragmente* as a "Literary Song Cycle"', in Suzanne M. Lodato, Suzanne Aspden and Walter Bernhart (eds.), *Word and Music Studies IV: Essays in Honor of Steven Paul Scher on Cultural Identity and the Musical Stage*, Amsterdam: Rodopi, 2002, 101–22.

Sheinbaum, John J., 'Adorno's Mahler and the Timbral Outsider', *Journal of the Royal Musical Association* 131 (2006), 38–82.

Sheppard, Richard, 'The Crisis of Language', in Malcolm Bradbury and James McFarlane (eds.), *Modernism 1890–1930*, Harmondsworth: Penguin, 1976, 323–36.

'German Expressionist Poetry', in Malcolm Bradbury and James McFarlane (eds.), *Modernism 1890–1930*, Harmondsworth: Penguin, 1976, 383–92.

Simms, Bryan, *The Atonal Music of Schoenberg*, Oxford University Press, 2000.

Solomon, Maynard, 'The Ninth Symphony: A Search for Order', in *Beethoven Essays*, Cambridge, Mass.: Harvard University Press, 1988, 3–32.

Solvik, Morten, 'Mahler's Untimely Modernism', in Jeremy Barham (ed.), *Perspectives on Gustav Mahler*, Aldershot: Ashgate, 2005, 153–71.

Spitzer, Michael, *Metaphor and Musical Thought*, Chicago University Press, 2004.

Steinberg, Michael P., *Listening to Reason: Culture, Subjectivity, and Nineteenth-Century Music*, Princeton University Press, 2004.

Stephan, Rudolf, 'Hans Werner Henze', *die Reihe* IV (1958), 32–7.

Straus, Joseph N., *Remaking the Past: Musical Modernism and the Influence of the Tonal Tradition*, Cambridge, Mass.: Harvard University Press, 1990.

Strauss, Walter A., *Descent and Return: The Orphic Theme in Modern Literature*, Cambridge, Mass.: Harvard University Press, 1971.

Stubbs, Jeremy, 'Goll versus Breton: The Battle for Surrealism', in Eric Robertson and Robert Vilain (eds.), *Yvan Goll–Claire Goll: Texts and Contexts*, Amsterdam: Rodopi, 1997, 69–82.

Subotnik, Rose Rosengard, *Deconstructive Variations: Music and Reason in Western Society*, Minneapolis: University of Minnesota Press, 1996.

Developing Variations: Style and Ideology in Western Music, Minneapolis: University of Minnesota Press, 1991.

Taruskin, Richard, 'Review of Kowalke, ed., *A New Orpheus*', *Kurt Weill Newsletter*, 4 (1986), 12–15.

'Revising Revision', in *The Danger of Music and Other Anti-Utopian Essays*, Berkeley: University of California Press, 2009, 354–81.

Stravinsky and the Russian Traditions, Oxford University Press, 1996.

Thomas, Calvin, 'A Knowledge That Would Not Be Power: Adorno, Nostalgia and the Historicity of the Musical Subject', *New German Critique* 48 (1989), 155–75.

Todorov, Tzvetan, *Theories of the Symbol*, trans. Catherine Porter, Oxford: Basil Blackwell, 1982.

Vennefrohne, Benedikt, *Die Sinfonien Hans Werner Henzes*, Hildesheim: Georg Olms Verlag, 2005.

Vilain, Robert and Chew, Geoffrey, 'Iwan Goll and Kurt Weill: *Der neue Orpheus* and *Royal Palace*', in Eric Robertson and Robert Vilain (eds.), *Yvan Goll–Claire Goll: Texts and Contexts*, Amsterdam: Rodopi, 1997, 97–126.

Vincent-Arnaud, Nathalie, 'Regards sur un paysage anglais: "Seascape" de W. H. Auden à Benjamin Britten', *LISA e-journal* 4 (2006), 159–69.

Vogt, Hans, *Neue Musik seit 1945*, Stuttgart: Philipp Reclam, 1972.

Wackers, Ricarda, *Dialog der Künste: Die Zusammenarbeit von Kurt Weill und Yvan Goll*, Münster: Waxmann, 2004.

'Eurydike folgt nicht mehr oder Auf der Suche nach dem neuen Orpheus', in Heinz-Klaus Metzger and Rainer Riehn (eds.), *Kurt Weill: Die frühen Werke 1916–1928*, Munich: edition text+kritik, 1998, 107–12.

Wagner, Richard, *Beethoven*, trans. William Ashton Ellis, London: Dodo Press, n.d.

Religion and Art, trans. William Ashton Ellis, Lincoln: University of Nebraska Press, 1994.

Weidinger, Alfred, *Kokoschka and Alma Mahler*, Munich: Prestel, 1996.

Weill, Kurt, *Musik und musikalisches Theater: Gesammelte Schriften*, ed. Stephen Hinton and Jürgen Schebera, Mainz: Schott, 2000.

Wenk, Arthur B., 'The Composer as Poet in *Das Lied von der Erde*', *19th-Century Music* 1 (1977), 33–47.

White, Alan, *Within Nietzsche's Labyrinth*, London: Routledge, 1990.

Whittall, Arnold, 'Along the Knife-Edge: The Topic of Transcendence in Britten's Musical Aesthetic', in Philip Reed (ed.), *On Mahler and Britten*, Woodbridge: Boydell Press, 1995, 290–8.

'Britten's Lament: The World of *Owen Wingrave*', *Music Analysis* 19 (2000), 148–66.

Exploring Twentieth-Century Music: Tradition and Innovation, Cambridge University Press, 2003.

'Henze's Haunted Sensibility', *The Musical Times* 147, no. 1895 (2006), 5–15.

'Individualism and Accessibility: The Moderate Mainstream', in Nicholas Cook and Anthony Pople (eds.), *The Cambridge History of Twentieth-Century Music*, Cambridge University Press, 2004, 364–94.

'The Signs of Genre: Britten's Version of Pastoral', in Chris Banks, Arthur Searle and Malcolm Turner (eds.), *Sundry Sorts of Music Books: Essays on the British Library Collections*, London: The British Library, 1993, 363–74.

'The Study of Britten: Triadic Harmony and Tonal Structure', *Proceedings of the Royal Musical Association* 106 (1979–80), 27–41.

'Tonality in Britten's Song Cycles with Piano', *Tempo* 96 (1971), 2–11.

'Webern and Atonality: The Path from the Old Aesthetic', *The Musical Times* 124 (1983), 733–7.

Willett, John, *The Theatre of Bertolt Brecht*, London: Methuen, 1977.

Williams, Alastair, 'Adorno and the Semantics of Modernism', *Perspectives of New Music* 37 (1999), 29–50.

New Music and the Claims of Modernity, Aldershot: Ashgate, 1998.

'Torn Halves: Structure and Subjectivity in Analysis', *Music Analysis* 17 (1998), 281–93.

Williamson, John, 'The Eighth Symphony', in Donald Mitchell and Andrew Nicholson (eds.), *The Mahler Companion*, Oxford University Press, 2002, 407–18.

'Fragments of Old and New in "Der Abschied"', *Nineteenth-Century Music Review* 8 (2011), 197–217.

'New Research Paths in Criticism, Analysis and Interpretation', in Jeremy Barham (ed.) *The Cambridge Companion to Mahler*, Cambridge University Press, 2007, 262–74.

Wintle, Christopher, *All the Gods: Benjamin Britten's 'Night-Piece' in Context*, London: Plumbago, 2006.

Wolin, Richard, 'Benjamin, Adorno, Surrealism', in Tom Huhn and Lambert Zuidervaart (eds.), *The Semblance of Subjectivity: Essays on Adorno's Aesthetic Theory*, Cambridge, Mass.: MIT, 1997, 93–122.

'Utopia, Mimesis, and Reconciliation: A Redemptive Critique of Adorno's Aesthetic Theory', *Representations* 32 (1990), 33–49.

Walter Benjamin: An Aesthetic of Redemption, New York: Columbia University Press, 1982.

Wood, Hugh, 'Britten's Hölderlin Songs', *The Musical Times* 104, no. 1449 (1963), 781–3.

Worton, Michael and Still, Judith (eds.), *Intertextuality: Theories and Practices*, Manchester University Press, 1990.

Youens, Susan, 'Schubert, Mahler and the Weight of the Past: *Lieder eines fahrenden Gesellen* and *Winterreise*', *Music & Letters* 67 (1986), 256–68.

'Words and Music in Germany and France', in Jim Samson (ed.), *The Cambridge History of Nineteenth-Century Music*, Cambridge University Press, 2002, 460–99.

Index